The Political Economy of the Middle East

Series Editor
Ashraf Mishrif, Humanities Research Centre, Sultan Qaboos University, Al Khaud, Oman

This series explores the nature of Middle Eastern political regimes and their approaches to economic development. In light of the region's distinctive political, social and economic structures and the dramatic changes that took place in the wake of the Arab spring, this series puts forward a critical body of high-quality, research-based scholarship that reflects current political and economic transitions across the Middle East. It offers original research and new insights on the causes and consequences of the Arab uprisings; economic reforms and liberalization; political institutions and governance; regional and sub-regional integration arrangements; foreign trade and investment; political economy of energy, water and food security; finance and Islamic finance; and the politics of welfare, labor market and human development. Other themes of interest include the role of the private sector in economic development, economic diversification, entrepreneurship and innovation; state-business relationships; and the capacity of regimes and public institutions to lead the development process.

The book series is Scopus Indexed.

Ashraf Mishrif
Editor

Economic Effects of the Pandemic

Implications for the Economy, Finance and Tourism

palgrave
macmillan

Editor
Ashraf Mishrif
Humanities Research Centre
Sultan Qaboos University
Muscat, Sultanate of Oman

ISSN 2522-8854 ISSN 2522-8862 (electronic)
The Political Economy of the Middle East
ISBN 978-981-97-4366-7 ISBN 978-981-97-4367-4 (eBook)
https://doi.org/10.1007/978-981-97-4367-4

This Palgrave Macmillan imprint is published by the registered company Springer Nature Singapore Pte Ltd.
The registered company address is: 152 Beach Road, #21-01/04 Gateway East, Singapore 189721, Singapore

To my Parents and Family

Acknowledgements

This book is the outcome of the papers presented at the international conference on the Impact of COVID-19 on the economy and society that took place at Sultan Qaboos University on 10–12 October 2022. Under the patronage of the Minister of Commerce, Industry and Investment Promotion, participation of senior officials from the World Trade Organization (WTO), United Nations Conference on Tade and Development (UNCTAD), and Oman Chamber of Commerce and Industry, this conference attracted over 100 scholars and researchers from 16 countries, with extensive participation from the government, the private sector, and the academic community.

The author and editor of this book would like to express his gratitude of Sultan Qaboos University for its financial and logistical support to organize this conference. I am also grateful to Oman Chamber of Commerce and Industry for their participation and continuous support to the OCCI Research Chair for Economic Studies. My thanks and appreciation go to all the authors who devoted their time and efforts to write their papers. My thanks to my research assistant Maryam Essa for her excellent support during the preparation of this book. Without their tireless efforts this book would not have been produced and come out in the market.

Special thanks to Vishal Daryanomal, editor of Palgrave Macmillan, and his colleagues for their outstanding support during the publication of this book. My thanks also go to the three anonymous reviewers who provided rigorous comments and feedback that helped us to improve the quality of the manuscript.

The publication of this book comes at a critical junction in the global economy. So, I hope that our analysis will assist policymakers, academics, students, and other stakeholders to understand and respond appropriately to the economic effects of the pandemic for a better future.

Contents

Notes on Contributors

Mustafa Hamid Salim Abid is Associate Professor in accounting and finance, Alzaiem Alazhari University, Khartoum North, Sudan.

Iman Al-Kendi is currently working as Head of Application Development Section at Central Bank of Oman. She earned her Ph.D. in Computer Science from Sultan Qaboos University, Sultanate of Oman in 2022. She received her M.Sc. in Computer Science from Sultan Qaboos University, Sultanate of Oman in 2017. She has worked as a visiting lecturer for more than one year at Sultan Qaboos University in Oman. She has experience as a business analyst for 4 years, also she has around 24 publications in different journals and conferences. She is a reviewer member in many Scopus journals.

Abdullaziz M. Al Rahbi is an experienced Economist currently serving as Acting Manager at the Financial Stability and Research Directorate at the Central Bank of Oman, where he has been a key team member since 2011. Specializing in macroeconomics and the banking industry, Abdullaziz holds a Master of Science in Economics from the prestigious Durham University Business School in the UK. With advanced exposure in External Sector and Monetary Policy Affairs. As the author of several papers, he continues to contribute significantly to economics and financial policy in Oman.

Amira Al Salhi is a dedicated statistician with a bachelor's degree in Statistics and Computer Science in 2013 from Sultan Qaboos University.

Currently, I am a master's student at Sultan Qaboos University, specializing in Data Science and Machine Learning. Since 2018, I worked as a statistician in the Geographic, Environment, Tourism, and Energy Statistics Department at the Statistical Center for the Cooperation Council for the Arab countries of the Gulf. Prior to this, from 2014 to 2018, I worked in the Planning and Statistics Department at the Civil Service Employees Pension Fund in the Sultanate of Oman.

Ibtihag Al-Siyabi Environment Statistician position in Statistical Centre for the Cooperation Council for the Arab Countries of the Gulf ("GCC-Stat") since 2015 until now. She graduated from Lancashire University in the UK with an Honor degree in Health, Safety and Environment Management Science in 2014. She also has a diploma degree in Database management system from Middle East college in 2022 and currently she is M.Sc. student in Sultan Qaboos University in the field of Environment science.

Ahmed Badran is Associate Professor of Public Policy and Department Head at Department of International Affairs, Qatar University. Dr. Badran holds a Ph.D. degree in Politics/Public Policy from the University of Exeter, the United Kingdom. Dr Badran has also worked as a Post-Doctoral Research Fellow at Aston Centre for Critical Infrastructure and Services (ACCIS), Aston Business School, Aston University, Birmingham, the UK. Dr. Badran's research interests extend to cover different areas of the Public Policy and regulatory governance in liberalised public utilities including telecoms, water, and energy sectors particularly in transition and developing economies.

Issac P. Elias is an Associate Professor of Finance and Accounting at the School of Business and Management of Christ University, Bangalore, India. His domain areas of research interests include Social Entrepreneurship, Social capital, Finance and Taxation. He has participated and presented research papers in many international research conferences. His recent publications include *Community based organizations and Social Capital Building among Women* (2021), *Entrepreneurial Activities of women Self-Help groups and Improvement in Quality of Life and Standard of Living of Members (2022)*, and *Relationship between Financial Stress and Financial Wellbeing of Micro and Small Businessmen: Evidence from India (2023)*.

Lim Thye Goh is a Senior Lecturer and the current Head of the Department of Economics at University Malaya's Faculty of Business and Economics. He earned a Ph.D. in Economics, a Master of Science in International Economics, and a Bachelor of Economics specialising in Finance and Investment Analysis from University Putra Malaysia. Dr. Goh's research interests are primarily in Development Economics, International Economics, Macroeconomics, and Applied Econometrics. He has received numerous research grants, most of which have been directed towards investigating issues related to development economics and sustainable growth. In addition, as an Associate Editor for the Journal of Institutions and Economics, he contributes to the academic community.

Ashraf Mishrif is the founding director and research chair of Oman Chamber of Commerce and Industry Research Chair for Economic Studies, Sultan Qaboos University, Oman. Prior to that he was Associate Professor at King's College London and taught at various universities including Qatar University, Ahmed bin Mohammed Military College Qatar, Anglia Ruskin University Cambridge, and the University of Greenwich, London, UK. He assumed several executive posts including Cultural Advisor for the Egyptian Embassy Cultural Bureau in London, Managing Director of the London-based consulting firm EU-Med International, and International Advisor and member of the Academic Board of Directors, Boston Business Management School, Singapore. He is an expert in economic development and the political economy of the Middle East, with a special focus on the Gulf region. He established and led several research clusters, masters and doctoral programs in political economy, foreign direct investment, international trade, economic diversification, and Euro-Arab economic relations. He provides advisory services to international organizations and governments including UNCTAD (Geneva), UNIDO (Vienna), UK Trade and Investment (London), Ministry of Economy (Oman), Islamic Development Bank (Saudi Arabia), and Social Fund for Development (Egypt), Chambers of Commerce, among others. He manages several strategic research projects and regional development programs, with a research budget of US$1.2 million and 32 research staff. He is Fellow of International Society for Development and Sustainability (Japan) and the Book Series Editor of Palgrave Macmillan Political Economy of the Middle East. He authored and edited several books and peer-reviewed papers, including two volumes on economic diversification and nationalization of the labour market in the GCC.

Shanu N. Nazar is Assistant Professor of Economics in Jain (Deemed-to-be University) with Ph.D. in Economics. He has five years of teaching experience. He has authored 3 textbooks in Economics and published several research papers in national and international journals.

Salfaraz Ali Shah Seyd is a distinguished economist with extensive experience in academia and public service. He served as a Minister/Advisor to the Chief Minister of KPK, Pakistan, overseeing Planning & Development, Energy & Power, and Minerals Development. While currently, he is affiliated with Cardiff School of Management, he previously has held positions at the American University in Cairo, ESLSCA Business School Paris, and the OSCE Academy in Bishkek. Being former central banker, his research focuses on Macroeconomics, Monetary Economics, and International Finance, with numerous peer-reviewed publications. Dr. Syed holds a PhD in Economics from the University of Sciences & Technologies, Lille, France.

V. K. Xavier is Professor of Economics at CMS Business School in Jain (Deemed-to-be University) with Ph.D. in International Finance. He is a passionate teacher and researcher in economics with 32 years of teaching experience in five reputed universities. He has authored 16 textbooks in Economics and published several research papers in national and international journals. He was the local organising secretary of 105th Indian Economic Association Annual conference. He is a committed academician, a scholar in economics and a social entrepreneur.

Jaynab Yousuf is a postdoctoral researcher in the Humanities Research Centre, Sultan Qaboos University. She obtained her Ph.D. in natural resources economics from the College of Agriculture and Maritime, Sultan Qaboos University.

Mulook Al Zadjali is currently working as Head of Cash settlement section, Investment sector at Central Bank of Oman. She graduated from Sultan Qaboos University with a Bachelor of Finance in 2010 and also completed her master's in financial planning from the University of New South Wales, Sydney Australia in 2016. She participated in international conferences with her research paper in International Conference on the leadership and management of projects in the digital age (ICLAMP

2022). She is a certified TOT trainer in the field of financial planning, Lean, strategic planning, etc.

List of Figures

Chapter 1

Chapter 4

Chapter 6

Chapter 7

Chapter 10

Chapter 11

List of Tables

Chapter 8

Chapter 9

Chapter 10

Chapter 11

Chapter 12

PART I

The Impact of COVID-19 on Economy

CHAPTER 1

COVID-19 Effects on the Global Economy: An Overview

Ashraf Mishrif

1 Introduction

The economic impact of COVID-19 was severe on the national, regional, and global markets. The closure of borders and lockdowns due to the pandemic disrupted the global value chains and affected most economic activities, including manufacturing facilities, factories, commercial centers, and business entities around the globe. The impact of the pandemic was also apparent in the health threats to human life and public health. According to the World Health Organization (WHO), over 768 million people were infected and over 7 million people lost their lives. As by August 2023, confirmed cases, and over 7 million deaths as by August 2023 (WHO, 2023). This triggered strict public health guidelines and policies to control the spread of the virus, including social distancing, lockdown, and boarder closure. Despite their effectiveness, these polices

A. Mishrif (✉)
Humanities Research Centre, Sultan Qaboos University, Muscat, Sultanate of Oman
e-mail: ashraf.mishrif@gmail.com

A. Mishrif (ed.), *Economic Effects of the Pandemic*, The Political Economy of the Middle East,
https://doi.org/10.1007/978-981-97-4367-4_1

measures resulted in a significant reduction in business, economic and financial activities.

According to the World Bank statistics (2023), global GDP fell from 2.6 in 2019 to –2.8 in 2020, which estimated a loss of US$2.59 trillion. The economic complication of COVID-19 is related to both the pandemic itself and its related restrictions and policies, most notably placing about one third of the global population under lockdown at the beginning of the pandemic. This lockdown resulted in a wide range of economic implications, which affected almost all economic sectors including production facilities, labor market, supply chain, financial sector across the world, subsequently resulting in a severe global economic shock and recession. Market mechanisms were also affected by the pandemic due to significant reductions in the demand for goods and services. On the supply side, major suppliers of manufacturing goods and powerful warehouses such as China, Taiwan, Japan, South Korea, and the USA closed their borders and stopped supplying goods and services, except medical supplies, causing huge reductions in stocks and fall in sales. The mobility restrictions during the pandemic negatively affected household consumptions and caused an economic slowdown across several sectors and industries, especially financial services, insurance, tourism, hospitality, aviation, transportation, and supply chains, as well as service sectors such as health and education (Brodeur et al., 2021; Roy, 2020).

Despite the notable success of the vaccination policy in controlling the spread of COVID-19, the global economy has yet to recover from the pandemic because of the slow progress made in the industrialized countries. For example, the Organization for Economic Cooperation and Development (OECD, 2023) estimated the growth of global GDP at around 2.6% in 2023, and a modest improvement of 2.9% in 2024, which is the lowest since the global financial crisis 2008. The full recovery process is likely to take longer than any other economic crisis because the pandemic caused a long-lasting economic consequence (Jackson, 2023).

Thus, the aim of this chapter is to provide an overview of the impact of COVID-19 on global economy and pave the way for further examination of the localized effects of the pandemic on national markets, economic sectors, and industries in the GCC and beyond. The next section provides an overview on the economic consequences of the pandemic, including energy markets and global value chains and international trade. This is followed by the objectives, rationale, and structure of the book.

2 Economic Consequences of the Pandemic

One of the most notable effects of the pandemic is the significant economic slowdown due to the pandemic's disruption in the global demand and supply. On the supply side, the infection or the fear infection of COVID-19 reduced labor productivity and resulted in the closure of many businesses, factories, and commercial centers. Most industrial and services providers were unable to maintain their activities due to the restrictions imposed by the border closures and lockdowns. On the demand side, the closure of companies and factories resulted in the workers' losing their jobs and main sources of income. Thus, higher unemployment, layoffs, morbidity, movement restriction, loss of income and reduced household consumption have all reduced demand in the local and global economy. The impact of the pandemic was much greater on the economic sectors that depended more on human interactions than other sectors, including hospitality and tourism sectors, which declined by up to 90% in 2020 and 2021 (Asare & Barfi, 2021).

On a global level, restrictions applied by governments and the related changes in people's behaviors negatively affected contact-intensive services, work pattern, and mobility. These changes were reflected in the decline in production and consumption, subsequently resulting in a sharp fall in global GDP from 2.6% in 2019 to –2.8% in 2020, indicating an economic contraction by 5.7% (The World Bank, 2023). This corresponded to about US$2.5 trillion loss in economic production in 2020. The impact of COVID-19 on global economy was uneven across different countries and sectors. This impact on the global economy worsened after February 2022 due to the economic spillover of Russia's war in Ukraine (Jackson, 2023). Figure 1 shows the changes in GDP between 2016 and 2023.

The impact of the pandemic was tougher on many Middle Eastern countries, particularly oil producing countries. Oil exporting countries were affected by a double crisis, the negative economic impact of the pandemic and the sharp fluctuation in the international oil prices due to reduced demand for energy in China and the industrialized nations, as explained below (IMF, 2020; IMF, 2023a, 2023b).

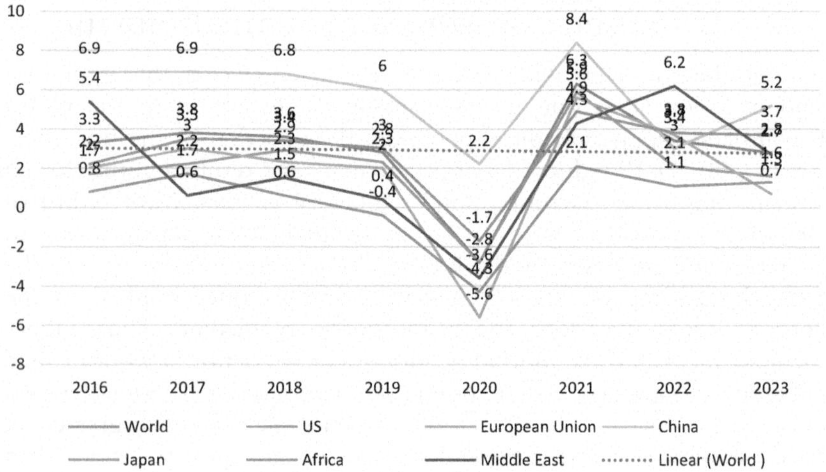

Fig. 1 Real GDP growth of major economies, 2016–2023 (*Source* IMF, 2023a, 2023b)

2.1 COVID-19 Effect on the Energy Sector

The energy markets were badly affected by the decrease in the demand for oil in China and the industrialized countries. The closure of factories, partial movement of transport vehicles and airlines, and drop in energy usage considerably reduced the demand for oil, subsequently increasing global oil supply and plummeting oil prices to their lowest levels in the past few decades (Rodrigues et al., 2021). The energy market was affected by not only the decline in production and manufacturing activities in China, as the largest global warehouse, but it also impacted by the decision of Russia and Saudi Arabia to increase oil production during the pandemic, causing a further reduction in the global oil prices (Hanieh, 2021).

According to the Oil Producing and Exporting Countries (OPEC, 2022), the world crude oil production declined by 6.15 mb/d (8.2%) in 2020, while OPEC countries crude oil production declined by 3.72 mb/d (12.7%), and non-OPEC countries declined by 2.43 mb/d (5.3%) in the same year compared to the previous year. Statistics also show that world oil demand was negatively affected by the pandemic and recorded a decline of 9.3 mb/d compared to 2019. In terms of oil export, OPEC countries oil export declined by 2.78 mb/d (12.4%), of which 14.43 mb/d (73.2%) was exported to Asia, mainly China and India, while only 3.13 mb/d was exported to OECD Europe. The global refinery quantity also declined sharply by over 9% reaching 78 mb/d amid the fall in demand during the pandemic. The effect of this is illustrated in Fig. 2, which shows that oil price declined sharply to US$ 41.47/b in 2020 compared to US$ 64.04 /b in 2019, before reaching the peak in 2022.

In 2021, the relaxation of lockdown restrictions allowed economic activities to gradually resume and generate a 4% increase in global economy demand. This rise in demand for goods and services observed a huge increase in coal and oil use, leading to sharp price upsurges in natural gas and coal compared to 2020, while oil prices increased from US$ 41.47/b in 2020 to just under US$ 70/b in 2021 (IEA, 2021). This rise in oil demand and oil prices continued to increase due to China's lifting its COVID-19 restrictions in late 2022, reaching above US$100 pb, before dropping to around US$80 pb due to a combination of demand and supply factors in 2023. On the demand side, China's manufacturing sector contracted, creating market concerns about the economic growth of China. Ther was also a growing concern related to the possibility of a US recession and the health of its banking sector after the closure of

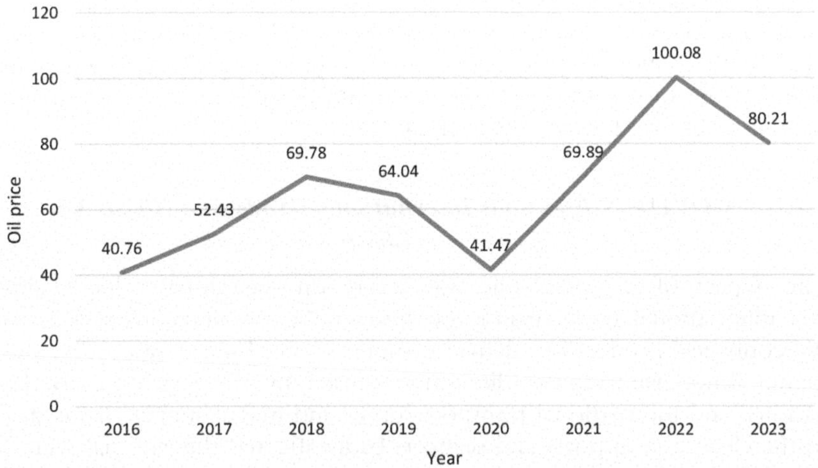

Fig. 2 Fluctuation in international oil prices, 2016–2023 (*Source* OPEC, 2023)

the First Republic Bank. On the supply side, the oversupply of oil from Russia remained unexpectedly high, which created pressure on curd oil prices. However, the decision of the OPEC+ members in April 2023 to cut their oil production until the end of 2023 was expected to balance between oil supply and demand (EIA, 2023).

When it comes to the GCC countries, the pandemic caused a significant decrease in demand. The sharp collapse in oil prices negatively affected the GCC economies, which depend heavily on oil revenues. These economies were affected by both the economic impact of the pandemic, the decrease in oil revenues, and the negative externalities of the pandemic and decreased income on the Gulf stock markets that are heavily dominated by local investors. To ease the negative impact of the pandemic, GCC governments introduced financial stimulus packages worth over US$120 billion. The total stimulus package of the UAE was US$ 34.3 billion, Saudi Arabia US$32 billion, Oman US$20.8 billion, Qatar US$20.6 billion, Bahrain US$11.4 billion, and Kuwait US$1.5 billion. These stimulus packages aimed at accelerating economic recovery and preventing further recession due to oil prices decline (Al Samman, 2022; Shamsudheen, 2022). When assessing the economic risk of the GCC countries, Saudi Arabia and the UAE were more vulnerable to oil risk than other GCC economies because of their proximity to the oil market, although all GCC markets held more systemic risk from the crude oil market. Saudi Arabia and the UAE also had the greatest stock market value in the region and were first and second among the Gulf States in terms of oil exports, the least affected countries were Kuwait, Oman, and Bahrain (Abuzayed & Al-Fayoumi, 2021).

2.2 COVID-19 Effects on International Trade and Global Value Chain

The impact of the pandemic was severe on the global value chains and international trade, mainly because of the simultaneous shocks to the countries' production, demand, supply chain, human resources, and capital flows. In fact, the disruption caused by the pandemic to the national and international transport routes and global supply chains due to the closure of airports and seaports badly affected the external sector, significantly lowering exports and imports of both goods and services (Barua, 2021). According to the World Trade Organization (WTO, 2023), the volume of world's merchandise trade sharply declined in 2020, which was the hardest ever decline in one year, falling by an average of 5.1% compared to the previous year. This decline in trade volume reached its lowest point of 15.5% in the second quarter of 2020, mainly due to the strict covid-19 restrictions amid the peak of the pandemic.

The effects of the partial suspension of international trade and global supply chain caused substantial decrease in imports, experts, and capital flow worldwide. China's decision to close its borders impacted negatively on the global supply chain that was mainly relying on Chinese raw materials and manufacturing output. This affected production and trade flow in China, which was responsible for over 60% of world's manufacturing and of world supply and demand. The disruptions in the Chinese logistics and transports systems also caused complications in other countries that suffered from shortage of inputs imported from China such as raw materials and spare parts. This underlines the importance of China in international trade and the extent to which any disruption to its economic cycle can spillover to its main trading partners, including the USA, the EU, the UK, Japan, and the Southeast Asian countries. In fact, the spread of the pandemic from China in 2019 resulted in a temporal cessation in most business activities of local and international firms in China and globally (Barlow et al., 2021).

Moreover, trade data reveals that merchandise trade volume fluctuated sharply during the pandemic period. Figure 2 illustrates the annual percentage changes in world merchandise trade volume between 2016 and 2023. Statistics show that the sharp decline in the percentage of merchandised trade volume from 4.9% in 2017 to minus –5.1% in 2020, before jumping to a peak of 9.4% in 2021. Trade data analysis also reveals that merchandise trade volume started to increase gradually from the third quarter of 2020, achieving a significant increase of 9.4% in the second quarter of 2021, which exceeded the pre-pandemic level (WTO, 2021a, 2022). The growth in trade volume was not only limited to manufactured goods, but trade in services also increased significantly and reached the pre-pandemic levels in the fourth quarter of 2021, reaching US$1.6 trillion. Overall, the global trade value reached over US$28 trillion in 2021, which was an increase of about 25% and 13% compared to 2020 and the pre-pandemic level in 2019 respectively. This increase in trade in 2021 was largely a result of commodity process increase, the ease in pandemic's restriction, and the strong recovery of demand (UNCTAD, 2022a, 2022b). Figure 3 also shows that the increase in trade in 2021 was followed by sharp decline in 2020 and a negative value of minus –1%

in the first quarter of 2023. Several factors contributed to this decline such as the persistent global inflation, the Russian war in Ukraine, the COVID-19 impact, and the unprecedented disruption in the global supply chain (WTO, 2022).

In terms of exports, COVID-19 had negative effects on the capacity of many countries to maintain the volume of exports to the international markets. For example, over 80 countries introduced export restrictions as an immediate response to the pandemic, which led to a remarkable decline in export and import of manufactured goods (Table 1). The world merchanded export declined by 8% to US$17.87 trillion and commercial service exports dropped by 20% to US$4.91 trillion in 2020 (Barlow et al., 2021; WTO, 2021a). As a result, major exporters of merchandized goods suffered economically, with China experiencing a dip of US$48 billion in February 2020, before recovering and increasing its exports by US$40 billion in July 2020, making China the only economy that achieved a growth in merchandise trade worldwide (Barlow et al., 2021; Wei et al., 2021; Zhang et al., 2022).

In the Middle East, the region was not an exception when it comes to the pandemic's impact on trade. The region recorded a decline in merchandise trade volume in the second quarter of 2020 by –19.7%, with a large one-year import contractions for merchandise trade volumes in the second quarter of 2020 by –20.1%, and merchandise export was also

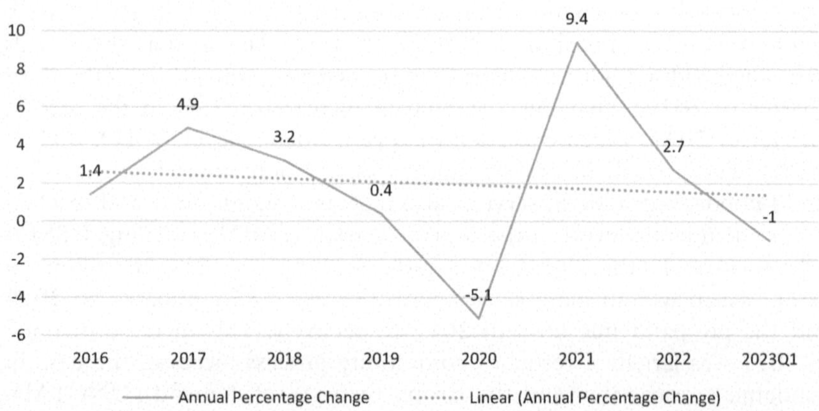

Fig. 3 World merchandise trade volume, 2016–2023 (*Source* WTO, 2023)

Table 1 World merchandise export by region 2016–2022 (Million US$)

	World	*United States*	*European Union*	*China*	*Japan*	*Africa*	*Middle East*
2016	16,035,818	1,451,011	4,969,739	2,097,632	645,052	361,148	819,970
2017	17,740,817	1,546,273	5,466,719	2,263,346	698,329	434,363	938,773
2018	19,549,257	1,663,982	5,992,950	2,486,695	738,143	508,966	1,172,492
2019	19,014,182	1,643,161	5,825,391	2,499,457	705,564	479,916	1,075,148
2020	17,648,303	1,424,935	5,475,129	2,589,952	641,319	394,404	811,563
2021	22,343,840	1,754,300	6,647,139	3,358,163	756,032	556,149	1,154,938
2022	24,904,489	2,064,787	7,147,789	3,593,601	746,920	655,239	1,635,577

Source WTO (2023)

down in this region in the second quarter of 2020. This was mainly caused by the persistent reduction in fuel consumption and a fall in prices during the pandemic. By the first quarter of 2021, trade started to show signs of recovery, but it lagged in poorer economies in the Middle East region. Also, countries depended on the export of natural resources recorded the weakest volumes of merchandise exports. However, merchandise export volumes increased by 8% in the Middle East by the first quarter of 2021 (WTO, 2021a). The region recorded the highest year-on-year growth in merchandise export by 78% in the second quarter of 2022, while achieving above world average in merchandise import value by 23% increase in the same period (WTO, 2022). Surprisingly, all regions recorder a negative growth in import, including the Middle East (–7%) in the first quarter of 2023 (Table 2). In contrast, export increased by 10% in the Middle East due to the increased price of oil and natural gas, which boosted domestic revenues and allowed for more good purchasing from outside (WTO, 2023).

Unlike other goods and services, the trade in medical goods increased from 4.7% in 2019 to 16.3% in 2020, with the trade in personal protective product growing the most by 47.2% and import of face mask increased by 80% to reach over US$141 billion in 2020 (WTO, 2021a). Many governments temporarily removed tariff duties and taxes on critical medical goods to decrease the cost of these products and make them more accessible for the public and the healthcare sector. The pharmaceutical industry also contributed to the rise in trade of medical goods to produce medications, supplements, and vaccines to control the virus. According to WTO

Table 2 World merchandise import by region 2016–2022 (Million US$)

	World	*United States*	*European Union*	*China*	*Japan*	*Africa*	*Middle East*
2016	16,206,454	2,250,154	4,621,875	1,587,925	607,728	500,101	711,039
2017	17,976,786	2,408,476	5,161,124	1,843,792	672,096	522,671	719,365
2018	19,818,778	2,614,221	5,752,013	2,135,748	748,488	588,868	732,337
2019	19,338,838	2,567,445	5,544,411	2,078,386	720,957	589,873	790,017
2020	17,881,471	2,406,932	5,156,031	2,065,964	635,460	491,747	688,517
2021	22,620,211	2,935,314	6,508,262	2,686,747	768,976	622,375	869,336
2022	25,621,162	3,376,200	7,462,582	2,715,999	897,242	723,663	1,045,732

Source WTO (2023)

(2021a, 2021b, 2021c), pharmaceutical companies worked on the manufacturing of vaccines sources around 9000 different materials from 300 suppliers in 30 countries. This does not only underline the complexity of the raw materials value chains, but it also underscores the extent of impact of COVID-19 on the global export of some raw materials used for vaccine production, which increased by 49%, reaching over US$15 billion in the first half of 2020.

2.3 *Pandemic Effects on the Tourism Sector*

COVID-19 affected all economic sectors to varying degrees. The impact was very severe on key services sectors such as education, health, tourism, and hospitality, and to a lesser extent on sectors such as agriculture, fisheries, and mining. The impact was also severe on the financial sector, as well be explained in Part 2 of this book. According to Boubaker et al. (2023), changes brought by the pandemic are expected to be long-lasting, altering many fundamental elements of the financial market. Undoubtedly, COVID-19 caused a severe decline in income, increased poverty, and raised inflation to unpresented levels, creating huge financial distress on individuals, households, firms, market, and the international financial system. While much of the scope of this book is devoted to the impact of the pandemic on major economic sectors, including the finance and banking sector, this subsection only highlights the pandemic impact on the tourism sector that was the hardest hit globally.

Tourism is probably one of the most affected sectors by the COVID-19 pandemic. Mobility restrictions, travel control, social distancing, and boarder closure, paralyzed the hospitality and tourism sectors (Viana-Lora & Nel-lo-Andreu, 2022). According to World Tourism Organization (2020), these factors made tourism one of the least attractive sectors for investment, with foreign investment declining by over 73% in the first six months 2020, from US$48 billion in 2019 to US$12 billion in 2020 (UNWTO, 2020a, 2020b). The number of tourist arrivals decreased by 74%, falling from 1461 million tourists in 2019 to 381 million in 2020, causing a loss of US$1.3 trillion in export revenue by tourism sector.

Figure 4 illustrates the severity of the pandemic on tourism and reveals that the impact of COVID-19 was much greater than other global public health and economic crises on the tourism sector in the past two decades. The near collapse of the tourism sector contributed to substantial loss of jobs, with about 200 million direct tourism jobs lost or many others were at risk (UNWTO, 2020a, 2020b). Further implications were identified in the increasing number of people living in poverty, especially in low-income countries, due to job losses and reduced income to sustain basic needs for their families (Henseler et al., 2022).

The impact of the pandemic on tourism was also uneven from time to time and from one country to another. In 2020, Asia and the pacific witnessed a decline in tourist arrivals by 82%, decrease in the Middle East by 73%, fall in Africa by 69%, and decrees in Europe and Americas by 68%. This decline was responsible for 900 million tourist arrivals fewer than in 2019. The decline in Asia and the pacific continued until it reached almost

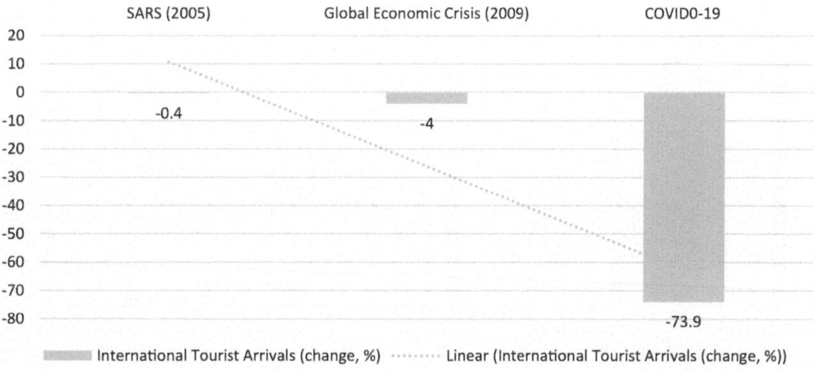

Fig. 4 Percentage changes in international tourist arrival during SARS, global financial crises, and COVID-19 (*Source* UNWTO, 2020a, 2020b)

a 100% in 2021, reflecting the severity of the crisis on this sector. Data also shows that China, which was the biggest tourist market in relation to number of visitors and spendings in Asia before the pandemic, experienced a sharp decline in visitors by 52% and 61% decrease in domestic tourism expenditure in 2020 compared to 2019 (Wu et al., 2022).

In terms of sector recovery, there was not any significant improvement in tourism in 2021, since travel restrictions were still high, and travelers lacked confidence in the fight against the virus. It was not until early 2022 that tourism began to improve with almost 60% of the pre-pandemic level and reaching over 900 million tourist arrivals. Figure 5 shows that this percentage was double the number of tourist arrivals in 2021, but still 37% less than the pre-pandemic level. The Figure also shows that the fastest recovery was in Europe, which recorded about 585 million tourist arrivals, accounting for almost 80% of the pre-pandemic level. The Middle East enjoyed the highest tourist arrivals, accounting for 83% of the pre-pandemic level. This rapid recovery could be attributed to many large events that were held in this region, including EXPO in UAE, FIFA World Cup in Qatar, and the Hajj pilgrimage in KSA. The Americas and Africa recovered by 65% of its pre-pandemic level, while Asia and the pacific recovered slowly, reaching 23% of the pre-pandemic visitors because of the belonged pandemic restrictions (UNWTO, 2023) (Fig. 6).

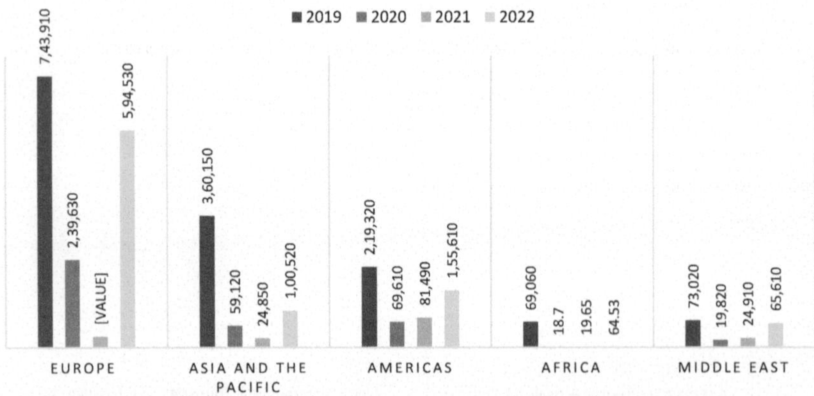

Fig. 5 International tourist arrival by region, 2019–2022 (*Source* UNWTO, 2023)

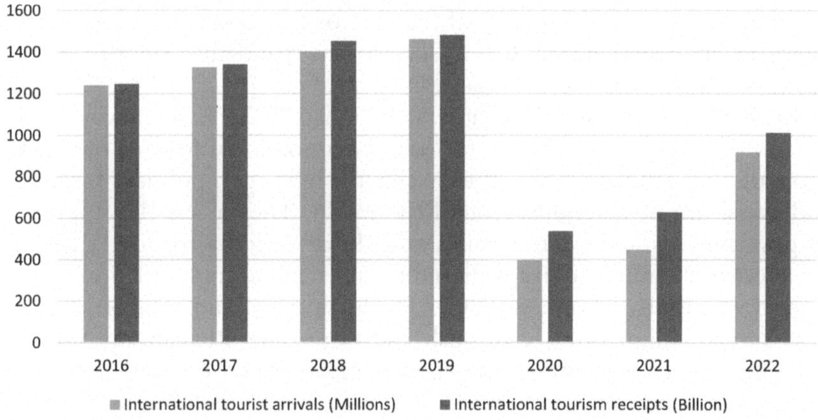

Fig. 6 International tourist arrival and tourism receipts, 2016–2022 (*Source* UNWTO, 2023)

Figure 6 confirms that the performance of the tourism sector has not reached the levels of the pre-pandemic period in both number of international tourist arrivals and tourism revenues.

3 The Objectives of the Book

This book aims to achieve the following objectives:

1. Explain the severity of the COVID-19 pandemic on the global economy.
2. Analyze the effect of the pandemic on key economic sectors.
3. Understand the impact of the pandemic on the finance and banking sectors in the Middle East and beyond.
4. Analyze the effects of the pandemic in the tourism sector.

4 Structure of the Book

This book is divided into three parts, each part focuses on one sector of the economy. Part 1 examines the impact of COVID-19 on the economy. Part 2 analyzes the impact of the pandemic on the finance and banking sectors. Part 3 addresses the economic effects of the pandemic on the tourism sector. Meanwhile, the editor of this books, Ashraf Mishrif, provides an overview on the effects of the pandemic on the global economy in an introductory chapter.

In Part 1, there are six chapters. In Chapter 2, V. K. Xavier, Issac Elias and Shanu Nazar analyse the world economic outlook in the backdrop of the pandemic, the Russia-Ukraine war, geo-political tensions, and social unrest emerging around the world. They assess the responses of governments and central banks with huge bailouts to beat a potential recession leading to excess liquidity and demand-pull inflation, while scarcity of inputs, labour, supply chain disruptions, and cost of production surged augmenting cost-push inflation. The Russian invasion of Ukraine further aggravated the supply-side shocks from sanctions and energy and food inflation surged—a 38-year high—to 6.7% in advanced economies and 8.7% in emerging markets and developing economies creating misery among people particularly in the low-income countries. They discussed the intersection between the geopolitical tensions, particularly the Russian-Ukrainian war, and economic performance and the impact of this link on inflation, unemployment, inequality, poverty, and social tension and the economic outlook in some developed and developing countries. They present a gloomy picture of the global economy, which is facing an extremely challenging near-term outlook due to sharply rising food, fertilizer and energy prices, and rising interest rates, capital outflows, currency depreciation and leading to unsustainable levels of external debt.

In Chapter 3, Ashraf Mishrif and Jaynab Yousuf examine the impact of COVID-19 on household consumption behavior during the pandemic. With restrictions in place to ensure containment of the virus and safeguard people's lives, household consumption and behaviour changed worldwide. They used the MANOVA testing method and descriptive statistics to assess the household consumption behaviour and perception in the Sultanate of Oman, and whether any shift or change in the consumption is permanent or transient, as well as the 'next normal' of consumer behaviour. They also investigate whether the change in household consumption is related to purchasing patterns of habit-forming goods, necessity, and luxury goods, shift towards a healthy diet, panic buying of toiletries and other necessary items.

In Chapter 4, Ibtihaj Al-Siyabi examines the impact of COVID 19 on water consumption in the GCC countries. She argues that during the pandemic people were encouraged and educated on the importance of making behavioural changes related to washing hands, and closures and suspension of certain activities. All of these measures have had an impact on how and where water was consumed. The most significant increase observed was in water consumption in households in many countries, including GCC countries. She also argues that the increase in water consumption might have serious implications on water resources and water security in GCC countries. She concludes by highlighting the need for efficient management of water resources and preparedness for any future crises.

In Chapter 5, Sarfaraz Ali Shah Syed delves into the extensive ramifications of the COVID-19 pandemic on macroeconomic expectations across a spectrum of sectors within economies. Expanding beyond prevailing research on consumer expectations and their interplay with macroeconomic indicators, his analysis encompasses sectors such as services, industry, finance, and retail, all of them were significantly disrupted by the pandemic's repercussions. He employs a latent factor model coupled with GMM techniques to construct scenarios representing heightened, diminished, and unchanged COVID-19 infections and fatalities. Simultaneously, he used the MMR model to scrutinize the intricate relationship between fatalities and the expectations held by economic agents in the European Union. The findings underscore a prevailing sense of pessimism across these varied sectors, bringing attention to a fascinating trend where nations with divergent fatality rates exhibit akin behavioural responses. The study uncovers that reductions in fatalities lack the equivalent positive sway on expectations, when contrasted with the negative sway generated by upswings.

In Chapter 6, Lim Thye Goh assesses the relationship between inflation and unemployment rate during the pandemic in Malaysia with reference to Oman. He explores the best possible options to revitalize the domestic economy and reduce unemployment and argues that correlation between inflation and unemployment rate is critical for policymakers to develop an effective macroeconomic policy to boost the country's economy. His empirical findings revealed four significant findings. First, inflation was significantly associated with the unemployment rate in the short run, but the effect was only temporary. Second, there was no trade-off between Malaysian inflation and unemployment in the long run. Third, the inflation rate was significantly related to Malaysia's unemployment rate, indicating that the pandemic gave the Phillips Curve a new lease on life. Fourth, inflation was asymmetrically correlated with Malaysia's unemployment rate during the pandemic. He also reveals that a decrease in inflation tended to increase unemployment by a larger margin, while an increase in inflation would result in a lower deviation in unemployment.

In Chapter 7, Ahmed Badran assesses the recovery of the green economy in the GCC with specific reference to Qatar in the post-COVID-19. He argues that the GCC governments responded to the pandemic by addressing the health effects and providing relief to the most affected businesses and workers, while supporting environmental goals. However, much more needs to be done to guarantee that recovery plans expedite the transition to a green economy, hence increasing resilience to external shocks. His analysis covers pandemic-related policies that could accelerate the transition to a greener, climate-resilient, and low-carbon economy. While focusing on Qatar as a case study, he explores three potential scenarios for GCC governments to ensure that economic recovery is aligned with their goals on climate change, biodiversity, and environmental conservation in general.

In Part 3, there are three chapters. In Chapter 8, Abdullaziz Al Rahbi analyses the impact of the pandemic on Oman's banking sector. He provides his analysis by utilizing various profitability indicators as performance metrics and examining the complex interplay between financial sector policy announcements and the banking sector's performance. He also analyses the pandemic's disruptive effects on banking operations. The findings reveal a significant strain on the banking system, primarily attributed to the unprecedented implementation of the countercyclical lending role during the crisis. Policy interventions, including monetary easing and liquidity enhancements, played a crucial role in mitigating the severe repercussions of the crisis on the financial sector. In Chapter 9, Iman Al-Kendi and Mulook Al Zadjali underscore the positive impact of Covid-19 on the practices and services of commercial banks in Oman. They use a comparative analysis approach to evaluate the service provisions provided by nine commercial banks on the local economy. Key indicators used for the comparison between banks are awareness and support, operational services, technical or e-services, and business continuity, which were useful in assessing the effectiveness of banks in dealing with their customers during Covid-19.

In Chapter 10, Mustafa Abid measures the impact of implementing the 2014 GFSM on public sector performance in Australia and Oman before and during the COVID-19 pandemic. He analysed the performance of the public sector using six indicators, which were divided to public finance indicators include gross operating balance (GOB), below-the-line transactions, and transfer payments excluding grants, and wealth and debt indicators including total debt, net financial value, and change in net worth. He found that the application of GFSM 2014 offered better understanding of the performance of the public sector through the analysis of public finance indicators and wealth and debt indictors that provide a more balanced view of the performance than other methods. He concludes by stressing the need to fully adhere to the GFSM 2014 analytical framework and its accounting rules and enhancing cooperation between the Ministry of Finance, the National Bureau of Statistics, and the Accounting Regulatory Authority to measure, present, and disclose the government's financial statistics.

In Part 3, there are two chapters addressing the Impact of COVID-19 on Tourism. In Chapter 11, Amira Al Salhi examines the effect of the pandemic on the tourism sector in the GCC countries. She argues that tourism is one of the economically important sectors, occupying the third place in terms of its contribution to the international economy after chemicals and fuels. This sector was negatively affected by the pandemic, with both the supply and demand for tourism badly affected due to restrictions imposed on travel destinations. She measures the impact of the pandemic on flight cancelation and suspension of most aviation activities and how this affected the number of travellers and performance of the aviation industry and the tourism sector in the GCC region. In Chapter 12, Isaac Elias compares the impact of COVID-19 on travel and tourism industry in India and Middle Eastern countries. He stresses the importance of tourism as a major contributor to gross domestic product (GDP), the largest service industry, where a greater number of women and youth are employed. The effect of the pandemic was severe on the tourism sector in India and many Middle Eastern countries, which are highly reliant on international tourism for economic growth. The impact could be greater as tourism is associated with many other sectors in terms of products and services, hence creating both direct and indirect effects on the economy. He ends by concluding that the tourism sector has not recovered to the level of the pre-COVID-19 period and countries should develop appropriate strategies to accelerate the recovery of this sector, even though there is uncertainty and challenges in the road ahead. In Chapter 13, Ashraf Mishrif concludes with some reflections on the pandemic experience and the lessons learned to minimize the effects of any similar crises in the future.

5 Conclusion

This chapter provided an overview of the impact of the COVID-19 pandemic on the global economy, with some reflections on the performance of the global economy in terms of growth levels, disruption of the global supply chains, logistics and international trade. It also explained the double-crisis created by the pandemic in the oil-exporting Arab Gulf countries, where the economy suffered from the economic effects of the pandemic and the sharp reduction in oil revenues that affected the financial position of these countries. In terms of sectoral development, this chapter selected the tourism sector as an exemplary model of the severity of the pandemic on the economy. The chapter revealed that the tourism sector was not sensitive to political instability and geopolitics, but it was also vulnerable to one of the most challenging public health crises in the past hundred years.

References

Abuzayed, B., & Al-Fayoumi, N. (2021). Risk spillover from crude oil prices to GCC stock market returns: New evidence during the COVID-19 outbreak. *The North American Journal of Economics and Finance, 58*, 101476.

Al Samman, H., & AKKAŞ, E. (2022). How do the crises of falling oil prices and COVID-19 affect economic sectors in the rentier economies? Evidence from the GCC countries. *Journal of Economy Culture and Society*.

Asare, P., & Barfi, R. (2021). The impact of Covid-19 pandemic on the global economy: Emphasis on poverty alleviation and economic growth. *Economics, 8*(1), 32–43.

Barlow, P., van Schalkwyk, M. C., McKee, M., Labonté, R., & Stuckler, D. (2021). COVID-19 and the collapse of global trade: Building an effective public health response. *The Lancet Planetary Health, 5*(2), e102–e107.

Barua, S. (2020). Understanding coronanomics: The economic implications of the coronavirus (COVID-19) pandemic. Available at SSRN 3566477.

Barua, S. (2021). Understanding coronanomics: The economic implications of the covid-19 pandemic. *The Journal of Developing Areas, 55*(3), 435–450. https://doi.org/10.1353/jda.2021.0073

Boubaker, S., Goodell, J. W., Kumar, S., & Sureka, R. (2023). COVID-19 and finance scholarship: A systematic and bibliometric analysis. *International Review of Financial Analysis, 85*, 102458.

Brodeur, A., Gray, D., Islam, A., & Bhuiyan, S. (2021). A literature review of the economics of COVID-19. *Journal of Economic Surveys, 35*(4), 1007–1044.

EIA expects lower crude oil prices for the second half of 2023 and for 2024. (n.d.). Independent Statistics and Analysis, Energy Information Administration. Retrieved August 22, 2023, from https://www.eia.gov/todayinenergy/detail.php?id=56560

Hanieh, A. (2021). COVID-19 and global oil markets. *Canadian Journal of Development Studies/revue Canadienne D'études Du Développement, 42*(1–2), 101–108.

Henseler, M., Maisonnave, H., & Maskaeva, A. (2022). Economic impacts of COVID-19 on the tourism sector in Tanzania. *Annals of Tourism Research Empirical Insights, 3*(1), 100042. https://doi.org/10.1016/j.annale.2022.100042

IEA (2021). World Energy Outlook 2021, International Energy Agency. https://www.iea.org/reports/world-energy-outlook-2021/executive-summary

IMF. (2020). Five charts that illustrate COVID-19's impact on the Middle East and Central Asia. International Monetary Fund. https://www.imf.org/en/News/Articles/2020/07/14/na071420-five-charts-that-illustrate-covid19s-impact-on-the-middle-east-and-central-asia

IMF. (2023a). *Real GDP growth.* International Monetary Fund. https://www.imf.org/external/datamapper/NGDP_RPCH@WEO/WEOWORLD/JPN/AFQ/EU/CHN/ARE

IMF. (2023b). *Real GDP growth.* International Monetary Fund. https://www.imf.org/external/datamapper/NGDP_RPCH@WEO/WEOWORLD/JPN/AFQ/EU/CHN/ARE

Jackson, C. (2023). Revisiting covid scarring in emerging markets. *IMF Working Papers, 2023*(162), 1. https://doi.org/10.5089/9798400252136.001

OECD. (2023a). *GDP growth.* Organization for Economic Co-operation and Development. https://www.oecd.org/economic-outlook/june-2023/

OPEC. (2022). *Annual report 2022.* Organization of the Petroleum Exporting Countries. https://www.opec.org/opec_web/static_files_project/media/downloads/AR%202022.pdf

OPEC. (2023b). *OPEC basket price.* Organization of the Petroleum Exporting Countries. https://www.opec.org/opec_web/en/data_graphs/40.htm

Rodrigues, M. V. G., Duarte, T. E., Dos Santos, M., & Gomes, C. F. S. (2021). Prospective scenarios analysis Impact on demand for oil and its derivatives after the COVID-19 pandemic. *Brazilian Journal of Operations & Production Management, 18*(2), 1–15. https://doi.org/10.14488/bjopm.2021.039

Roy, S. (2020). Economic impact of Covid-19 pandemic. *A Preprint, 1*, 29.

Shamsudheen, S. V., Khattak, M. A., Muneeza, A., & Huda, M. (2022). COVID-19 and GCC stock market performance: An analysis of the boon (financial stimulus package) and curse (oil price plunge) effects. *International*

Journal of Islamic and Middle Eastern Finance and Management, 15(2), 223–235.
The World Bank. (2023). GDP growth (annual %). https://data.worldbank.org/indicator/NY.GDP.MKTP.KD.ZG?end=2022&start=2019&view=chart
UNWTO. (2020a). Covid-19 and tourism, a year in review. World Tourism Organization. https://www.unwto.org/covid-19-and-tourism-2020
UNWTO. (2020b, October). *UNWTO world tourism barometer and statistical annex*. World Tourism Organization. https://www.e-unwto.org/doi/abs/10.18111/wtobarometereng.2020.18.1.6
UNWTO. (2021a, May). *UNWTO world tourism barometer and statistical annex*. World Tourism Organization. https://www.e-unwto.org/loi/wtobarometereng
UNWTO. (2021b). *World tourism barometer, 2023*. World Tourism Organization. https://www.e-unwto.org/doi/abs/10.18111/wtobarometereng.2023.21.1.1
UNWTO. (2021c). *Tourism investments trends and challenges during COVID-19*. The World Trade Organization. https://www.unwto.org/events/tourism-investments-trends-and-challenges-during-covid-19
UNCTAD. (2022a). *Global trade update 2022*. United Nations Conference on Trade and Development. https://unctad.org/system/files/official-document/ditcinf2022d4_en.pdf
UNCTAD. (2022b). *Global trade hits record high of $28.5 trillion in 2021, but likely to be subdued in 2022*. United Nations Conference on Trade and Development. https://unctad.org/news/global-trade-hits-record-high-285-trillion-2021-likely-be-subdued-2022
UNWTO (2023). *Global and regional tourism performance*. World Tourism Organization. https://www.unwto.org/tourism-data/global-and-regional-tourism-performance
Wei, P., Jin, C., & Xu, C. (2021). The influence of the COVID-19 pandemic on the imports and exports in China, Japan, and South Korea. *Frontiers in Public Health, 9*, 682693.
WEO. (2022). World Economic Outlook. https://www.imf.org/en/Publications/WEO/Issues/2022/10/11/world-economic-outlook-october-2022
WEO. (2023). World Economic Outlook. https://www.imf.org/en/Publications/WEO/Issues/2023/07/10/world-economic-outlook-update-july-2023
World Economic Outlook. (2019). World Economic Outlook, April 2019 growth slowdown, precarious recovery. https://www.imf.org/en/Publications/WEO/Issues/2019/03/28/world-economic-outlook-april-2019
World Health Organization. (2023). https://covid19.who.int/
WTO. (2021a). *World trade statistical review 2021*. World Trade Organization. https://www.wto.org/english/res_e/statis_e/wts2021_e/wts2021_e.pdf

WTO. (2021b). *Information note on trade in intermediate goods: Second quarter 2021.* World Trade Organization. https://www.wto.org/english/news_e/news21_e/stat_03nov21_e.pdf

WTO. (2021c). *Spotlight COVID-19 and world trade.* World Trade Organization. https://www.wto.org/english/res_e/booksp_e/anrep_e/anrep21_spotlight_covid_e.pdf

WTO. (2022). *World trade statistical review 2022.* World Trade Organization. https://www.wto.org/english/res_e/publications_e/wtsr_2022_e.htm

WTO. (2023). *World trade statistical review 2023.* World Trade Organization. https://www.wto.org/english/res_e/publications_e/wtsr_2023_e.htm

Wu, D. C., Cao, C., Liu, W., & Chen, J. L. (2022). Impact of domestic tourism on economy under COVID-19: The perspective of tourism satellite accounts. *Annals of Tourism Research Empirical Insights, 3*(2), 100055. https://doi.org/10.1016/j.annale.2022.100055

Viana-Lora, A., & Nel-lo-Andreu, M. G. (2022). Bibliometric analysis of trends in COVID-19 and tourism. *Humanities and Social Sciences Communications, 9*(1).

Zhang, W. W., Dawei, W., Majeed, M. T., & Sohail, S. (2022). COVID-19 and international trade: Insights and policy challenges in China and USA. *Economic Research-Ekonomska Istraživanja, 35*(1), 1991–2002.

CHAPTER 2

Pandemic, War and Geo-Political Risk: The Outlook for Global Economy

V. K. Xavier, Issac P. Elias, and Shanu N. Nazar

1 Introduction

COVID-19 pandemic was an unwanted gift from the nature causing devastating impact on the global economy. Having originated in China, it spread across the world in multiple waves and mutation, hitting all groups of people, sparing no human habitat, gender, age, income, colour, caste and creed. The loss of lives and livelihood was unprecedented in history.

This chapter is submitted for oral presentation in International Conference Impact of Covid-19 on Economy and Society from 10–12 October 2022 organised by Sultan Qaboos University, Muscat.

V. K. Xavier (✉)
Faculty of Management, CMS Business School, Jain Deemed-to-be University, Bengaluru, India
e-mail: xavier_vk@cms.ac.in

I. P. Elias
Department of Management Studies, Christ University, Bengaluru, India

A. Mishrif (ed.), *Economic Effects of the Pandemic*, The Political Economy of the Middle East,
https://doi.org/10.1007/978-981-97-4367-4_2

The world gross domestic product, income, employment, and international trade plummeted with rising multi-dimensional poverty, inequality and inflation. The world GDP declined due to multiple lockdowns to contain the spread of the virus, scarcity of inputs, labour and supply chain disruptions (World Economic Forum, 2023). The governments and central banks responded with huge bailouts to beat the potential recession leading to excess liquidity in the system causing demand-pull inflation. The demand and cost-push factors chased each other and inflation rose to a level not seen over the last four decades.

The liquidity adjustment mechanisms and global crisis control mechanisms extended hardly for two years. Meanwhile the Russian invasion of Ukraine on 24 February 2022 and consequent sanctions on Russia—on individuals, banks, businesses, monetary exchange, bank transfer, exports, and imports—aggravated the supply side shocks. In addition, social unrests occurred in many countries leading to geo-political tensions and the near-term outlook for the global economy has turned negative (Global Economic Outlook, 2023).

In order to target the inflation, the policy reversed to monetary tightening and rising interest rates leading to capital outflows, currency depreciation and meltdown in foreign exchange reserves. The pertinent questions we ask are what are the lessons learnt from the pandemic? Why inflation surged to unprecedented inflation? What policy interventions are needed to address skewflation, capital outflow, currency depreciation and exchange reserve meltdown? What is the outlook for the global economy? The global economy is facing an extremely challenging near-term outlook due to sharply rising food, fertilizer and energy prices, and rising interest rates, capital outflows, currency depreciation and leading to unsustainable levels of external debt.

1.1 Literature Review and Rationale of the Study

There are studies in the academia to quantify the war impact. "Correlates of War" the study done by Small and Singer in 1982 highlights the socio-economic impact. A data set that includes a judgment as to the magnitude of a war has been developed by the Center for Systemic Peace (Marshall &

S. N. Nazar
Department of Economics, St. Joseph's College of Commerce, Bengaluru, India
e-mail: nn.shanu@jainuniversity.ac.in

Elzinga-Marshall, 2017), covering the period 1946 to 2017. Magnitude 6 and 7 wars roughly correspond to the wars included in the Correlates of War data set. The studies conducted by Murdoch, J. C., and Sandler highlighted the war impact on GDP of US economy. However, all these studies do not cover the open economy impact—if the country is not a participant in the war—but how much they have to suffer.

The available literature on impact of COVID-19 pandemic address the health impact rather than economic impact. The study conducted by Prince Asare Vitenu-Sackey and Richard Barfi highlights poverty alleviation and economic growth in the purview of COVID-19 pandemic. This paper attempts to highlight the near-term outlook for the global economy in the purview of the Pandemic, war and geo-political risk. The standard data were collected from World Economic Forum reports, Reports of World Trade Organisation, World Bank, International Monetary Fund and Global Economic Forum.

2 Impact of COVID-19 Pandemic

The COVID-19 pandemic impacted both the people who contracted the disease and who did not. People who were spared by the pandemic lived in anxiety, fear, and loss of confidence. Over 7 million people suffered a painful death due to the disease. Those who survived the pandemic suffer from loss of jobs, reduction in income and distressed sale of assets. Innocent children are orphaned due to the death of their parents. The loss of lives and livelihoods substantially reduced the income levels and increased the absolute level of poverty (food intake), changed the lifestyles (giving up luxury and comforts) that people have enjoyed while in employment. The decline in discretionary consumption negatively affected the investment expenditure. The breakdown in the supply chain and logistics led to scarcity of goods and services, inflation, and loss of purchasing power of money. The scarcity in respect of fuel, food grain and health services caused immense misery particularly on the common man.

The impact of the pandemic was severe on the informal sector workers although the formal sector experienced the similar situation. The misery of migrant labourers is ineffable as these workers and their families had been uprooted from their workplace and living space and decided to go back to their birthplaces. Their journey was extremely painful as they had to trek long distances due to lack of transport facilities. They had no money to meet the cost of the transport wherever it was available. While walking back to their birthplaces, these workers had to carry their luggage and many a time, they had to piggyback the old and the sick and their children during the journey. Hunger and illness took their toll on many of them. The pandemic was a clear tragedy forced upon the people who migrated in search of a fortune.

Apart from the economic life of the people, the pandemic impacted the social life and mental wellness. A new phenomenon of untouchability emerged from the pandemic that was legally permitted and administratively enforced. Those who contracted the disease had to be indeed isolated within their homes. In that sense, they became untouchables within the family and from social circle. Upon death, their dead bodies faced undignified burials deprived of any religious rites and ceremonies. Many a time, the dead bodies of those who died an account of the pandemic were wrapped up in cloth and tossed into a common pit—the most undignified way of disposing of the dead bodies by any religion. Even healthy people suffered some degree of indignity outside their homes. Wearing masks and social distancing were made compulsory. There were restrictions to enter hotels, theatres, marriage halls, schools, colleges, and places of worship. All group activity and social functions attracted regulations. These are some kind of untouchable practices that arose from the Pandemic. Besides, the Pandemic impacted the earning capacity of the workers as they had to follow the COVID-Protocol. Although the workers of the formal sector were allowed to work from home, the workers in the informal sector who had to be physically present in the workplace such as construction, agriculture and industry lost their jobs and daily wages.

3 COVID-19 Interventions

As the COVID-19 Pandemic spread disproportionately, governments across the world adopted a series of measures—preventive, curative and rehabilitative in nature. The preventive measures are intended to build immunity in people. The most important was to develop vaccines and administer them to persons in age of 15 and above years. Scientists across the world indulged in developing effective vaccines. Having succeeded in this effort within a few months, the authorities vaccinated people at different periods. The general feeling was that those who got vaccinated could be prone to virus attack, although the outcome could be mild and less fatal. The curative measures included putting the health infrastructure in place—hospital beds, oxygen cylinders, health equipment and health workers (doctors and nurses). Despite the efforts put up by the governments, there were cases of non-availability of beds, oxygen, and essential health equipment, particularly during the first and second waves of the pandemic breakout. Luckily, during the third wave, when the Omicron pandemic broke out there were reasonably adequate health facilities. As for the rehabilitative measures, the government's role was minimal and confined to counselling the patients—how they should conduct themselves at home and the diet to be taken and how to follow-up, what medical care has to be taken and watch out for any past disease symptoms that indicate functioning of the internal organs. A laudable action by the government was the care of the orphaned children who lost both or one of their parents due to which they had no chance to survive or pursue education. The government identified such children and admitted them to Child homes and provided them with food, shelter and education opportunities.

There have been complaints from people that the hospitals, particularly private hospitals exploited the patients by overcharging the medical services. There were many cases where people suffered on account of inadequate health facilities, ICUs, oxygen, and health workers including doctors and nurses who simply made themselves scarce. Many cases were reported that patients had to move from one hospital to another on account of a lack of beds and many were lying on the roads uncared for. NGOs and people with concern came forward to help the migrant labourers during the first wave. They offered help in the form of transport facilities, food, and burial of the dead. The lorry drivers gave a lift to the migrant labourers travelling by foot. The availability of food and water at different points of travel was a great solace to migrant workers on their move towards their respective villages.

4 Russia-Ukraine War and Geo-Political Tensions

While the global economy was yearning to recover from the COVID-19 pandemic, the Russian invasion of Ukraine on 24 February 2022 came as a surprise to aggravate the global crisis. It has created the largest refugee crisis in Europe since World War II. Around 7.1 million Ukrainians have escaped the country and a third of its population was displaced causing global food shortages. Russia received widespread international condemnation. The United Nations General Assembly passed a resolution condemning the invasion and demanding a full withdrawal of Russian forces; the International Court of Justice ordered Russia to suspend military operations; the Council of Europe expelled Russia; many countries-imposed sanctions on Russia and Belarus (which supported invasion). The sanctions had affected the economy of Russia and the world economy. The Russian invasion of Ukraine created manmade havoc not only on Ukraine's economic and social infrastructure but also created further supply chain disruptions to the flow of international trade in fuel and food supply. The sanctions imposed on Russian crude and food halted a significant portion of supply to Europe, America, and Asian countries. Russia being a dominant supplier of crude and natural gas, its elimination led to energy price escalation and cost-push inflation. Ukraine being a large supplier of edible oil to Asian countries including India, there has been a sharp rise in the price of edible oil and wheat.

New geo-political tensions and social unrest have emerged around the world. The social unrest in developed countries (Canada, New Zealand, the US, Austria, the Netherland) and developing countries (Chile, Algeria, Iran, Iraq, Lebanon, Brazil, Belarus, Sri Lanka, Ethiopia, Burkina Faso, Tajikistan, and Sudan) and added the geo-political tensions in Asia (China and Taiwan) have worsened the near-tern world economic outlook. The sovereign debt crisis (Sri Lanka, Pakistan and Zimbabwe) has a potential domino effect. Crisis in Sri Lanka was forced upon due to multiple factors—deliberate reduction of tax (value added tax) to appease vote-bank politics, pandemic hitting tourism revenue to near-zero which contributes one-tenth of Sri Lanka's GDP, enforced organic farming policy dwindled Sri Lanka's food production and export of tea and cotton textiles. Sri Lankan Rupiah unprecedentedly depreciated forcing a sovereign debt default that was inevitable from the original sin—inability of a country to borrow in its own currency.

5 Analysis and Discussions

This section attempts to substantiate the above fundamental arguments with empirical evidence. For this the researchers have focused on dimensions of estimators/sections as described below. Section 1 provides regression-based analysis of the current account. Section 2 gives regression-based analysis of the 2021 REER index. Section 3 gives regression-based analysis of the 2021 REER Level. Section 4 provides external sustainability analysis.

5.1 Current Account Regression-based Analysis

The tables in this section present the results from the EBA analysis of 2021 current account balances (CA, as percentage of GDP). Table 1 decomposes the 2021 CA balances into cyclical and short-term components (related to the business cycle, the commodity price cycle and short-term exchange rate movements) and cyclically-adjusted component. The latter is further decomposed into a cyclically adjusted CA "norm" (a benchmark calculated using desirable P^* policy settings), the observed gap with respect to said norm that arises from the estimated contributions of four policy gaps, and a regression residual. The last column is the Total CA Gap, the sum of the overall policy gaps and the residual. The CA numbers in Table 1 include small adjustments that have been applied uniformly across economies (in terms of an economy's own GDP) to ensure multilateral consistency. Thus, the cross-economy sum of the CA norm levels, when measured in U.S. dollars, matches the sum of the actual 2021 CA levels of all 52 EBA economies.

Table 2 breaks down the policy gap contributions by the four policies covered in the EBA CA analysis (fiscal balance, public expenditure on health, the interaction between reserve accumulation and capital controls, and private credit). For each policy gap, the reported estimates include both the total contribution and the subcomponent that is "domestic" (i.e., arising from an economy's own policies). Tables 3–6 show in detail the derivation of the contribution of each policy gap. The abbreviation "wo" is used to denote the world average counterparts of the variables (in all cases, world averages are obtained as GDP-weighted averages of the relevant variables). Table 7 shows the derivation of the cyclical components of the current account. Table 8 shows the estimated coefficients of the EBA model.

Table 1 EBA regression analysis of 2021 current accounts (in percent of GDP, includes multilateral consistency adjustments)

Country	*Actual CA*	*Cyclical contributions (incl. ToT)*[a]	*Cyclically adjusted CA*	*Cyclically adjusted CA Norm*[b]	*Contribution of identified policy gaps*	*Unexplained residual*	*Total gap, including residual*
Argentina	1.4	0.9	0.5	0.2	0.7	−0.4	0.3
Australia	3.5	1.8	1.7	−0.9	−1.1	3.6	2.6
Belgium	−0.4	−0.4	0.0	3.1	−0.7	−2.4	−3.1
Brazil	−1.7	1.1	−2.8	−1.6	0.3	−1.5	−1.2
Canada	0.0	0.4	−0.4	2.6	−1.2	−1.8	−3.0
China	1.8	−0.4	2.2	0.8	1.3	0.1	1.4
France	0.4	0.1	0.2	0.3	−0.4	0.3	−0.1
Germany	7.4	−0.1	7.6	3.3	−0.8	5.1	4.3
India	−1.2	0.4	−1.6	−1.9	1.1	−0.8	0.3
Indonesia	0.3	1.8	−1.5	−0.8	0.7	−1.5	−0.7
Italy	2.4	0.3	2.2	3.4	0.2	−1.4	−1.2
Japan	2.9	0.0	2.9	3.9	−1.8	0.9	−0.9
Korea	4.9	−0.7	5.6	5.0	0.1	0.5	0.6
Malaysia	3.8	1.2	2.6	−0.1	1.3	1.4	2.7
Mexico	−0.4	1.1	−1.5	−1.2	1.3	−1.6	−0.2
Netherlands	9.0	−0.2	9.2	5.1	1.9	2.2	4.1
Poland	−0.6	−0.3	−0.3	−2.4	2.7	−0.6	2.1

Country	*Actual CA*	*Cyclical contributions (incl.ToT)[a]*	*Cyclically adjusted CA*	*Cyclically adjusted CA Norm[b]*	*Contribution of identified policy gaps*	*Unexplained residual*	*Total gap, including residual*
Russia	6.9	–0.2	7.1	4.4	1.8	0.8	2.6
South Africa	3.6	2.3	1.3	2.6	0.5	–1.7	–1.3
Spain	0.9	1.0	–0.1	0.0	0.2	–0.3	–0.1
Sweden	5.5	0.2	5.3	1.2	0.2	3.9	4.1
Switzerland	9.3	–0.6	9.9	6.8	0.0	3.0	3.1
Thailand	–2.2	0.6	–2.8	1.4	–1.2	–3.0	–4.2
Turkey	–1.7	–1.1	–0.6	–0.8	1.6	–1.4	0.2
UK	–2.6	–0.6	–2.0	–0.7	–0.4	–0.9	–1.3
United States	–3.6	–0.4	–3.2	–1.3	–1.1	–0.8	–1.9
Euro Area[c]	2.4	0.1	2.3	0.6	–0.1	1.8	1.7

Source IMF (2020)

[a]Sum of estimated contributions of output cycle and commodity terms of trade cycle

[b]Current account norm determined by regression evaluated at observed fundamentals and desirable policy settings (and zero cyclical contributions)

[c]Euro area current account gaps and policy gap contributions are calculated as GDP-weighted averages of values for the 11 largest Euro area economies. The CA norm is corrected for reporting discrepancies in intra-area transactions, since the CA of the entire Euro area is about 1.41 percent of GDP less than the sum of the individual 11 countries' CA balances (for which no such correction is available)

Table 2 EBA-estimated policy gap contributions to 2021 current accounts (in percent)

Country	*All (sum)*		*Fiscal balance*		*Health exp.*		*Δ Reserves * KC*		*Credit*	
	Total	*Dom.*	*Total*	*Dom.*	*Total*	*Dom.*	*Total*	*Dom.*	*Total*	*Dom.*
Argentina	0.7	–0.3	0.8	–0.5	0.0	0.0	0.0	0.2	–0.1	0.0
Australia	–1.1	–2.0	–0.9	–2.2	–0.1	–0.1	–0.1	0.1	0.0	0.2
Belgium	–0.7	–1.7	–0.2	–1.5	–0.1	–0.1	–0.1	0.1	–0.3	–0.2
Brazil	0.3	–0.7	1.1	–0.2	0.2	0.2	–0.3	–0.1	–0.7	–0.5
Canada	–1.2	–2.2	0.1	–1.1	–0.9	–1.0	–0.1	0.1	–0.2	–0.1
China	1.3	0.3	0.2	–1.1	0.1	0.1	0.3	0.5	0.7	0.8
France	–0.4	–1.3	0.0	–1.3	–0.2	–0.2	–0.2	0.0	0.0	0.1
Germany	–0.8	–1.8	0.5	–0.7	–0.3	–0.3	–0.1	0.1	–1.0	–0.9
India	1.1	0.1	0.4	–0.9	0.1	0.1	–0.1	0.1	0.7	0.8
Indonesia	0.7	–0.2	0.9	–0.4	0.4	0.4	–0.4	–0.2	–0.2	–0.1
Italy	0.2	–0.8	–0.5	–1.8	0.0	0.0	–0.2	0.0	0.8	0.9
Japan	–1.8	–2.8	–0.6	–1.9	0.0	0.0	–0.1	0.1	–1.1	–1.0
Korea	0.1	–0.9	1.3	0.1	0.3	0.3	–0.2	0.0	–1.4	–1.3
Malaysia	1.3	0.3	0.6	–0.7	0.6	0.6	0.6	0.8	–0.6	–0.4
Mexico	1.3	0.3	1.2	0.0	0.1	0.1	0.0	0.2	–0.1	0.0
Netherlands	1.9	0.9	1.0	–0.3	–0.1	–0.2	–0.2	0.0	1.2	1.4
Poland	2.7	1.7	1.0	–0.2	0.3	0.2	0.5	0.7	0.8	1.0

Country	*All (sum)*		*Fiscal balance*		*Health exp.*		*Δ Reserves * KC*		*Credit*	
	Total	*Dom.*	*Total*	*Dom.*	*Total*	*Dom.*	*Total*	*Dom.*	*Total*	*Dom.*
Russia	1.8	0.9	0.3	−1.0	0.3	0.3	0.7	0.9	0.5	0.7
South Africa	0.5	−0.5	0.5	−0.7	−0.1	−0.1	−0.3	−0.1	0.4	0.5
Spain	0.2	−0.7	0.7	−0.5	0.0	0.0	−0.1	0.1	−0.4	−0.3
Sweden	0.2	−0.8	1.0	−0.3	−0.1	−0.1	−0.1	0.1	−0.6	−0.5
Switzerland	0.0	−0.9	1.4	0.2	−0.1	−0.1	0.5	0.7	−1.9	−1.8
Thailand	−1.2	−2.2	0.1	−1.2	0.1	0.1	−0.4	−0.2	−1.1	−0.9
Turkey	1.6	0.6	1.4	0.1	−0.4	−0.4	0.1	0.3	0.5	0.6
United Kingdom	−0.4	−1.3	−0.2	−1.5	−0.7	−0.7	−0.1	0.1	0.7	0.8
United States	−1.1	−2.0	−0.7	−2.0	0.0	0.0	−0.1	0.1	−0.3	−0.1
Euro Area (agg)[a]	−0.1	−1.1	0.3	−1.0	−0.1	−0.1	−0.1	0.1	−0.1	0.0

Source IMF (2020) Authors' Calculation
[a]Euro area policy gap contributions are GDP-weighted averages of the 11 largest Euro area economies

Table 3 Breakdown of 2021 policy gap contribution: fiscal balance/GDP (in percent)

Country	*Overall contribution*	*Beta*	*Policy gap*[a]	(P–P*)	P	P*	P_wo	P*_wo
Argentina	0.8	0.31	2.5	–1.6	–3.1	–1.5	–5.7	–1.6
Australia	–0.9	0.31	–3.0	–7.1	–7.1	0.0	–5.7	–1.6
Belgium	–0.2	0.31	–0.8	–4.9	–5.3	–0.4	–5.7	–1.6
Brazil	1.1	0.31	3.5	–0.6	–4.1	–3.5	–5.7	–1.6
Canada	0.1	0.31	0.4	–3.7	–4.4	–0.7	–5.7	–1.6
China	0.2	0.31	0.6	–3.5	–5.4	–1.9	–5.7	–1.6
France	0.0	0.31	–0.1	–4.2	–5.3	–1.1	–5.7	–1.6
Germany	0.5	0.31	1.7	–2.4	–2.9	–0.5	–5.7	–1.6
India	0.4	0.31	1.2	–2.9	–8.7	–5.8	–5.7	–1.6
Indonesia	0.9	0.31	2.8	–1.3	–3.8	–2.5	–5.7	–1.6
Italy	–0.5	0.31	–1.7	–5.8	–5.3	0.5	–5.7	–1.6
Japan	–0.6	0.31	–2.0	–6.1	–6.6	–0.5	–5.7	–1.6
Korea	1.3	0.31	4.4	0.3	0.3	0.0	–5.7	–1.6
Malaysia	0.6	0.31	1.8	–2.3	–4.8	–2.5	–5.7	–1.6
Mexico	1.2	0.31	4.1	0.0	–2.8	–2.8	–5.7	–1.6
Netherlands	1.0	0.31	3.2	–0.9	–1.9	–1.0	–5.7	–1.6
Poland	1.0	0.31	3.4	–0.7	–1.7	–1.0	–5.7	–1.6
Russia	0.3	0.31	0.8	–3.3	0.5	3.8	–5.7	–1.6

Country	*Overall contribution*	*Beta*	*Policy gap*[a]	(P–P*)	P	P*	P_wo	P*_wo
South Africa	0.5	0.31	1.7	–2.4	–3.8	–1.4	–5.7	–1.6
Spain	0.7	0.31	2.3	–1.8	–3.8	–2.0	–5.7	–1.6
Sweden	1.0	0.31	3.2	–0.9	–0.5	0.3	–5.7	–1.6
Switzerland	1.4	0.31	4.7	0.6	–0.4	–1.0	–5.7	–1.6
Thailand	0.1	0.31	0.3	–3.8	–6.1	–2.3	–5.7	–1.6
Turkey	1.4	0.31	4.4	0.3	–4	–4.3	–5.7	–1.6
United Kingdom	–0.2	0.31	–0.7	–4.8	–7.2	–2.4	–5.7	–1.6
United States	–0.7	0.31	–2.3	–6.4	–8.1	–1.7	–5.7	–1.6
Euro Area (agg)	0.3	0.31	0.9	–3.2	–3.9	–0.6	–5.7	–1.6

Source IMF (2020) Authors' Calculation
[a] *(P–P_wo) – (P* –P* _wo)*

Table 4 Breakdown of 2021 policy gap contribution: public expenditure on health/GDP (in percent)

Country	*Overall contribution*	*Beta*	*Policy gap* [b]	(P–P*)	P	P*	P_wo	P*_wo	P* *Benchmark from Regression*[c]
Argentina	0.0	–0.30	–0.1	0.0	6.5	6.5	6.7	6.6	4.6
Australia	–0.1	–0.30	0.3	0.4	7.6	7.2	6.7	6.6	7.1
Belgium	–0.1	–0.30	0.3	0.3	8.2	7.9	6.7	6.6	7.5
Brazil	0.2	–0.30	–0.6	–0.5	3.9	4.4	6.7	6.6	3.5
Canada	–0.9	–0.30	3.1	3.2	10.2	7.0	6.7	6.6	7.2
China	0.1	–0.30	–0.4	–0.3	3.7	4.0	6.7	6.6	3.9
France	–0.2	–0.30	0.5	0.6	9.9	9.3	6.7	6.6	8.0
Germany	–0.3	–0.30	1.0	1.1	10.7	9.6	6.7	6.6	8.2
India	0.1	–0.30	–0.3	–0.3	1.5	1.8	6.7	6.6	1.5
Indonesia	0.4	–0.30	–1.5	–1.4	1.6	3.0	6.7	6.6	2.6
Italy	0.0	–0.30	–0.1	0.0	7.6	7.6	6.7	6.6	7.9
Japan	0.0	–0.30	–0.1	0.0	9.1	9.1	6.7	6.6	9.2
Korea	0.3	–0.30	–1.0	–0.9	5.1	6.1	6.7	6.6	6.1
Malaysia	0.6	–0.30	–2.2	–2.1	2.0	4.1	6.7	6.6	4.3
Mexico	0.1	–0.30	–0.5	–0.4	3.2	3.6	6.7	6.6	3.7
Netherlands	–0.1	–0.30	0.4	0.5	9.3	8.8	6.7	6.6	8.0
Poland	0.3	–0.30	–0.9	–0.8	5.5	6.3	6.7	6.6	6.5
Russia	0.3	–0.30	–1.0	–0.9	4.6	5.5	6.7	6.6	5.6

Country	*Overall contribution*	*Beta*	*Policy gap* [b]	(P–P*)	P	P*	P_wo	P*_wo	P* *Benchmark from Regression*[c]
South Africa	–0.1	–0.30	0.3	0.4	4.5	4.1	6.7	6.6	2.8
Spain	0.0	–0.30	–0.1	0.0	6.4	6.4	6.7	6.6	6.8
Sweden	–0.1	–0.30	0.2	0.3	9.3	9.0	6.7	6.6	8.3
Switzerland	–0.1	–0.30	0.2	0.3	7.8	7.5	6.7	6.6	8.0
Thailand	0.1	–0.30	–0.4	–0.3	3.8	4.1	6.7	6.6	4.3
Turkey	–0.4	–0.30	1.3	1.4	5.0	3.6	6.7	6.6	4.7
UK	–0.7	–0.30	2.3	2.3	10.2	7.9	6.7	6.6	7.4
US	0.0	–0.30	–0.1	0.0	8.4	8.4	6.7	6.6	7.6
Euro Area	–0.1	–0.30	0.4	0.5	9.0	8.5	6.7	6.6	7.8

Source IMF (2020) Authors' Calculation

[a]This variable is lagged in estimation, thus 2020 values are shown; before small M.C. adjustment

[b]*(P–P_wo) – (P* –P*_wo)*

[c]Fitted value from cross-country regression of public health expenditure on relative per capita income, old age dependency, and income inequality (Gini coefficient). For reference, desk value may differ

Table 5 Breakdown of 2021 policy gap contribution: (Change in FX reserves)/GDP (in percent)

Country	*Overall contribution*	*Beta*	*Policy gap* [b]	(P_KC) – (P_KC)*	(P_KC)	(P_KC)*	(P_KC)_wo	(P_KC)*_wo	*Components*			
									P	P*	KC	KC*
Argentina	0.0	0.63	0.0	0.3	0.6	0.3	0.3	0.0	0.9	1.0	0.64	0.29
Australia	–0.1	0.63	–0.2	0.1	0.1	0.0	0.3	0.0	1.0	0.0	0.12	0.12
Belgium	–0.1	0.63	–0.1	0.2	0.2	0.0	0.3	0.0	1.4	0.0	0.14	0.14
Brazil	–0.3	0.63	–0.5	–0.2	–0.2	0.0	0.3	0.0	–0.5	0.0	0.46	0.29
Canada	–0.1	0.63	–0.2	0.1	0.1	0.0	0.3	0.0	1.0	0.0	0.08	0.08
China	0.3	0.63	0.5	0.8	0.8	0.0	0.3	0.0	1.1	0.0	0.72	0.29
France	–0.2	0.63	–0.3	0.1	0.1	0.0	0.3	0.0	0.9	0.0	0.07	0.07
Germany	–0.1	0.63	–0.1	0.2	0.2	0.0	0.3	0.0	0.9	0.0	0.25	0.25
India	–0.1	0.63	–0.1	0.2	0.2	0.0	0.3	0.0	0.2	0.0	0.78	0.29
Indonesia	–0.4	0.63	–0.6	–0.3	–0.3	0.0	0.3	0.0	–0.6	0.0	0.46	0.29
Italy	–0.2	0.63	–0.3	0.0	0.0	0.0	0.3	0.0	1.2	0.0	0.03	0.03
Japan	–0.1	0.63	–0.2	0.1	0.1	0.0	0.3	0.0	1.8	0.0	0.05	0.05
Korea	–0.2	0.63	–0.3	0.0	0.0	0.0	0.3	0.0	0.5	0.0	0.07	0.07
Malaysia	0.6	0.63	1.0	1.3	1.3	0.0	0.3	0.0	2.3	0.0	0.58	0.29
Mexico	0.0	0.63	0.0	0.3	0.3	0.0	0.3	0.0	0.8	0.0	0.44	0.29
Netherlands	–0.2	0.63	–0.3	0.0	0.0	0.0	0.3	0.0	1.1	0.0	0.03	0.03
Poland	0.5	0.63	0.8	1.2	1.2	0.0	0.3	0.0	2.8	0.0	0.41	0.29

Country	*Overall contribution*	*Beta*	*Policy gap* [b]	(P_KC) – (P_KC)*	(P_KC)	(P_KC)*	(P_KC)_wo	(P_KC)*_wo	*Components*			
									P	P*	KC	KC*
Russia	0.7	0.63	1.2	1.5	1.5	0.0	0.3	0.0	3.7	0.0	0.41	0.29
South Africa	–0.3	0.63	–0.5	–0.2	0.7	0.9	0.3	0.0	1.1	3.0	0.61	0.29
Spain	–0.1	0.63	–0.2	0.2	0.2	0.0	0.3	0.0	1.0	0.0	0.17	0.17
Sweden	–0.1	0.63	–0.2	0.1	0.1	0.0	0.3	0.0	0.9	0.0	0.15	0.15
Switzerland	0.5	0.63	0.9	1.2	1.2	0.0	0.3	0.0	6.3	0.0	0.19	0.19
Thailand	–0.4	0.63	–0.6	–0.3	–0.3	0.0	0.3	0.0	–0.6	0.0	0.53	0.29
Turkey	0.1	0.63	0.2	0.5	0.9	0.4	0.3	0.0	2.3	1.2	0.39	0.29
UK	–0.1	0.63	–0.2	0.1	0.1	0.0	0.3	0.0	0.9	0.0	0.10	0.10
US	–0.1	0.63	–0.2	0.1	0.1	0.0	0.3	0.0	0.6	0.0	0.20	0.20
Euro Area	–0.1	0.63	–0.2	0.1	0.1	0.0	0.3	0.0	1.0	0.0	0.14	0.14

[a] Before small Multilateral Consistency adjustment

[b] [(*P_KC*) (*P_KC*)_*wo*] – [(*P_KC*)* – (*P_KC*)* _*wo*]

Table 6 Breakdown of 2021 policy gap contribution: private credit/GDP (HP detrended) (in percent)

Country	*Overall contribution*	*Beta*	*Policy gap*[a]	(P–P*)	P	P*	P_wo	P*_wo
Argentina	–0.1	–0.10	0.8	–0.4	–0.4	0.0	–0.8	0.4
Australia	0.0	–0.10	–0.5	–1.7	–1.7	0.0	–0.8	0.4
Belgium	–0.3	–0.10	3.4	2.2	2.2	0.0	–0.8	0.4
Brazil	–0.7	–0.10	6.8	5.6	5.6	0.0	–0.8	0.4
Canada	–0.2	–0.10	2.4	1.2	1.2	0.0	–0.8	0.4
China	0.7	–0.10	–7.5	–8.7	–8.7	0.0	–0.8	0.4
France	0.0	–0.10	0.1	–1.1	–1.1	0.0	–0.8	0.4
Germany	–1.0	–0.10	10.2	8.9	8.9	0.0	–0.8	0.4
India	0.7	–0.10	–7.5	–8.7	–8.7	0.0	–0.8	0.4
Indonesia	0.2	–0.10	1.9	0.7	0.7	0.0	–0.8	0.4
Italy	0.8	–0.10	–8.6	–9.8	–9.8	0.0	–0.8	0.4
Japan	–1.1	–0.10	11.2	9.9	18.9	9.0	–0.8	0.4
Korea	–1.4	–0.10	14.7	13.5	13.5	0.0	–0.8	0.4
Malaysia	–0.6	–0.10	5.8	4.5	4.5	0.0	–0.8	0.4
Mexico	–0.1	–0.10	1.0	–0.2	–0.2	0.0	–0.8	0.4
Netherlands	1.2	–0.10	–12.9	–14.1	–14.1	0.0	–0.8	0.4
Poland	0.8	–0.10	–8.7	–10.0	–10.0	0.0	–0.8	0.4
Russia	0.5	–0.10	–5.7	–6.9	–6.9	0.0	–0.8	0.4

Country	*Overall contribution*	*Beta*	*Policy gap*[a]	(P–P*)	P	P*	P_wo	P*_wo
South Africa	0.4	–0.10	–3.7	–4.9	–4.9	0.0	–0.8	0.4
Spain	–0.4	–0.10	4.2	3.0	2.0	–1.0	–0.8	0.4
Sweden	–0.6	–0.10	6.5	5.3	5.3	0.0	–0.8	0.4
Switzerland	–1.9	–0.10	19.5	18.3	18.3	0.0	–0.8	0.4
Thailand	–1.1	–0.10	11.0	9.8	9.8	0.0	–0.8	0.4
Turkey	0.5	–0.10	–4.8	–6.0	–6.0	0.0	–0.8	0.4
UK	0.7	–0.10	–7.2	–8.4	–8.4	0.0	–0.8	0.4
US	–0.3	–0.10	2.7	1.5	1.5	0.0	–0.8	0.4
Euro Area	–0.1	–0.10	1.5	0.3	0.0	–0.3	–0.8	0.4

Source IMF (2022); Authors' Calculation
[a] $(P–P\_wo) − (P^* − P^*\_wo)$

Table 7 Estimated contribution to current account of output gap and TOT gap in 2021 (in percent)

Country	*ToT gap * openness coefficient contribution*		*= Data*	*0.29*	*REER log-change (lagged) coefficient = contribution*	*−0.01 Data*	*Contribution sum*
	*tgap*open*	*tgap*open*	*tgap*	*open2y*	*L.REER log chg*	*L.REER log chg*	
Argentina	0.2	0.7	4.6	16.2	0.0	2.3	0.9
Australia	1.9	6.5	30.7	21.1	0.0	−0.8	1.8
Belgium	−0.2	−0.7	−0.9	85.8	0.0	1.4	−0.4
Brazil	0.7	2.6	13.5	19.1	0.3	−23.1	1.1
Canada	0.3	1.1	3.5	30.7	0.0	−1.1	0.4
China	−0.5	−1.7	−9.0	18.7	0.0	2.0	−0.4
France	−0.1	−0.4	−1.2	31.8	0.0	1.0	0.1
Germany	−0.3	−0.9	−2.0	44.8	0.0	1.3	−0.1
India	−0.3	−1.2	−5.2	22.6	0.0	0.3	0.4
Indonesia	0.7	2.6	13.1	19.6	0.0	−1.3	1.8
Italy	−0.4	−1.2	−3.9	31.6	0.0	0.5	0.3
Japan	−0.4	−1.5	−7.7	18.8	0.0	0.9	0.0
Korea	−0.8	−2.6	−6.4	40.6	0.0	−1.9	−0.7
Malaysia	0.4	1.2	1.9	65.3	0.1	−3.7	1.2
Mexico	−0.2	−0.7	−1.6	41.1	0.1	−7.9	1.1
Netherlands	−0.1	−0.3	−0.4	78.1	0.0	1.9	−0.2
Poland	0.0	0.0	0.0	58.4	0.0	0.7	−0.3

Country	*ToT gap * openness coefficient contribution*		*= Data*	*0.29*	*REER log-change (lagged) coefficient = contribution*	*−0.01 Data*	*Contribution sum*
	*tgap*open*	*tgap*open*	*tgap*	*open2y*	*L.REER log chg*	*L.REER log chg*	
Russia	0.2	0.6	2.3	26.1	0.1	−7.7	−0.2
South Africa	0.8	2.7	9.5	27.9	0.1	−9.7	2.3
Spain	−0.2	−0.6	−1.8	34.2	0.0	0.5	1.0
Sweden	0.2	0.7	1.5	44.4	0.0	2.4	0.2
Switzerland	−0.4	−1.2	−1.9	63.3	−0.1	3.7	−0.6
Thailand	−0.3	−1.2	−2.1	57.4	0.0	−2.7	0.6
Türkiye	−0.4	−1.4	−3.8	35.2	0.2	−10.6	−1.1
UK	−0.2	−0.8	−2.9	27.6	0.0	0.2	−0.6
US	0.1	0.3	2.4	12.9	0.0	1.3	−0.4
Euro Area	−0.2	−0.7	−1.6	45.9	0.0	1.0	0.1

Source IMF (2022); Authors' Calculation

Table 8 EBA analysis of the CA: coefficients

	(1) *Previous model*	*(2)* *Refined model*
Temporary and Cyclical Factors		
Output gap	−0.356***	−0.297***
Commodity terms of trade, interacted with trade openness	0.161***	0.291***
REER annual log-change (lagged)		−0.015***
Macroeconomic Fundamentals		
Net foreign asset (NFA) position	0.023***	0.036***
NFA, interacted with high debt dummy	−0.006	
Output per worker	0.023	0.034***
Expected GDP growth	−0.302***	−0.296***
Reserve currency status (RCS)	−0.030***	
Structural Fundamentals		
Old-age dependency ratio (OAD)	−0.069	−0.096**
Population growth	−0.692*	−0.797**
Share of prime-aged savers	0.138**	0.124**
Life expectancy	−0.005***	−0.004***
Life expectancy, interacted with OAD	0.013***	0.013***
Institutional quality	−0.047**	−0.046**
Oil and gas reserves	0.310***	0.304***

	(1) *Previous model*	(2) *Refined model*
Policy Variables		
Fiscal policy	0.329***	0.307***
Health spending	–0.399***	–0.298**
FXI, interacted with capital controls	0.754***	0.631***
Credit gap	–0.104***	–0.096***
Output per worker, interacted with capital openness	0.041*	
Global risk aversion, interacted with capital openness	0.020	
Global risk aversion, interacted with capital openness and RCS	0.002	
Observations	1367	1480
R-squared	0.550	0.525
Root MSE	0.031	0.032
Number of economies	49	52

Source Authors' calculation

* Significant at 10 percent; ** significant at 5 percent; *** significant at 1 percent based on Driscoll- Kraay standard errors (not shown)

5.2 *REER Regression-Based Analysis: Index REER*

This section contains results from the EBA analysis of 2021 (year average) REER index values. The summary table (Table 9) identifies a Total (Index) REER Gap as the sum of two parts: a gap that arises from the estimated contributions of policy gaps, and a gap that is the regression residual. As with the CA gaps, the REER gap estimates are adjusted for multilateral consistency. Table 10 breaks down the policy gap contributions into the four policies covered by EBA's REER regression-based analysis (health expenditure, reserves accumulation interacted with capital controls, private credit, and the real short term interest rate interacted with capital openness). The contributions of each policy gap are calculated analogously to the procedure used for the CA analysis, and as with the CA tables, the reported estimates show both the total contribution and the subcomponent that is "domestic" for each policy gap. Finally, Table 11 shows the estimated coefficients of the Index REER model (Tables 12–14).

5.3 *REER Regression-Based Analysis: Level REER*

This section contains results from the EBA analysis of 2021 (year average) levels of the REER. The key difference with respect to the results presented in Section II is that the regression analysis uses a measure of the level of the economy's real exchange rate as the dependent variable (rather than a REER index, which contains no information about the relative prices across economies). In addition, the Level REER regression only identifies the contributions of three policy variables to the REER gap (health expenditure, reserves accumulation interacted with capital controls, and the real short term interest rate interacted with capital openness). The structure and presentation of the tables are similar to that of Sect. 2.

Table 9 EBA regression analysis of the 2021 REER using the REER-index model (in percent)

	Net contributions of policy gaps							
	Total REER Gap[a]	*Sum*	*Health exp.*	*Reserves*	*Private credit*	*Real interest rate*	*Residual*[a]	*Memo: Dec'2021 REER, % dev. from 2020 avg REER (GDS)*
Argentina	7.6	−0.5	−0.1	−0.3	−0.1	−0.1	8.2	16.1
Australia	−2.3	2.1	0.4	0.3	−0.2	1.6	−4.4	3.3
Belgium	12.0	2.1	−0.3	0.1	0.3	2.0	10.0	0.0
Brazil	−36.4	0.1	−1.3	0.9	0.6	−0.1	−36.5	−3.9
Canada	6.7	4.9	6.0	0.2	0.1	−1.4	1.8	3.2
China	10.5	−2.1	−0.8	−1.1	−1.2	1.0	12.7	5.6
France	−2.1	2.7	0.4	0.4	−0.1	2.1	−4.8	−2.6
Germany	7.7	4.7	1.6	0.1	1.1	1.9	3.0	−0.5
India	10.1	−0.5	−0.8	0.2	−0.9	1.0	10.6	0.5
Indonesia	1.9	−0.6	−2.8	1.1	0.0	1.1	2.5	−0.1
Italy	8.6	0.5	−0.8	0.4	−1.1	1.9	8.0	−1.3
Japan	−20.1	2.7	0.0	0.5	1.0	1.2	−22.8	−11.9
Korea	−0.8	1.7	−1.3	0.6	1.4	1.0	−2.5	−1.9
Malaysia	−22.4	−4.5	−4.1	−2.1	0.4	1.4	−18.0	−2.2
Mexico	−9.1	−1.9	−1.0	−0.3	−0.1	−0.4	−7.3	3.6
Netherlands	21.9	1.0	0.1	0.4	−1.5	1.9	21.0	0.5
Poland	−1.0	−2.6	−2.5	−1.7	−1.0	2.7	1.5	−0.3

(continued)

Table 9 (continued)

	Net contributions of policy gaps							
	Total REER Gap[a]	*Sum*	*Health exp.*	*Reserves*	*Private credit*	*Real interest rate*	*Residual*[a]	*Memo: Dec'2021 REER, % dev. from 2020 avg REER (GDS)*
Russia	−11.2	−3.3	−2.3	−2.3	−0.7	1.9	−7.9	2.8
South Africa	1.2	2.6	0.2	0.9	−0.5	2.0	−1.4	4.7
Spain	8.8	1.8	−0.9	0.1	0.4	2.2	7.0	1.4
Sweden	−11.1	2.5	−0.3	0.2	0.6	2.0	−13.6	0.4
Switzerland	10.5	2.3	−0.2	−1.8	1.8	2.6	8.2	−1.6
Thailand	6.0	2.7	−0.6	1.2	0.9	1.3	3.2	−8.6
Turkey	−41.1	−1.7	2.1	−0.5	−0.6	−2.8	−39.4	−29.6
United Kingdom	−7.5	3.7	4.0	0.3	−0.9	0.3	−11.2	3.8
United States	1.6	−0.7	−0.9	0.3	0.1	−0.2	2.3	1.7
Euro Area	6.8	2.5	0.2	0.2	0.1	2.0	4.2	−1.3

Source IMF (2022)

[a]For multilateral consistency, adjusted by the weighted average of the 2021 regression residuals (subtracting −4.8 percent)

Table 10 Estimated policy gap contributions in the 2021 REER-index model (in percent)

	All (sum)		*Health exp.*		*Δ in reserves*		*Private credit*		*Interest rate*	
	Total	*Dom.*	*Total*	*Dom.*	*Total*	*Dom.*	*Total*	*Dom.*	*Total*	*Dom.*
Argentina	−0.5	−2.4	−0.1	0.0	−0.3	−0.6	−0.1	0.0	−0.1	−1.8
Australia	2.1	0.3	0.4	0.8	0.3	−0.2	−0.2	−0.2	1.6	0.0
Belgium	2.1	0.4	−0.3	0.6	0.1	−0.4	0.3	0.2	2.0	−0.1
Brazil	0.1	−1.7	−1.3	−1.0	0.9	0.4	0.6	0.6	−0.1	−1.7
Canada	4.9	3.1	6.0	6.1	0.2	−0.2	0.1	0.1	−1.4	−2.9
China	−2.1	−3.4	−0.8	−0.6	−1.1	−1.5	−1.2	−0.9	1.0	−0.5
France	2.7	0.9	0.4	1.1	0.4	−0.1	−0.1	−0.1	2.1	0.0
Germany	4.7	2.4	1.6	2.1	0.1	−0.4	1.1	0.9	1.9	−0.1
India	−0.5	−2.3	−0.8	−0.5	0.2	−0.3	−0.9	−0.9	1.0	−0.6
Indonesia	−0.6	−2.3	−2.8	−2.6	1.1	0.5	0.0	0.1	1.1	−0.2
Italy	0.5	−1.1	−0.8	0.0	0.4	−0.1	−1.1	−1.0	1.9	−0.1
Japan	2.7	0.8	0.0	0.0	0.5	−0.2	1.0	1.0	1.2	0.0
Korea	1.7	0.0	−1.3	−1.2	0.6	−0.1	1.4	1.3	1.0	0.0
Malaysia	−4.5	−5.9	−4.1	−4.0	−2.1	−2.6	0.4	0.5	1.4	0.1
Mexico	−1.9	−3.4	−1.0	−0.7	−0.3	−0.7	−0.1	0.0	−0.4	−2.0
Netherlands	1.0	−0.6	0.1	1.0	0.4	−0.1	−1.5	−1.4	1.9	−0.1
Poland	−2.6	−4.3	−2.5	−1.6	−1.7	−2.2	−1.0	−1.0	2.7	0.4

(continued)

Table 10 (continued)

	All (sum)		*Health exp.*		*Δ in reserves*		*Private credit*		*Interest rate*	
	Total	*Dom.*	*Total*	*Dom.*	*Total*	*Dom.*	*Total*	*Dom.*	*Total*	*Dom.*
Russia	−3.3	−5.1	−2.3	−1.7	−2.3	−2.8	−0.7	−0.7	1.9	0.1
South Africa	2.6	1.0	0.2	0.8	0.9	0.5	−0.5	−0.5	2.0	0.3
Spain	1.8	−0.1	−0.9	0.0	0.1	−0.3	0.4	0.3	2.2	−0.1
Sweden	2.5	0.8	−0.3	0.6	0.2	−0.3	0.6	0.5	2.0	0.0
Switzerland	2.3	0.6	−0.2	0.6	−1.8	−2.2	1.8	1.8	2.6	0.4
Thailand	2.7	1.1	−0.6	−0.6	1.2	0.6	0.9	1.0	1.3	0.1
Türkiye	−1.7	−3.8	2.1	2.7	−0.5	−1.0	−0.6	−0.6	−2.8	−4.9
United Kingdom	3.7	1.6	4.0	4.4	0.3	−0.2	−0.9	−0.8	0.3	−1.8
United States	−0.7	−1.8	−0.9	0.0	0.3	−0.2	0.1	0.2	−0.2	−1.7

Source IMF (2022)

Table 11 EBA analysis of the index REER: coefficients

	(1) *Previous model*	*(2)* *Refined model*
Cyclical Factors		
Output Gap	0.392**	0.516**
Commodity terms of trade (log, index)	0.184***	0.160***
Macroeconomic Fundamentals		
Net foreign asset (NFA) position	–0.109***	–0.105***
Output per worker	0.217***	0.241***
Expected GDP growth	2.012***	3.112***
Financial Home bias (lagged)	0.193***	0.258***
Reserve currency status (RCS)	–0.068	
Structural Fundamentals		
Population growth	2.003	
Trade Openness	–0.208***	–0.153
Share of administered prices in CPI	–1.713***	
Policy Variables		
Real interest rates, interacted with capital openness	0.697***	0.875***
Health spending	2.040***	1.886**
Credit gap	0.093***	0.099**
Global risk aversion, interacted with capital open	–0.164***	
Global risk aversion, interacted with capital open	0.483**	
FXI, interacted with capital controls	–2.479**	–1.901*
Observations	1004	1105
Adjusted R-squared	0.553	0.557
RMSE	0.086	0.090
Cragg-Donald Wald F statistic		36.509
Number of Economies	40	41

Source IMF (2022)

* Significant at 10 percent; ** significant at 5 percent; *** significant at 1 percent based on heteroskedastic and autocorrelation-consistent standard errors (not shown)

Table 12 EBA regression analysis of the 2021 REER using the REER-level model (in percent)

	Total REER gap[a]	*Net contributions of policy gaps*				*Residual*[a]
		Sum	*Health exp.*	*Reserves*	*Real interest rate*	
Argentina	−8.7	−1.6	−0.1	−1.2	−0.2	−7.0
Australia	24.6	4.8	0.7	1.3	2.8	19.7
Belgium	26.1	3.3	−0.5	0.3	3.5	22.7
Brazil	−19.6	1.8	−2.5	4.5	−0.1	−21.4
Canada	−7.2	10.2	11.4	1.1	−2.3	−17.4
China	10.5	−5.3	−1.6	−5.4	1.7	15.7
France	8.2	6.1	0.7	1.7	3.6	2.1
Germany	−7.9	6.9	3.0	0.5	3.3	−14.7
India	8.5	1.0	−1.5	0.8	1.7	7.5
Indonesia	−18.1	1.9	−5.2	5.3	1.9	−20.0
Italy	10.8	4.0	−1.5	2.1	3.4	6.8
Japan	−18.4	4.3	0.1	2.2	2.0	−22.8
Korea	4.2	2.2	−2.5	2.9	1.8	2.0
Malaysia	−29.1	−15.7	−7.8	−10.3	2.4	−13.4
Mexico	7.7	−4.2	−1.9	−1.6	−0.7	11.9
Netherlands	6.0	5.5	0.1	2.0	3.4	0.6
Poland	−20.2	−8.4	−4.7	−8.3	4.6	−11.8

	Total REER gap[a]	*Net contributions of policy gaps*				*Residual*[a]
		Sum	*Health exp.*	*Reserves*	*Real interest rate*	
Russia	–33.8	–12.4	–4.3	–11.4	3.3	–21.4
South Africa	15.9	8.4	0.3	4.6	3.5	7.5
Spain	26.4	2.6	–1.7	0.5	3.7	23.8
Sweden	–14.8	3.9	–0.6	1.0	3.5	–18.7
Switzerland	16.8	–4.9	–0.5	–8.9	4.4	21.7
Thailand	–2.8	6.8	–1.1	5.7	2.2	–9.5
Turkey	–50.5	–3.1	4.0	–2.3	–4.8	–47.4
United Kingdom	5.6	9.4	7.6	1.4	0.5	–3.9
United States	8.9	–0.5	–1.7	1.6	–0.4	9.4
Euro Area	7.1	5.0	0.4	1.2	3.4	2.0

Source IMF (2022)

[a]For multilateral consistency, adjusted by the weighted average of the 2021 regression residuals (subtracting –9.4 percent)

Table 13 Estimated policy gap contributions in the 2021 REER-level model

	All (sum)		*Health exp.*		*Δ in reserves*		*Interest rate*	
	Total	*Dom.*	*Total*	*Dom.*	*Total*	*Dom.*	*Total*	*Dom.*
Argentina	−1.6	−6.1	−0.1	0.0	−1.2	−3.0	−0.2	−3.1
Australia	4.8	0.3	0.7	1.4	1.3	−1.1	2.8	−0.1
Belgium	3.3	−0.8	−0.5	1.2	0.3	−1.8	3.5	−0.1
Brazil	1.8	−2.8	−2.5	−1.9	4.5	2.0	−0.1	−3.0
Canada	10.2	5.7	11.4	11.5	1.1	−0.8	−2.3	−5.0
China	−5.3	−9.1	−1.6	−1.1	−5.4	−7.1	1.7	−0.8
France	6.1	1.5	0.7	2.1	1.7	−0.6	3.6	−0.1
Germany	6.9	1.7	3.0	3.9	0.5	−2.1	3.3	−0.1
India	1.0	−3.6	−1.5	−0.9	0.8	−1.7	1.7	−1.0
Indonesia	1.9	−2.8	−5.2	−5.0	5.3	2.7	1.9	−0.4
Italy	4.0	−0.5	−1.5	0.0	2.1	−0.4	3.4	−0.1
Japan	4.3	−0.8	0.1	0.0	2.2	−0.8	2.0	0.0
Korea	2.2	−2.7	−2.5	−2.3	2.9	−0.3	1.8	0.0
Malaysia	−15.7	−19.8	−7.8	−7.5	−10.3	−12.5	2.4	0.2
Mexico	−4.2	−8.0	−1.9	−1.4	−1.6	−3.2	−0.7	−3.4
Netherlands	5.5	1.3	0.1	1.8	2.0	−0.4	3.4	−0.1
Poland	−8.4	−13.0	−4.7	−2.9	−8.3	−10.7	4.6	0.7

	All (sum)		*Health exp.*		*Δ in reserves*		*Interest rate*	
	Total	*Dom.*	*Total*	*Dom.*	*Total*	*Dom.*	*Total*	*Dom.*
Russia	–12.4	–17.0	–4.3	–3.2	–11.4	–13.9	3.3	0.1
South Africa	8.4	4.2	0.3	1.4	4.6	2.3	3.5	0.5
Spain	2.6	–1.7	–1.7	0.0	0.5	–1.5	3.7	–0.1
Sweden	3.9	–0.3	–0.6	1.1	1.0	–1.3	3.5	–0.1
Switzerland	–4.9	–9.1	–0.5	1.1	–8.9	–10.9	4.4	0.7
Thailand	6.8	1.9	–1.1	–1.1	5.7	2.8	2.2	0.2
Türkiye	–3.1	–8.2	4.0	5.1	–2.3	–4.8	–4.8	–8.5
United Kingdom	9.4	4.4	7.6	8.3	1.4	–0.8	0.5	–3.1
United States	–0.5	–4.0	–1.7	0.0	1.6	–1.1	–0.4	–2.9

Source IMF (2022)

Table 14 EBA analysis of the level REER: coefficients

	(1) *Previous model*	*(2)* *Refined model*
Cyclical Factors		
Commodity terms of trade, interacted with trade o	0.064***	0.054
Macroeconomic Fundamentals		
Net foreign asset (NFA) position	0.056***	0.112***
Output per worker	0.171***	0.247***
Expected GDP growth	1.961**	3.308***
Reserve currency status (RCS)	–0.357***	–0.174**
Capital stock per employed person (lagged)	0.110***	
Traded/Non Traded productivity (log, lagged)	0.184***	0.180***
Structural Fundamentals		
Old-age dependency ratio (OAD)	0.362*	0.894***
Population growth	2.570	9.081***
Institutional quality	0.653***	0.587***
Trade Openness	–0.336***	–0.400***
VAT revenue, percent of GDP	0.662	1.209**
Share of administered prices in CPI	–2.809***	
Policy Variables		
Real interest rates, interacted with capital openness	0.585*	1.511***
FXI, interacted with capital controls	–3.561*	–9.290***
Health spending	4.196***	3.580***
Credit gap	0.032	
Global risk aversion, interacted with capital openness	–0.150	
Global risk aversion, interacted with capital open	0.829	
Observations	990	1078
Adjusted R-squared	0.893	0.801
RMSE	0.146	0.194
Cragg-Donald Wald F statistic	66.224	40.831
Number of Economies	39	40

Source IMF (2022)

* Significant at 10 percent; ** significant at 5 percent; *** significant at 1 percent based on heteroskedastic and autocorrelation-consistent standard errors (not shown)

6 Conclusion

The biggest challenge for emerging market economies that have been hit by multiple shocks (Pandemic, war and geopolitical tensions) is that capital tends to flee to safer havens in developed economies. When the first shock hit, emerging market economies had little fiscal space. The advanced economies spent around 28 percent of GDP to support their citizens and businesses during the pandemic, while the share of emerging market economies was about 6–7 percent and for low-income countries, it was around 2–3 percent of GDP. The pandemic and subsequent efforts to recover exhausted their fiscal space, leaving them on weaker ground. The Russia-Ukraine war started with stubborn inflation that forced aggressive monetary policy measures by central banks. The appreciation of the dollar in the US and the depreciation of currencies in emerging markets put further upward pressure on capital inflows into the US. But emerging market economies with robust forex reserves and good macroeconomic policies weathered the onslaught of the pandemic war and inflation.

Economies like India believe that inflation is not transitory in nature and policy action was needed at the earliest. As far as India is concerned, the Pandemic had mixed blessings. While it was terrible for people and the economy, the country put digitalization on steroids. India adopted a better fiscal policy and placed both taxation and public expenditure on digital platforms. This resulted in improvements in tax collection and targeting the subsidies. Financial inclusion really worked, and more attention was paid to the quality of education.

Different economies responded to the pandemic in different ways. While India focused on supply side interventions and infrastructure expenditure, many economies put money directly into the pockets of people. In the case of India, it was less money in the pockets of people but was well targeted due to digitalization. One general lesson of the pandemic is that countries that build social safety nets fare much better in times of shocks as they immediately deploy them for targeted support. The greatest advantage that India gained at the start of COVID was the digital identity and public infrastructure. While there was support, it wasn't over the top.

When the next crisis hit, India didn't have much of a buffer as it built up a healthy foreign exchange reserves and vaccinated the population with digital India. The country lost a lot of people as a result of its weak health system. The pandemic opened the eyes of the country's leaders and led them to invest more in health systems rather than just vaccines. India effectively used its financial resources in the aftermath of the COVID Pandemic as accelerated digitalization and digital public infrastructure helped to improve tax collection and target the expenditure to the needy.

References

Asare, V.-S., & Barf, R. (2021). The impact of COVID-19 pandemic on the global economy: Emphasis on poverty alleviation and economic growth. *The Economics and Finance Letters, 8*(1), 32–43.

Aziz, A. (2022). Impact of Covid-19 pandemic on the social and economic life of religious minorities in Karnataka: A concept note, seminar on religious minorities in Karnataka. National Law School of India University.

Chandrappa, C. (2022). The status of Buddists in Karnataka, Seminar on religious minorities in Karnataka. National Law School of India University.

Desai, R. G. (2022). Impact of Covid-19 pandemic on the social and economic life of Jain minorities in Karnataka; some case studies, Seminar on religious minorities in Karnataka. National Law School of India University.

George, S. (2022). From fear, hate and stigmatization to cooperation and caring: Covid-19 and the shifting discourses of resilience in the public sphere influenced by the faith-based organisation in India, Seminar on religious minorities in Karnataka. National Law School of India University.

https://www.eiu.com/n/campaigns/global-economic-outlook-sept2023/?utm_source=google&utm_medium=paid-search&utm_campaign=sept-23-global-outlook-wp&gclid=CjwKCAjwnOipBhBQEiwACyGLuqdkCsdtTy327F1lH0wt354bkBw0BMY668o8v6aHR3Xc4z8HeHO95hoCSX8QAvD_BwE

Ikenberry, G. J. (2020). *A world safe for democracy: Liberal internationalism and the crises of global order*. Yale University Press.

International Monetary Fund (2022). *World Economic Outlook Report 2022*. Washington DC.https://www.imf.org/en/Publications/WEO/Issues/2022/10/11/world-economic-outlook-october-2022

Marshall, M. G., & Elzinga-Marshall, G. (2017). *Global report 2017: Conflict, governance and state fragility*. Center for Systemic Peace.

Murdoch, J. C., & Sandler, T. (2004). Civil wars and economic growth: Spatial dispersion. *American Journal of Political Science, 48*(1), 138–151.

Singh, B. (2022). Impact of Covid-19 pandemic on the social and economic life of Sikh minority communities, Seminar on religious minorities in Karnataka. National Law School of India University.

Small, M., & Singer, J. D. (1982). *Resort to arms: International and civil war, 1816–1980*. Sage.

Vakil, S. (2022). Impact of Covid on Parsi community, Seminar on religious minorities in Karnataka. National Law School of India University.

World Economic Forum (2023). Annual Report 2023. https://www.weforum.org/publications/annual-report-2022-2023/

CHAPTER 3

Impact of Covid-19 on Household Consumption Behavior

Ashraf Mishrif and Jaynab Yousuf

1 Introduction

The pandemic has undoubtedly affected people's lifestyles all around the globe. On March 11, 2020, the World Health Organization (WHO) declared the outbreak of the infectious disease COVID-19 as a pandemic (WHO, 2020). In the absence of a vaccine or an immediate response to curb the spread of the disease, countries were forced to take preventive measures such as lockdowns and social distancing (Kaplan et al., 2020; Verma & Naveen, 2021). This brought about drastic changes and shifts in consumer food shopping and household consumption behaviors. There was evidence of a deep-set lack of trust in the supply food chain and some even speculate that such changes in behavior will persist in the food industry trajectory even after COVID is long gone (Chenarides et al., 2021). Surely the pandemic has emphasized consumers'

A. Mishrif (✉) · J. Yousuf
Humanities Research Center, Sultan Qaboos University, Muscat, Sultanate of Oman
e-mail: ashraf.mishrif@gmail.com

A. Mishrif (ed.), *Economic Effects of the Pandemic*, The Political Economy of the Middle East,
https://doi.org/10.1007/978-981-97-4367-4_3

spending behavior when hit with risks and crises. Valaskova et al. (2015) defined consumer behavior as an "important decision-making process of searching, purchasing, using, evaluating and disposing of products and services". There have been studies conducted previously indicating behavioral changes and changes in utility patterns in consumers during times of crisis (Flatters & Wilmott, 2009; Hoon Ang et al., 2001).

In Oman the government set up the Supreme Committee who were responsible with implementing measures to combat and curb against the spread of the disease on a national level. Like other countries, Oman adhered to the recommendations by WHO to maintain food supply and safety of the population. During the period of full lockdown, online delivery and take-away services were operating along with supermarkets and pharmacies and other places supplying essential items. People were assured that the food supply chain would remain fully functional, and that food supply and stocks would not be disrupted (Table 1). People were also advised not to panic buy and hoard necessary items as the government repeatedly assured the people that they would not face any shortages regarding essential supplies, as this was observed in other countries (Mao, 2020; Sterman & Dogan, 2015).

However, these measures taken by the government may have affected peoples' consumption behavior and household consumptions patterns. Since this outbreak is rather new and although due to vaccination policies, it has seen a decline in the number of infections and spread, yet people are still finding their ways around dealing with it. In the face of the current situation there is a dire need for data and information to assess the extent to which changes have taken place in the household consumption patterns (positive and negative) and whether this change is here to stay for the long haul. After all, little is clearly known about how individuals change their consumption habits in the face of a pandemic. Moreover, it also challenges policy makers to set measures in place that would benefit individuals and business entities and the economy. Therefore, given the above arguments, the aim of this paper is to attempt to close this gap by investigating the impact of Covid-19 on the household consumption patterns in Oman and to also assess whether the change is a permanent or a transient one. Since the pandemic is only a little over two years old, there are not a lot of studies done with the current perspective at hand. A substantial amount of scientific work yet needs to be done in the area. Hence, the chapter intends to fill the gap in the knowledge and data pool, especially with respect to the case of the Sultanate.

Table 1 Main measures to prevent the spread of COVID-19 in Oman

Date	*Measures*
July 21, 2020	Closure of all public places and shops and prohibited the movement of people from 7:00 p.m. to 6:00 a.m. from July 28, 2020, to August 8, 2020
August 7, 2020	Extended the closing date to August 15, 2020, but modify the closing hours from 9:00 p.m. to 5:00 a.m.
October 11, 2020	Prohibiting mobility and closing all public places and stores from 8:00 p.m. to 5:00 a.m. till Saturday, October 24, 2020
March 25, 2021	The timings of closure decision were 8:00 p.m. to 5:00 a.m., and continued until the morning of Thursday, April 8, 2021
June 20, 2021	Made barring individuals and vehicles from moving and closing all public venues and commercial activity (allowing home delivery) from 8:00 p.m. to 4:00 a.m.
July 20, 2021	Prohibiting people and vehicles from moving from 5:00 p.m. to 4:00 a.m., with the option of resuming commercial activities and delivery services until July 31, 2021, and ensuring a four-day closure during the blessed Eid Al-Adha
July 29, 2021	Reduction of the closing hours from 10:00 p.m. to 4:00 a.m. This closure eventually terminated at daybreak, Saturday, August 21, 2021

Source Supreme Committee for Monitoring COVID-19, various statements in 2020–2021

The chapter would be using primary data which was obtained through online questionnaire surveys of 414 households in Oman. The survey was conducted from December 2020 until March 2021. A descriptive analysis will be done for the demographic part of the questionnaire. The rest of the paper is sectioned as follows: literature review highlighting the positive and negative impacts on consumer behavior due to Covid-19 and studies that have dealt with studying consumer behavior in the face of a crisis. The materials and method section will discuss the design and participants, the data, and the tools of analysis. The results and discussion section will present the key findings of the chapter whose implications will be discussed with respect to policy suggestions as well. The paper will present the concluding remarks in the last section.

2 Literature Review

2.1 Positive Impacts of Covid-19

Although the pandemic has been a global nightmare for the most parts, yet it has inadvertently steered some positive changes into people's lives in terms of an improved lifestyle through healthy eating (Carroll et al., 2020; Zwanka & Buff, 2021), practicing mindfulness and increased family time. It also led to a shift in healthy lifestyle for children as parents had more time to focus on and spend with their children due to lockdown measures and stay at home orders. Maestre et al. (2021) confirmed that quarantine and lockdown measures forced families to spend more time with each other at home engaging in healthy cooking and other activities. Also, this led to an increased shift in the purchase of dairy products and fresh produce. Mahmoud et al. (2021) also pointed out how because of the precautionary measures, including closures and home quarantine, individuals, families, and children spend most of the day together, which has strengthened the bond between parents and children as a result. It was found that staying at home increased parents' awareness about healthy nutrition for their children as the covid-19 pandemic was for them an opportunity to use the time to raise their children in a healthy life.

Hesham et al. (2021) and Ben Hassen et al. (2020) pointed out that adults, especially parents started thinking about switching to a healthy life to protect themselves from the risks of infection with this deadly virus. Hesham et al. (2021) also reported that females were more committed to a healthier lifestyle than males and people between the ages 12–86 increased their consumption of fresh vegetables and meat from the supermarkets (Dumitras et al., 2021) which also showed a change in their purchasing habits from unhealthy to healthy foods. The pandemic also saw how people became more reliant in preparing their own meals at home and sustained the habit of eating in even after the effects of the pandemic subsided.

2.2 Negative Impacts of Covid-19

An apparent adverse effect of Covid was the indulgence on panic buying (Verma & Naveen, 2021). Social networking sites aggravated the whole situation by spreading news and rumors about the situation everywhere which further caused panic among people leading them to stockpile necessity goods excessively (Barua, 2021). Also, due to border closures and some products not being available, people buy groceries and other supplies in large quantities. Güngördü Belbağ (2022) reported how people rushed to stores when the news of Covid-19 first broke out to stockpile clothes and groceries. When people indulged in panic buying and hoarding behavior, it gave them a sense of safety. In the United States, the government also at one point in time encouraged people to stockpile so as not to depend on them for charities in case of shortages to avoid spending large sums of money on aid (Loxton et al., 2020). Such consumption behavior during the pandemic, however, was not witnessed in the Sultanate. Ben Hassen et al. (2020) commented that people in Oman did not engage in a panic buying rush and thus, did not undergo feelings of fear or insecurity about the availability of food and non-food items.

Several studies since the outbreak of the virus and since WHO's declaration of the virus as a pandemic documented changes in food purchasing and eating behaviors (AlTarrah et al., 2021). Other studies associated the panic buying behavior more with the fear of not having enough food than concerns of food shortages (Baker et al., 2020). The pandemic saw an apparent increase in the demand for fast food consumption across the globe (Ashby, 2020). This shift in the demand for fast food had several implications for people. During the crisis, they saw food consumption deteriorate since people were not allowed to move around freely due to lockdowns and other restrictive measures. Those who were in quarantine and were infected also resorted to food consumption, especially fast food to fulfill their physical (hunger) and psychological void. Moreover, when some of the restrictions were lifted and lockdowns were lifted, people turned towards dining outside, preferably to fast food joints to rejoice (Carroll et al., 2020).

2.3 Changes in Consumer Behavior

According to Valaskova et al. (2015) consumer behavior can be explained in three approaches: physical based on the relation between the psyche and the behavior of the consumer, sociological based which is related to the reactions and behavior of the consumer in different situations and economic approach which is based on the basic knowledge of the micro economy where consumers express their needs and requirements. Pertaining to this argument, it has been observed that people are not being the same and having different reactions to negative circumstances or crises (Amalia et al., 2012), new trends in consumer behavior can be seen at such times. Mehta et al. (2020) confirmed that during times of crises consumer's attitude and perception to risk are the most important factors and Hoon Ang et al. (2001) added that personality characteristics too influence consumer behavior.

Coibion et al. (2020) studied the causal effects of lockdown on consumer spending using survey data to find out that lockdowns not only negatively affected consumption as well as employment but also affected people's expectations of the economy. Using similar methods (high frequency data) Chronopoulos et al. (2020) examined changes in household spending patterns in the UK to find out groceries shopping, and stockpiling became apparent. Chang and Meyerhoefer (2020) found out that in Taiwan with increases in the number of Covid cases, the demand for online food shopping services also increased. Similar findings were also observed by Alexander and Karger (2020).

Although the above-mentioned studies rather focus on the various impacts Covid-19 has had on consumer behavior, there are yet not a lot of work done on the effects since the effect of Covid has simmered down and the world is trying to get back a sense of the new normal. Moreover, Oman in particular lacks information and more importantly data in such areas. Keeping the limitations of the chapter in mind, it attempts to bridge data and information the void in the scientific pool.

3 Materials and Method

3.1 Study Design and Participants

A cross-sectional study was conducted between 14 December 2020 until 2 June 2022 to survey the impact of COVID-19 on households in Oman. Target population included all adults over the age of 18 years who resided in the Sultanate of Oman during the pandemic. The online questionnaire was prepared in Google Forms and disseminated to all students and staff of the Sultan Qaboos University through public relations. Participants were asked to share it with their acquaintances and peers to reach the largest number of the population to ensure that the survey reaches a wide range of people. During the pandemic online questionnaire survey was considered the most appropriate and safest method for social distancing to limit the spread of COVID-19. Also, e-mails and personal relationships helped to spread the survey widely, faster, and effectively. Moreover, the objectives and purpose of the survey and study were explained to the participants at the beginning of the questionnaire. The identities of the respondents were kept confidential and only data pertaining to the objectives of the study were used. The total number of participants in the study was 414 participants from different groups of society and age.

3.2 *Questionnaire*

The questionnaire was developed by researchers at the Humanities Research Center of Sultan Qaboos University in the Sultanate of Oman. The questionnaire was designed using relevant information from literature and current circumstances that pertained during the time of the study and was published in both languages to cater towards the different backgrounds of the respondents. A pilot study was conducted on 10 researchers within the centers to examine the acceptability and clarity of the questionnaire and the time taken to complete the questionnaire. Minor modifications were made to the questionnaire because of the feedback of the pilot study. A total of 73 questions in the questionnaire were analyzed for the purposes of meeting the objective of the chapter.

Data on demography and social background were obtained through questions on gender, nationality, age, educational qualification, residence (Governorate), marital status, number of family members, number of working members. The section also had questions on the total number of people infected with COVID-19 in the family and their family income. An important section of the questionnaire that has a direct link to the objective of the study consisted of questions on the effects on family expenses due to the pandemic. Respondents were asked about how the electricity bills at home changed during the Covid-19 period, how internet bills changed during Covid-19, whether their family gave up buying unnecessary items to reduce monthly expenses, whether they reduced spending on weddings and social gatherings due to the pandemic, whether their spending on vehicle oil reduced and if their spending on vehicle maintenance decreased. The same section also included questions on if their travel expenses decreased during the period of border closures and movement restrictions, whether their spending on consumables increased, and if the cost of covid-19 treatment and medication is high. The questionnaire also consisted of questions on whether the pandemic led to an additional cost to purchase sterilization and prevention supplies (masks, sterilizers) to protect against Covid-19 and whether their private spending increased for treating family members in private hospitals. Respondents were asked if the exorbitant costs of masks at the beginning of the pandemic have exhausted the family budget. To get a better understanding on if changes due to the pandemic have sustained even after the situation has relaxed, respondents were asked if family members have learned to budget and spend wisely due to COVID-19 and finally, family plans have changed due to COVID-19 and that they have moved towards self-reliance and preferring home cooked meals than dining out or ordering in from restaurants.

3.3 Tools of Analysis

For the purposes of carrying out the study and meeting the objectives, this chapter applied a combination of descriptive analysis and statistical testing to assess the various impacts on household consumption behavior during Covid-19. Data on demography and socio-economic profile of the respondents were analyzed using descriptive statistics through frequency and percentage. Various aspects that capture changes in consumption pattern and behavior were tested against gender and nationality. Variables that depicted whether the change is persistent were also tested against gender and nationality. Similar technique has been used in a study in Kuwait (AlTarrah et al., 2021) and Qatar (Ben Hassen et al., 2020).

A multivariate analysis of variance (MANOVA) test was used to assess changes in consumer behavior during covid-19, in terms of gender and nationality against variables that measured impact on family expenses. MANOVA is normally used when multiple levels of independent variables influence more than one dependent variable, either in combination or alone (Reinhart, n.d.). Also, a descriptive analysis was done to calculate frequencies and percentages of the demographic profile and social background of the respondents. The statistical analysis was performed using IBM SPSS statistics version 26.

4 Results

4.1 Demographic Characteristics

A total of 414 responses were obtained from the questionnaire surveys. Table 2 presents the frequencies and percentages of all the demographic factors of the respondents.

Table 2 Descriptive statistics of respondents' demographic factors

Category	*Variables*	*Frequency*	*Percentage*
Gender	Male	89	21.5
	Female	323	78
Nationality	Omani	389	94
	Non-Omani	23	5.6
Age	18–28	180	43.5
	29–38	146	35.3
	39–48	57	13.8
	49–58	16	3.9
	59 and above	13	3.1
Qualification	Below High School	10	2.4
	High School	61	14.7
	Diploma	64	15.5
	Bachelors	216	52.2
	Masters	36	8.7
	PhD	25	6
Residence	Muscat	167	40.3
	Al Dakhiliya	86	20.8
	Musandam	1	0.2
	Al Buraimi	8	1.9
	Al Dhahira	26	6.3
	Al Batinah South	21	5.1
	Al Batinah North	78	18.8
	Al Sharqiya North	14	3.4
	Al Sharqiya South	10	2.4
	Dhofar	1	0.2
Marital Status	Married	259	62.6
	Unmarried	146	35.3
	Widower	4	1
	Divorced	3	0.7
No. of family members	1–3	97	23.4
	4–6	166	40.1
	7–9	87	21
	10 and above	62	15
No. of working members	None	46	11.1
	1–3	320	77.3
	4–6	29	7
	7–9	14	3.4
	10 and above	3	0.7
Monthly Income (OMR)	>350	43	10.4

(continued)

Table 2 (continued)

Category	*Variables*	*Frequency*	*Percentage*
	351–499	40	9.7
	500–999	108	26.1
	1000–1499	86	20.8
	1500–1999	48	11.6
	<2000	87	21

Of the 414 respondents 78% were females while 21.5% were males. Most of the respondents were Omanis (94%) while only 5.6% of them were non-Omanis. Respondents were also asked about their marital status, number of members in the house and the number of working members in the house.

4.2 *Statistical Analysis*

For the MANOVA test was used to test changes in consumer behavior during Covid-19 against two dependent variables: gender and nationality. Changes in consumer behavior were assessed through the following 14 variables:

FMSPF: self-reliance in preparing food rather than depending on restaurants.
FLSW: members of the household learnt to budget and spend wisely during covid-19.
HCMB: high costs of masks and sterilizers stretched family budget.
IETPH: expenditure of treating family members in private hospital increased during covid-19.
ESSMC: testing kits caused extra spending.
CHTM: covid-19 treatment and medication cost were high.
ISG: expenditure on groceries increased during the pandemic.
RTE: lockdowns and mobility restrictions reduced travelling expenses.
RSVM: vehicle maintenance decreased during the pandemic.
RSCF: expenditure on car fuel decreased during covid-19.
RSG: restrictions minimized expenditure on gatherings and weddings.

FGUIC: giving up on unnecessary spending to balance the budget.
CIB: internet bill increased during the pandemic.
CEB: electricity bill increased during the pandemic.

Table 3 shows the output of the multivariate tests of all the 14 independent variables on the combined dependent variables gender and nationality. Only significant variables have been reported and the implications will be discussed in the discussion section. The multivariate tests results show whether the predictor variables have a significant main effect with the dependent variable(s). For this study, we will be only presenting the Wilk's Lambda effect. However, results of the other effects can be presented upon request. We decided to use Wilk's Lambda because the data is clean. Variables FMSPF, FLSW, HCMB, IETPH, ESSMC, CHTM and FGUIC were found to be statistically significant (at 10%, 5% and 1%). This implies that there was sufficient evidence to reject the null hypothesis that there is no significant difference between the two dependent variables on the above-mentioned predictor variables.

Table 4 shows the results of the tests of between subject-effects. It basically shows the interaction of the predictor variables with the dependent variables. The development of self-reliance in preparing food rather

Table 3 Multivariate tests results

Effect	*Value*	F	*Hypothesis df*	*Error df*	*Sig*
Intercept	0.940	11.484^b	2.000	358.000	0.000
FMSPF	0.943	2.655^b	8.000	716.000	0.007
FLSW	0.958	1.934^b	8.000	716.000	0.052
HCMB	0.940	2.815^b	8.000	716.000	0.004
IETPH	0.953	2.194^b	8.000	716.000	0.026
ESSMC	0.949	2.386^b	8.000	716.000	0.015
CHTM	0.944	2.624^b	8.000	716.000	0.008
ISG	0.984	0.747^b	8.000	716.000	0.650
RTE	0.966	1.580^b	8.000	716.000	0.127
RSVM	0.977	1.030^b	8.000	716.000	0.412
RSCF	0.977	1.056^b	8.000	716.000	0.392
RSG	0.967	1.505^b	8.000	716.000	0.152
FGUIC	0.921	3.764^b	8.000	716.000	0.000
CIB	0.984	1.473^b	4.000	716.000	0.209
CEB	0.988	1.088^b	4.000	716.000	0.361

than depending on restaurants during Covid-19 was found to be statistically significant (at 5%) with respect to gender but not with respect to nationality. This implies that there is significant difference in self-reliance of preparing food between male and female but not in case of Omanis and non-Omanis. Similarly, the fact that members of the household learnt how to budget and spend wisely was also found to be statistically significant (at 10%) in case of male and female but not in the case of nationality.

Respondents were asked whether the high costs of sterilizers and masks stretched their budget, and it was found to be statistically significant in cases of gender (0.040) and nationality (0.015). It implies that high costs of safety and precautionary measures did put a dent on the budget in cases of male and female and for Omanis and non-Omanis. Testing kits causing extra spending presented similar findings. It was found to be significant in cases of both the dependent variables (0.040 and 0.066 respectively). This finding can also be linked to the variable "giving up on unnecessary spending to balance the budget" which produced similar results. Both respondents being male and female and Omani and non-Omani were affected significantly affected by covid-19 circumstances that they had to give up on unnecessary spending to balance their budget.

In cases of lockdowns and mobility restrictions reducing travelling expenses and restrictions reducing expenditure on gatherings and weddings, the results were statistically significant (at 10% and 5% respectively) in case of gender while treatment and medication cost was found to be statistically significant (at 5%) with respect to Omanis and non-Omanis.

The results of the multivariate tests and the between subject-effects tests validate the findings of each other since the variables were found to be statistically significant in both tests. Also, the findings in Table 4 have implications in terms of how covid-19 brought about changes in consumer behavior and purchasing patterns. Certain variables being significant also strongly indicated the interconnectedness between each other and depicted the changes in consumers' consumption patterns because of the pandemic. These implications are discussed in detail in the discussion section.

Table 4 Tests of between subjects-effects

Source	*Dependent Variable*	*df*	F	*Sig*
Corrected Model	Gender	52	2.229	0.000
	Nationality	52	1.674	0.004
Intercept	Gender	1	22.437	0.000
	Nationality	1	0.734	0.392
FMSPF	Gender	4	4.841	0.001
	Nationality	4	0.512	0.727
FLSW	Gender	4	3.042	0.017
	Nationality	4	0.825	0.510
HCMB	Gender	4	2.527	0.040
	Nationality	4	3.118	0.015
IETPH	Gender	4	3.015	0.018
	Nationality	4	1.369	0.244
ESSMC	Gender	4	2.534	0.040
	Nationality	4	2.228	0.066
CHTM	Gender	4	1.878	0.114
	Nationality	4	3.361	0.010
ISG	Gender	4	1.439	0.221
	Nationality	4	0.058	0.994
RTE	Gender	4	2.015	0.092
	Nationality	4	1.139	0.338
1RSVM	Gender	4	0.900	0.464
	Nationality	4	1.148	0.334
RSCF	Gender	4	0.371	0.829
	Nationality	4	1.739	0.141
RSG	Gender	4	2.664	0.032
	Nationality	4	0.354	0.841
FGUIC	Gender	4	4.878	0.001
	Nationality	4	2.704	0.030
CIB	Gender	2	0.631	0.532
	Nationality	2	2.302	0.102
CEB	Gender	2	1.564	0.211
	Nationality	2	0.618	0.539
Error	Gender	359		
	Nationality	359		
Total	Gender	412		
	Nationality	412		
Corrected Total	Gender	411		
	Nationality	411		

5 Discussion

The aim of this paper was to investigate the impact of Covid-19 on household consumptionbehavior and patterns and to also assess whether the change in consumption behavior is a permanent or a transient one. To accomplish the objective several variables were chosen so as to decipher them as a form of change in consumption behavior. Consumption behavior need not necessarily be depicted through consumption of commodities alone, but also through any changes in consumers' whole consumption basket. A total of 14 variables were selected from an online questionnaire that was conducted during covid-19 to assess the impact of the pandemic on households. Amongst these 14 variables, 3 of them namely "self-reliance in preparing food rather than depending on restaurants", "members of the household learnt to budget and spend wisely during covid-19" and "giving up on unnecessary spending to balance the budget". The rest of the variables were included to represent changes in consumer behavior due to the pandemic. The authors intended on including other variables for the analysis. However, the authors were faced with the issue of no responses for those variables and thus, could not include them in the analysis.

Although the concept of analysis was used following the works of AlTarrah et al. (2021) and Ben Hassen et al. (2020), the predictor variables that were used to represent changes in consumer behavior are different than the ones used to those studies. This is so because the nature and purpose of the questionnaire survey that was used here in the Sultanate was to use data for accomplishing various objectives of the project simultaneously, all associated with the impact of Covid-19. Thus, drawing similar comparisons with previous literature would be a bit challenging. Also, it highlights the ultimate purpose of the paper which is to reduce the gap in the literature pool, since to the best of the authors' knowledge study of this nature has not been conducted in the Sultanate. Moreover, consumer behavior studies generally produce data that is useful for future and further studies in the field.

To assess changes in consumer behavior, it was seen that consumers generally shifted their consumption patterns (as items in their consumption basket). This was evident as respondents incurred high costs in spending of masks and sterilizers which stretched their budget and added on it was the costs associated with treating family members in private hospitals, buying testing kits and medication related to covid-19. The fact that they were statistically significant, with respect to gender and/or nationality proves the substantial impact it had on people's spending patterns. Moreover, to accommodate for the increase in their expenditures on safety and precautionary measures, people ended up redirecting their expenditures on purely need or necessity-based shopping. In addition, due to lockdowns, movement restrictions and quarantine restrictions, people had to mostly stay at home. The emotional distress of being stuck at home led to increased food consumption which in turn led to increased expenditure on groceries. However, due to the same restrictions, peoples' expenditures on vehicle maintenance, gas, travelling and gatherings and weddings reduced significantly.

To determine whether these changes in consumption pattern are permanent or transient one, it was seen that because of covid-19 people started relying on cooking at home rather than ordering in or dining out. This was a substantial outcome, especially with respect to males and females. Also, since family members learnt to spend wisely and give up on buying unnecessary items, the implication of this outcome is twofold. First, it validates the findings of the first objective, i.e., the changes in consumer behavior. Second, it addresses the second objective. If the effects of covid-19 are here to stay, these changes would remain. However, now that we see ease in restrictions and the spread and effects of the disease, we can perhaps also notice people moving back to the life pre covid-19. In other words, people's spending on eating out, ordering in, travelling, gatherings and weddings have sort of come back to what used to be before the pandemic. Thus, it can be concluded that the changes in consumer behavior were a transient one.

These findings can be translated into several suggestions. An apparent shift/change in consumers' behavior due to the pandemic revealed that not only did people's reliance on necessity items increase, but they tend to indulge into panic and bulk buying during times of crises. At such times, prices are bound to increase, and governments could provide some sort of concession schemes to certain classes/groups of consumers. As an example, Oman's government helped consumers during the peak of the pandemic by not only maintaining supply of essentials and necessity goods, but also providing various kinds of support schemes. Since these shifts are normally seen with changes in the economic condition, changes in policies need to be more dynamic and accommodating for such unforeseen events.

6 Conclusion

The purpose of this study was to assess the impact of covid-19 on consumer behavior and to determine whether the change was a permanent or transient one. The changes in consumer behavior were assessed through changes in buying patterns of medications, sanitizers, and masks (during the peak of the pandemic and when restrictions were into place), groceries, vehicle maintenance and gas, electricity, and internet bills and so on. It was also found that these changes took place due to covid-19 and when the infection rate was high. However, as the situation started getting better, people started to gradually move back to their lives before the pandemic. Thus, it can be said that these changes were transient ones.

To meet the objectives of the study, a combination of descriptive statistics and MANOVA was conducted using STATA 26. Primary data was gathered through an online questionnaire survey on households,that was carried out during covid-19. The total number of respondents was 414. The variables used for the study were selected and divided according to addressing the objectives of the study. The concept of the methodology was taken from studies conducted in Kuwait and Qatar. However, the variable groups that were used in those studies were completely different, and thus, the findings of this study are one of its kind, especially in the Sultanate of Oman. The limitation of this study remains to be its geographical reach. The study was conducted using data obtained from the Sultanate alone. However, that also paves way for further research, which could even include a combined effect of the pandemic on the Gulf States or the Arab region.

Another take away of the findings of this study is that peoples' reactions and responsiveness in dire situations are always an area of interest because through these studies, the economy can prepare itself for the absorptive capacity of shock. The government of Oman did an impeccable job in maintaining supplies of food and medical requirements. This also calls for the need for redirection of dependence on natural resources and fossil fuels. Although Oman was no exception of being a recipient of a global crisis, yet its rapid response to the pandemic and apt decision making helped keep the situation under control respective to its neighboring economies. Nevertheless, the government could set up policies that would safeguard the welfare of entities involved in food and beverage industry, logistics (transportation) and supply chain and the medical sector of the nation so that in case of a future crisis, the reliance on outside sources does not disrupt the governance.

References

Alexander, D., & Karger, E. (2020). Do stay-at-home orders cause people to stay at home? Effects of stay-at-home orders on consumer behavior. *The Review of Economics and Statistics*, 1–25.

AlTarrah, D., AlShami, E., AlHamad, N., AlBesher, F., & Devarajan, S. (2021). The impact of coronavirus COVID-19 pandemic on food purchasing, eating behavior, and perception of food safety in Kuwait. *Sustainability, 13*(16), 8987.

Amalia, P., Mihaela, D., & Ionuţ, P. (2012). From market orientation to the community orientation for an open public administration: A conceptual framework. *Procedia-Social and Behavioral Sciences, 62*, 871–875.

Ashby, N. J. (2020). Impact of the COVID-19 pandemic on unhealthy eating in populations with obesity. *Obesity, 28*(10), 1802–1805.

Baker, S. R., Farrokhnia, R. A., Meyer, S., Pagel, M., & Yannelis, C. (2020). How does household spending respond to an epidemic? Consumption during the 2020 COVID-19 pandemic. *The Review of Asset Pricing Studies, 10*(4), 834–862.

Barua, S. (2021). Understanding coronanomics: The economic implications of the COVID-19 pandemic. *The Journal of Developing Areas, 55*(3), 435–450.

Ben Hassen, T., El Bilali, H., & Allahyari, M. S. (2020). Impact of COVID-19 on food behavior and consumption in Qatar. *Sustainability, 12*(17), 6973.

Carroll, N., Sadowski, A., Laila, A., Hruska, V., Nixon, M., Ma, D. W., & Guelph Family Health Study. (2020). The impact of COVID-19 on health behavior, stress, financial and food security among middle to high income Canadian families with young children. *Nutrients, 12*(8), 2352.

Chang, H.-H., & Meyerhoefer, C. 2020). *COVID-19 and the demand for online food shopping services: Empirical evidence from Taiwan* (Working Paper, National Taiwan University).

Chenarides, L., Grebitus, C., Lusk, J. L., & Printezis, I. (2021). Food consumption behavior during the COVID-19 pandemic. *Agribusiness, 37*(1), 44–81.

Chronopoulos, D. K., Lukas, M., & Wilson, J. O. (2020). Consumer spending responses to the COVID-19 pandemic: An assessment of Great Britain. Available at SSRN 3586723.

Coibion, O., Gorodnichenko, Y., & Weber, M. (2020). *The cost of the covid-19 crisis: Lockdowns, macroeconomic expectations, and consumer spending* (No. w27141). National Bureau of Economic Research.

Dumitras, D. E., Harun, R., Arion, F. H., Chiciudean, D. I., Kovacs, E., Oroian, C. F., & Muresan, I. C. (2021). Food consumption patterns in Romania during the COVID-19 pandemic. *Foods, 10*(11), 2712.

Flatters, P., & Willmott, M. (2009). Understanding the post-recession consumer. *Harvard Business Review, 87*(7/8), 106–112.

Güngördü Belbağ, A. (2022). Impacts of Covid-19 pandemic on consumer behavior in Turkey: A qualitative study. *Journal of Consumer Affairs, 56*(1), 339–358.

Hesham, F., Riadh, H., & Sihem, N. K. (2021). What have we learned about the effects of the COVID-19 pandemic on consumer behavior? *Sustainability, 13*(8), 4304.

Hoon Ang, S., Sim Cheng, P., Lim, E. A., & Kuan Tambyah, S. (2001). Spot the difference: Consumer responses towards counterfeits. *Journal of Consumer Marketing, 18*(3), 219–235.

Kaplan, G., Moll, B., & Violante, G. L. (2020). *The great lockdown and the big stimulus: Tracing the pandemic possibility frontier for the US* (No. w27794). National Bureau of Economic Research.

Loxton, M., Truskett, R., Scarf, B., Sindone, L., Baldry, G., & Zhao, Y. (2020). Consumer behaviour during crises: Preliminary research on how coronavirus has manifested consumer panic buying, herd mentality, changing discretionary spending and the role of the media in influencing behaviour. *Journal of Risk and Financial Management, 13*(8), 166.

Maestre, J. P., Jarma, D., Jia-Rong, F. Y., Siegel, J. A., Horner, S. D., & Kinney, K. A. (2021). Distribution of SARS-CoV-2 RNA signal in a home with COVID-19 positive occupants. *Science of the Total Environment, 778*, 146201.

Mahmoud, A. B., Hack-Polay, D., Fuxman, L., & Nicoletti, M. (2021). The Janus-faced effects of COVID-19 perceptions on family healthy eating behavior: Parent's negative experience as a mediator and gender as a moderator. *Scandinavian Journal of Psychology, 62*(4), 586–595.

Mao, Y. (2020). Combating COVID-19 through collaborative governance: Lessons from East Asia. *Chinese Public Administration Review, 11*(2), 132–141.

Mehta, S., Saxena, T., & Purohit, N. (2020). The new consumer behaviour paradigm amid COVID-19: Permanent or transient? *Journal of Health Management, 22*(2), 291–301.

Reinhart, A. M. (n.d.). Communication and media studies, sociology. In *The SAGE encyclopedia of communication research methods*. https://methods.sagepub.com/reference/the-sage-encyclopedia-of-communication-research-methods/i9318.xml

Sterman, J. D., & Dogan, G. (2015). "I'm not hoarding, I'm just stocking up before the hoarders get here": Behavioral causes of phantom ordering in supply chains. *Journal of Operations Management, 39*, 6–22.

Valaskova, K., Kramarova, K., & Bartosova, V. (2015). Multi criteria models used in Slovak consumer market for business decision making. *Procedia Economics and Finance, 26*, 174–182.

Verma, M., & Naveen, B. R. (2021). COVID 19 impact on buying behaviour. *Vikalpa, 46*(1), 27–40.

WHO. (2020, March 11). WHO director-general's opening remarks at the media briefing on COVID-19. https://www.who.int/dg/speeches/detail/who-director-general-s-opening-remarks-at-the-mediabriefing-on-covid-19---11-march-2020. Accessed 7 August 2022.

Zwanka, R. J., & Buff, C. (2021). COVID-19 generation: A conceptual framework of the consumer behavioral shifts to be caused by the COVID-19 pandemic. *Journal of International Consumer Marketing, 33*(1), 58–66.

CHAPTER 4

Impact of COVID 19 on Water Consumption in GCC Countries: Lessons to be Learned for Future Crises

Ibtihaj Al-Siyabi

1 Introduction

The outbreak of coronavirus disease was in Wuhan, China in 2019. When the World Health Organisation (WHO) declared it as a pandemic, the disease had already spread to 114 countries, and by the middle of January more than 300 million people were infected (Almulhim & Aina, 2022). As a mitigation measure, people were educated about handwashing using soap and water and its importance in preventing the transmission of the disease. Other hygiene practices at home such as bathing, showering, washing/wiping surfaces and floors and cleaning also had their share of focus in recommendations related to addressing the pandemic (Cahill et al., 2021). Another measure taken by countries was lockdowns and

I. Al-Siyabi (✉)
GCCStat, Muscat, Sultanate of Oman
e-mail: iAlsiyabi@gccstat.org

A. Mishrif (ed.), *Economic Effects of the Pandemic*, The Political Economy of the Middle East,
https://doi.org/10.1007/978-981-97-4367-4_4

closure of facilities such as schools, restaurants, retail stores and non-essential services. National lockdowns included the different sectors of industry and commerce in addition to the governmental bodies and authorities. Restrictions were imposed on international travel as well. Consequently, people were forced to spend more time in their homes. As a result of the stay-at-home policy, employees worked from home, and educational institutions shifted to online learning.

Though these measures were vital, they had implications on water demand and water consumption in residential areas. With people staying at home or working from home, and with increasing the frequency and duration of handwashing, water consumption increased especially in residential areas in different countries including the GCC countries as reported by several studied conducted on individual countries (Abulibdeh, 2021; Almulhim & Aina, 2022; Kalbusch et al., 2020; Lüdtke et al., 2021; Marshallsay, 2020; Menneer et al., 2021; Rizvi et al., 2021).

This pandemic has made nations and governments realise the importance of pure, clean water in households. It has shed light on the water insecurities as well, and the associated measure of handwashing was a challenge for water scarce countries. According to ESCWA (2020), in the Arab region "over 362 million people live with less than 1000 cubic metres of fresh water per person per year". The GCC countries are in water scarce regions with limited renewable water sources. They are classified as having "absolute water scarcity" as per ESCWA report (2020), Fig. 1. Nevertheless, the annual per capita of water consumption in GCC countries is 560 liters per person per day (LPCD) whilst the world average is 180 LPCD (Albannay et al., 2021). Due to the limited water resources and abundance of fossil fuels resources, the GCC countries resort to desalination as a means of generating freshwater using seawater. However, this raises concerns about energy consumption and depletion of resources as generating more water is associated with more consumption of fossil fuels (Abulibdeh, 2021).

This study investigates the changes in water consumption in the GCC countries during COVID-19 by examining statistics compiled by the Statistical Centre for the Cooperation Council for the Arab Countries of the Gulf-GCC-Stat. Results of the study would be significant for decision makers to develop integrated regional strategies for water production and supply at times of crises, and to develop strategies for a more sustainable water management in the region.

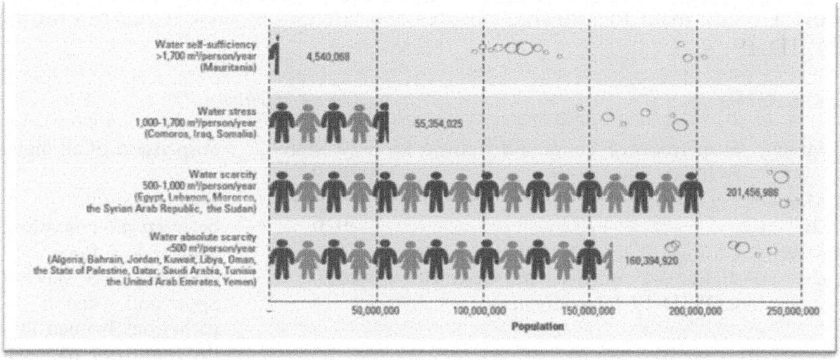

Fig. 1 Water scarcity in the Arab region, total annual renewable water resources per person

2 Literature Review

In late 2019, a case of respiratory disease was reported in the city of Wuhan, China. It was caused by a novel coronavirus later to be known as SARS-CoV-2, and it gave the disease its name of COVID-19. The World Health Organisation declared the disease as a pandemic on 11 March 2020 after the number of confirmed cases had reached 118,320 in 114 countries (Alandijany et al., 2020). The first COVID-19 cases in the GCC countries were in UAE as reported on 29 January 2020 by the Ministry of Health and prevention. In late February, cases were reported in other four countries, namely Bahrain, Kuwait, Oman and Qatar, while the first case of this disease was reported in Saudi Arabia on 2 March 2020 (Alandijany et al., 2020).

The GCC countries responded to COVID-19 by a series of measures in alignment with measures taken worldwide. All the member states put restrictions on people's mobility by imposing lockdowns, closures and ban of travel. Campaigns were also held to encourage citizens and residents to stay at home and minimize social interaction. Table 1 details the main lockdowns, closures and curfews in GCC countries and their dates.

In addition to resorting to closures and lockdowns was a common global practice as a mitigation precaution to control and minimize the spread of the disease, people were advised to observe the hygiene practices related to washing hands with pure water and soap as the best way to prevent themselves from COVID-19. Frequent handwashing with

Table 1 The main lockdowns, closures and curfews in GCC countries during COVID-19

Saudi Arabia		*Oman (Continued)*	
4 March, 2020	Suspension of Umra and tourism for residents and citizens	29 March, 2020	Suspension of all flights
8 March, 2020	Lockdown of Al Qatif	1 April, 2020	Ban of transfer between governorates
9 March, 2020	Closure of schools and universities, flights suspended to and from 19 COVID-19 hit countries	20 April, 2020	Muscat lockdown extended to 8 May. Sport and social gatherings banned in the month of Ramadan
14 March, 2020	Sport events suspended	4 May, 2020	Muscat lockdown extended to 29 May.
17 March, 2020	Closure of mosques	*Kuwait*	
25 March, 2020	Ban of transfer between provinces. Lockdown of main cities: Makkah, Madinah, and Riyadh	1 March, 2020	Closure of schools and universities
29 March, 2020	Lockdown of Jeddah Curfew 3 pm to 6 am.	12 March, 2020	Public holiday announced till 26 March
2 April, 2020	24-hour curfew in Makkah and Madinah for 24 hours	13 March, 2020	Some international flights suspended
6 April, 2020	24-hour curfew in additional 9 cities	20 March, 2020	Closure of shops, mosques and restaurants
11 April, 2020	Curfew extended	*Bahrain*	
Qatar		24 Feb, 2020	Closure of schools and universities
9 March, 2020	Closure of schools and universities, flights suspended to and from 15 COVID-19 hit countries	23 March, 2020	Closure of mosques
14 March, 2020	More international flights suspended	24 March, 2020	Curfew: 6 pm to 5 am
16 March, 2020	Closure of mosques	26 March, 2020	Closure of shops and restaurants

(continued)

Table 1 (continued)

Saudi Arabia		*Oman (Continued)*	
21 March, 2020	Restaurants, cafes, beaches and corniche closure	22 April, 2020	Social and sport gatherings banned for a month
Oman		*UAE*	
14 March, 2020	Closure of schools and universities	8 March, 2020	Closure of schools and universities
17 March, 2020	Closure of mosques Large gatherings banned	15 March, 2020	Closure of cinemas, parks and gyms
		25 March, 2020	Flights to and from the country suspended
		26 March, 2020	Curfew at night
		4 April, 2020	24-hour curfew in Dubai

Source Alandijany et al. (2020)

water and soap was clearly suggested by WHO to prevent transmission of the virus (Almulhim & Aina, 2022). Other hygiene practices were also encouraged including bathing, showering, washing/wiping surfaces and floors and cleaning in general. Following these directions, governments started spreading awareness and educating people about the necessity to increase the duration and frequency of handwashing (Menneer et al., 2021). Awareness campaigns were organised by the Gulf Health Council in addition to those organised by the individual member states to advocate the importance of hygiene and handwashing. The Gulf Health Council released more than 251 awareness products and conducted campaigns targeting residents of other nationalities in five different languages, English, Bengali, Urdu, Hindi and Indonesian (GCC-Stat & Gulf Health Council, 2021). The survey by Al Awaidy et al. (2021) revealed that all GCC countries had "transparent communication" at different levels, national and subnational, and that the six countries had "100% compliance with the infection prevention and control requirements" as per the strategic response disseminated by the WHO.

Following the guidance of WHO and governments, people increased handwashing with water and soap while spending more time at home due to lockdowns, closures or as a preventive measure to protect themselves.

Thus, the role of homes has changed and expanded to include activities that previously took place outside. Activities such as work, entertainment and even physical exercise were done at home due to restrictions imposed on mobility. Cahill et al. (2021) pointed out that domestic balconies, gardens and terraces became places for leisure and recreation as well as places for growing plants which increased the domestic water consumption. These precautions had an impact on water usage and have brought attention to the necessity of accessible, clean water and to water insecurities. The United Nations Economic and Social Commission for Western Asia (ESCWA) (2020) predicted an increase in water demand for washing hands in households by about 9 to 12 litres per person a day due to mitigation measures related to COVID-19. This estimated predicted increase represents a 5% increase in water demand in a household. In the Arab region collectively, this increase equals 4 to 5 million cubic metres per day, Fig. 2.

Expected increase in daily domestic water requirements because of increased handwashing owing to COVID-19 in the Arab region (million cubic metres per day)

Increase in water consumption was reported by studies in different parts of the world. Marshallsay (2020) reported an increase of 35% in England with variations depending on the city. For example, in Cornwall an increase of 17% was reported because of a study conducted on 280 households by Menneer et al. (2021). The increase reported in Northern Germany was 14% (Lüdtke et al., 2021) while in Brazil, usage of domestic

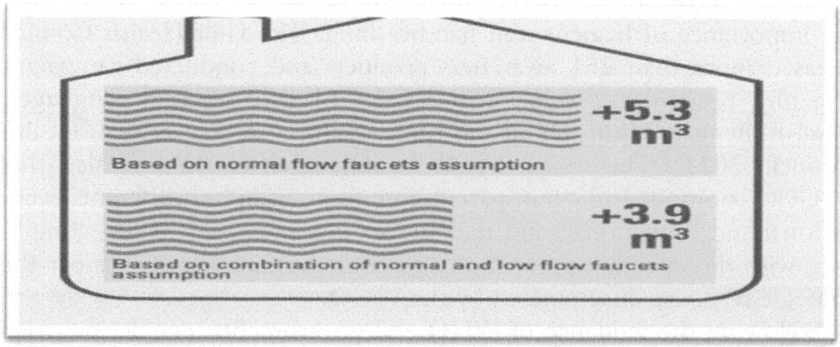

Fig. 2 Predicted in water demand for washing hands in households (*Source* ESCWA, 2020)

water increased by 11% in the lockdown period as opposed to the period before lockdown (Kalbusch et al., 2020).

Studies have been conducted to investigate how the lockdown period due to COVID-19 affected people's lifestyle, behaviour and resources consumption in the individual member states of the GCC. Abulibdeh (2021) studied the consumption of water and electricity in residential areas (villas and flats) in Doha, Qatar in four main phases. The study drew attention to the water-electricity nexus and compared the water and electricity consumption in the residential sector over a period of 12 months divided in four of time phases: Pre-lockdown (January and February 2020), Lockdown (March to May 2020), Easing lockdown (June to September 2020) and Post-lockdown (October to December 2020) with the consumption in the same periods of time in the years before, namely 2018 and 2019. The comparison revealed an increase in consumption in the pre-lockdown period which continued in the lockdown phase. The increase was 9% (minimum) based on the building type, flat or villa. Another revelation was that blocks characterized by high density of population and workforce had the highest consumption (Abulibdeh, 2021), especially that expiates were not able to travel to their home countries due the international travel ban. The household size is a determining factor in water consumption in the GCC countries because the national families are large with up to three generations in addition to sibling (Albannay et al., 2021).

Rizvi et al. (2021) found out that water consumption increased in residential buildings in Dubai during the lockdown period because of "Stay Home" campaign and that the increase correlated positively with the number of occupants in the building. It was also noticed that the highest peak of water consumption was still in the morning even though people worked online. However, smaller peaks were also observed, for example during lunchtime. In England, the per household consumption for the households covered in the study by Abu-Bakar et al. (2021) rose by 13%, 22%, 29% in March, April, and May 2020 respectively compared to the same months of the previous year. They also pointed out that water consumed in the evening peak decreased by 52% while multiple peak water consumption increased by 93% in the third and fourth weeks of March 2020 (Abu-Bakar et al., 2021). The annual water consumption in Abu Dhabi in 2020 was exceptional as members of the ame family stayed at home for most of the year. The water consumption in 2020 was 937 cubic meters/year compared to the respective consumption of 581 and

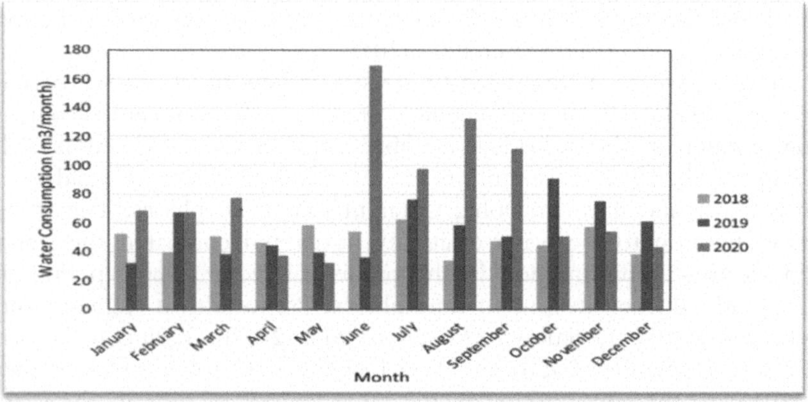

Fig. 3 Monthly water consumption per connection in Abu Dhabi 2018–2020

666 in 2018 and 2019. Though the monthly consumption of water in 2020 (Fig. 3) shows a rise in March 2020, the consumption in the subsequent months of April and May was low because during these two months meter readings were not taken, and estimated low values were recorded. However, the actual meter reading show that the highest consumption of all months was in June (Albannay et al., 2021). Increase in water consumption in households during the lockdown was also reported by Almulhim and Aina (2022) whose study revealed an increase of more than 50% in Dammam City in the eastern side of Saudi Arabia. Other significant findings of the study were the unwillingness of respondents to adopt measures to save water, the higher level of water use of females compared to males and for Saudis compared to expats.

3 Results

Statistics compiled by the Statistical Centre for the Cooperation Council for the Arab Countries of the Gulf, GCC-Stat, show an increase in water consumption in 2020 compared to 2019 in Bahrain, Kuwait, United Arab Emirates (UAE) (Sharjah), Oman, Qatar and Saudi Arabia of 6.3%, 4.4%, 3.9%, 2.3%, 1.1% and 0.1% respectively (Fig. 4). Similarly, water consumption from Water Supplies Authorities by household users increased in 2020 between 9.8% (Oman) and 0.1% (Saudi Arabia) comparing to 2019 (Fig. 5).

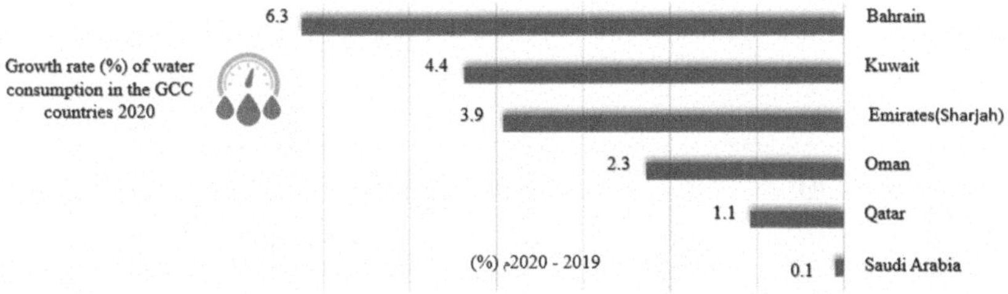

Fig. 4 The Growth Percentage of water consumption in GCC countries, 2020 (*Sources* Author's calculations)

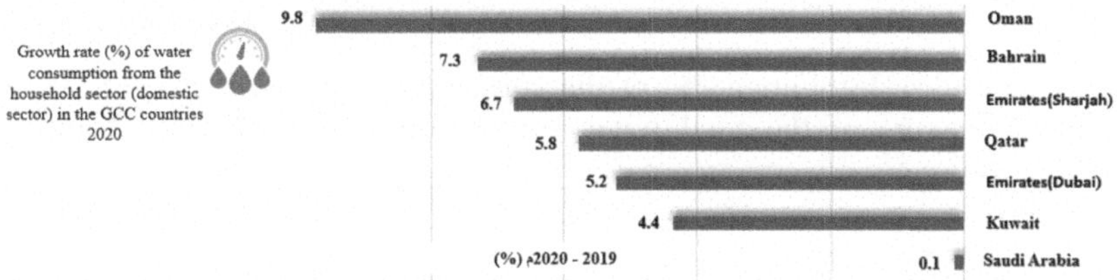

Fig. 5 Growth rate (%) of water consumption from the household sector (domestic sector) in the GCC countries 2020 (*Sources* Author's calculations)

Water consumption in the residential sector constituted 75%, 72.3%, 71.4%, 65.3%, 53.7% and 50.1% of the total water consumption in Kuwait, Qatar, Saudi Arabia, UAE (Dubai plus Sharjah) Bahrain and Oman respectively (Fig. 6). The high proportion of residential water consumption in 2020 compared to the other sectors is linked to the measures against the pandemic which mandated the closure of non-essential commercial and industrial activities. This increase was reflected on the consumption per capita per day.

Water consumption from household sector per capita per day increased in UAE (Sharjah) by 3.3% from 126 to 130 liters, in UAE (Dubai) by 3.2% from 268 to 276 liters, in Bahrain by 7.8% from 264 to 284 liters, in Qatar by 5.7% from 436 to 461 liters, in Kuwait by 4.1% from 313 to 326 liters, and the highest change in capita indicator is in Oman by 9.8% from 97 to 107 liters comparing to other countries (Fig. 7).

In Qatar the monthly water consumption increased in different rates in most of the months of 2020. In the months that witnessed closures and

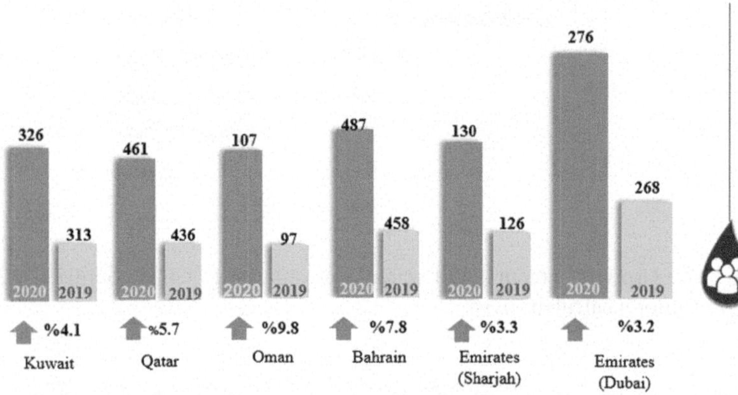

Fig. 6 Relative distribution (%) of the consumption of the household sector (domestic sector) of the total water consumption, 2020 (*Sources* Author's calculations)

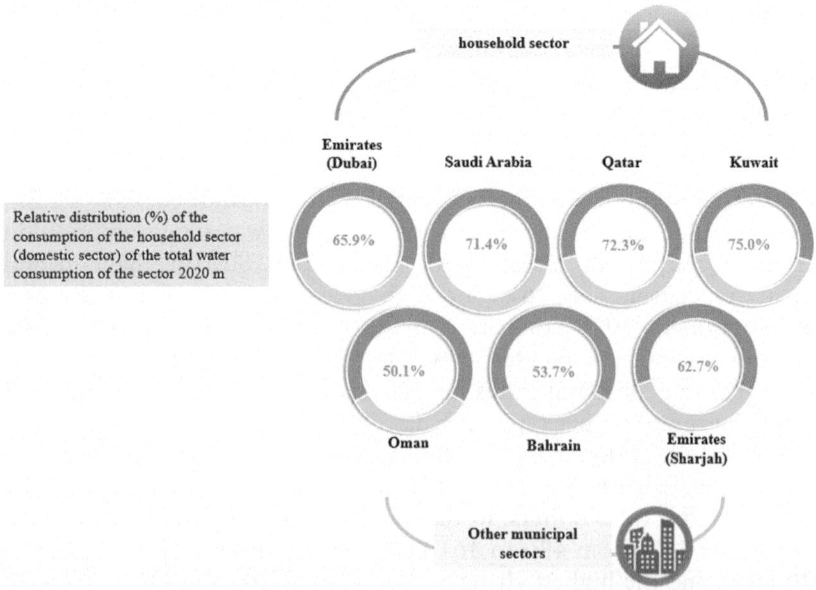

Fig. 7 Water consumption from Household sector per capita per day in 2020 and 2019 in GCC countries (*Source* Author's calculations)

lockdowns, i.e. March and April, the water consumption increased by 4% and 3% respectively. The increase in these two months is attributed to the preventive measures taken against COVID-19, mainly handwashing, stay at home guidance, and lockdowns/closures. However, these increases were not the highest compared to other months of the same year. It is noticeable that the water consumption increased significantly at the months prior to lockdown, January and February, and in October, Table 2.

The situation in Kuwait is like that of Qatar. Though freshwater consumption increased in March, April, and May 2020, this increase was lower than that of other months. Freshwater consumption in March 2020 increased by 4.3%, April by 2.9% and May by 2.1% compared to consumption in the same months of 2019 while it increased to higher percentages in other months such as February, July, August and September, Table 3.

Figures of daily consumption of freshwater in Kuwait in 2020 are higher than those in 2019 for all the months (except December), Table 4, leading to an overall annual and monthly increase as in Table 3.

Kuwait also makes use of brackish water which is conveyed to consumers through a separate network of pipes parallel to that of freshwater. Brackish water is used for multiple purposes such as landscaping, irrigation, household uses, and construction work. Brackish water net

Table 2 Total monthly water consumption in Qatar in 2019 & 2020

Month	*2019 (Million cubic meters)*	*2020 (Million cubic meters)*	*Change (%)*
January	33.9	52.1	35
February	30.6	49.5	38
March	50.9	53.3	4
April	50.1	51.6	3
May	55.5	55.5	0
June	56.9	60.0	5
July	59.2	62.0	4
August	58.9	62.6	6
September	58.1	59.7	3
October	40.8	59.6	32
November	54.4	55	1
December	52.3	53.9	3

Source PSA (2020)

Table 3 Total net consumption of freshwater in Kuwait in 2019 & 2020

Month	*2019 (Million gallons)*	*2020 (Million gallons)*	*Change (%)*
January	11,053	11,546	4.2
February	10,112	11,068	8.6
March	11,897	12,434	4.3
April	12,000	12,364	2.9
May	13,323	13,619	2.1
June	13,285	14,137	6
July	13,804	14,652	5.7
August	13,684	14,635	6.4
September	13,492	13,859	2.6
October	13,471	13,674	5.5
November	11,970	12,011	0.34
December	11,664	11,628	0.3 decrease

Source MEWRE (2021)

Table 4 Kuwait daily average consumption of freshwater 2019–2020

Month	*2019 (Million Gallons)*	*2020 (Million Gallons)*	*Change (%)*
January	382.3	400.4	4.5
February	387.6	410.4	5.5
March	410.9	432.3	4.9
April	428.4	443.9	3.5
May	460.8	472.8	2.5
June	475.1	506.8	6.2
July	479.4	509.2	5.8
August	475.3	507.1	6.2
September	484.2	497.4	2.6
October	463.9	473.3	1.9
November	427.0	432.2	1.2
December	403.9	403.8	0.02 decrease

Source MEWRE (2021)

consumption in 2020 was higher than 2019 by 6.2% while the daily consumption increased by 5.4%, Table 5. Considering the second quarter, April to June, the net consumption of brackish water in 2020 was higher than that of 2019 by 2%.

Table 5 Total annual net consumption of brackish water in Kuwait in 2019 & 2020

Year	*Net consumption*	*Daily average consumption*
2019	12,001	32.9
2020	12,474	34.8
	6.2% increase	5.4 increase

Source MEWRE (2021)

Table 6 Sharjah monthly sold water quantities in residential sector

Month	*2019 (Gallons)*	*2020 (Gallons)*	*Change (%)*
January	1,382,062	1,399,576	1.25
February	1,451,568	1,392,792	4.2 Decrease
March	1,314,281	1,379,564	4.7
April	1,373,568	1,592,055	13.7
May	1,431,965	1,626,680	11.9
June	1,564,953	1,676,934	6.6
July	1,469,708	1,572, 559	6.5
August	1,347,811	1,587,008	15
September	1,481,096	1,534,610	3.5
October	1,408,971	1,524,151	7.5
November	1,474,120	1,500,232	1.7
December	1,353,762	1,418,645	4.5

Source SEWGA (2020)

In Sharjah, the three months of March, April, and May 2020 witnessed a respective increase of 4.7%, 13.7%, and 11.9%. There were significant increases in the other months of June, July and August, Table 6.

4 Discussion

Most countries including the member states of GCC imposed lockdowns and closures in the months of March and April. This resulted in people spending more time at home. Additionally, to protect themselves against COVID-19 infection and as instructed by the WHO and government officials, people increased the frequency and duration of handwashing. This impacted water consumption in the residential sector in GCC countries. Examining the statistics compiled by GCC-Stat shows that there was an overall increase in residential water consumption in GCC countries in

2020 compared to 2019. It is also evident that consumption increased in the months of March, April and May. The increase in these months is explained by the fact that they coincided with the lockdowns, closures, and stay-at-home guidance. However, it is notable that in Kuwait and Qatar the increase declined gradually in three months. This trend is also observed in the daily consumption of freshwater in Kuwait. This is due to the relaxation of preventive measures in May compared to the previous two months. In Sharjah, the trend is different as the rise in April was the peak of the three-month period. This trend in Sharjah can be explained by the fact that lockdowns were imposed in UAE on 23 March 2020, which reflected on water consumption in April. The increase in the consumption of brackish water in Kuwait can be attributed to the increase in hygiene practices at homes and in gardening or planting.

The overall increase in residential consumption in 2020 is not attributed solely to the preventive precautions as monthly statistics show an increase in other months as well. Factors contributing to this are varied. Gulf countries are known for their hot climate for most of the year, and for their long summers. This leads to higher water consumption for washing, showering and laundry in households. For example, in Abu Dhabi, the highest consumption was recorded in June due to the hot climate and travel ban. There are other additional factors that reflect on water consumption in GCC countries such as the household size and income and educational awareness.

5 Conclusion

The purpose of this chapter is to examine the impact of lockdowns and closures on residential water consumption in the GCC countries. In general, water consumptions increased in GCC countries in 2020 in comparison to 2019. Though the monthly statistics show an increase in the months of March and April that coincided with lockdowns and closures, there were other significant increases in residential water consumption in other months of the year. Reasons vary to include population growth, hot climate, and the high standard of living. This always calls for sustainable management of resources, water and energy, in the countries of the region as the increase of water consumption in the GCC countries is directly linked to that of electricity due to the dependence of the countries on desalination.

6 Recommendations

To acknowledge the significance of the role of statistics compiled at times of risk in predicting behavior of water consumption so that plans can be prepared to face similar situations in the future.

1. When compiling statistics of water consumption at times of risk, it is important to consider the socioeconomic factors to achieve a better government planning for water supply and production.
2. To use statistics to understand the changes and trends in using water to help decision makers in forming strategies and schemes for water supply.
3. For governments to priorities availing and sustainably managing water for all in line with SDG 6.
4. To always manage resources in a sustainable way not only at times of risk but.
5. To conduct studies to investigate peak times of water demand, and then use the results for a more sustainable and informed water supply process. Instead of a continuous water supply which leads to more energy consumption, water would be supplied at peak hours.
6. To conduct studies to explore locations of high consumption and the factors associated with it to enable decision makers to put contingency plans to ensure that sufficient supply is provided to these areas.
7. To use the experience of COVID-19 to raise awareness about water conversation through campaigns that educate the public about the different practices that lead to conserving water.

References

Abu-Bakar, H., Williams, L., & Hallett, S. H. (2021). Quantifying the impact of the COVID-19 lockdown on household water consumption patterns in England. *npj Clean Water, 4*, 1–9. https://www.nature.com/articles/s41545-021-00103-8

Abulibdeh, A. (2021). Spatiotemporal analysis of water-electricity consumption in the context of COVID-19 pandemic across six socioeconomic sectors in Doha City, Qatar, *Applied Energy, 304*. https://www.sciencedirect.com/science/article/pii/S0306261921011867?via%3Dihub

Al Awaidy, S., Khamis, F., Al Attar, F., Abdul Razzaq, N., Al Dabal, L., Al Enani, M., Alfouzan, W., Al Maslamani, M., Al Romaihi, H., Al Salman, J., Altawalah, H., Langrial, S., Al Ariqi, L., & Mohamed, O. (2021). COVID-19 in the Gulf Cooperation Council member states: An evidence of effective response. *Oman Medical Journal, 36*(5). https://www.ncbi.nlm.nih.gov/pmc/articles/PMC8441050/

Alandijany, T., Faizo, A., & Azhar, E. (2020). Coronavirus disease of 2019 (COVID-19) in the Gulf Cooperation Council (GCC) countries: Current status and management practices. *Journal of Infection and Public Health, 13.* https://reader.elsevier.com/reader/sd/pii/S187603412030486X?token=47D5DAE812683196936A2E2B3E9734CCD5B84875C1A8F2FA32E9658B94B7CEAF5741D4FAD0E934871BEBA396E3ED7832&originRegion=eu-west-1&originCreation=20220912092759

Albannay, S., Kazama, S., Oguma, K., Hashimoto, T., & Takizawa, S. (2021). Water demand management based on water consumption data analysis in the Emirate of Abu Dhabi, *Water, 13.* https://www.researchgate.net/publication/355233040_Water_Demand_Management_Based_on_Water_Consumption_Data_Analysis_in_the_Emirate_of_Abu_Dhabi

Almulhim, A. I., & Aina, Y. A. (2022). Understanding household water-use behavior and consumption patterns during COVID-19 lockdown in Saudi Arabia. *Water, 14*, 314. https://doi.org/10.3390/w14030314

Cahill, J., Hoolohan, C., Lawson, R., & Brown, A. L. (2021). COVID-19 and water demand: A review of literature and research evidence, *WIREs Water, 9.* https://wires.onlinelibrary.wiley.com/doi/full/10.1002/wat2.1570

Cranfield University. (2021). Research reveals household water consumption changes during lockdown. https://www.cranfield.ac.uk/press/news-2021/research-reveals-household-water-consumption-changes-during-lockdown

Dubai Statistics Center (DSC). (2020). Manufacturing, energy and water themes: Quantity of water consumed and number of consumers by type of consumption—2020 (Excel file). https://www.dsc.gov.ae/en-us/Themes/Pages/Manufacturing-Energy-Water.aspx?Theme=29

Gulf Cooperation Council (GCC) Countries Statistic Center (GCC-Stat). (2020). Impact of COVID-19 pandemic on sustainable development strategic goals. https://www.gccstat.org/ar/statistic/publications/impacts-of-sustainable-development_publishing

Gulf Cooperation Council (GCC) Countries Statistic Center (GCC-Stat). (2021). Water statistics in GCC countries Bulletin 2020. https://www.gccstat.org/ar/statistic/statistics/environment

Gulf Cooperation Council (GCC) Countries Statistic Center (GCC-Stat). (2022). Water statistics in GCC countries Bulletin 2021, Unpublished.

Gulf Cooperation Council (GCC) Countries Statistic Center (GCC-Stat), & Gulf Health Council. (2021). Toward recover effects of COVID-19 pandemic in the GCC health, social, and economic aspects. https://gccstat.org/images/gccstat/docman/publications/covid-19report.pdf

Information & eGovernment Authority (IGA). (2022). Water statistics from 2000–2021 (Excel file), data unpublished.

Kalbusch, A., Henning, E., Brikalski, M. P., de Luca, F. V., Konrath, A. C. (2020). Impact of coronavirus (COVID-19) spread-prevention actions on urban water consumption. *Resources, Conversation and Recycling, 163*. https://reader.elsevier.com/reader/sd/pii/S0921344920304158?token=711AAFEF170CB663EA7115B723948DC11C36CE0FB7FBC93CCE1EF3E27BAC0FCAC348B9748D0BA0718B36549D914D9F82&originRegion=eu-west-1&originCreation=20220912090453

Lüdtke, D. U., Luetkemeier, R., Schneemann, M., & Liehr, S. (2021). Increase in daily household water demand during the first wave of the COVID-19 pandemic in Germany. *Water, 13*, 260. https://www.mdpi.com/2073-4441/13/3/260/pdf

Marshallsay, D. (2020, June 30). New waterwise article! The effect of the coronavirus lockdown on water use. https://artesia-consulting.co.uk/new-waterwise-article-the-effect-of-the-coronavirus-lockdown-on-water-use/

Menneer, T., Qi, Z., Taylor, T., Peterson, C., Tu, G., Elliot, L. R., Morrissey, K., & Mueller, M. (2021). Changes in domestic energy and water usage during the UK COVID-19 lockdown using high resolution temporal data. *International Journal for Environment, Research and Public Health, 18*(13), 6818. https://doi.org/10.3390/ijerph1813681

Ministry of Electricity & Water & Renewable Energy (MEWRE). (2021). Statistical year book 2020 water. https://www.mew.gov.kw/media/rckpzmm4/%D9%83%D8%AA%D8%A7%D8%A8-%D8%A7%D9%84%D8%A7%D8%AD%D8%B5%D8%A7%D8%A1-%D8%A7%D9%84%D8%B3%D9%86%D9%88%D9%8A-%D8%A7%D9%84%D9%85%D9%8A%D8%A7%D9%87-compressed.pdf

National Center for Statistics and Information (NCSI). (2021). Water statistics bulletin. https://ncsi.gov.om/Elibrary/LibraryContentDoc/bar_Water%202021_a40577cc-a89c-4c45-8301-2054380b071f.pdf

Planning and Statistics Authority (PSA). (2020). Glance Qatar monthly statistics. https://www.psa.gov.qa/ar/statistics1/pages/topicslisting.aspx?parent=General&child=QMS

Rizvi, S., Rustum, R., Deepak, M., Wright, G. B., & Arthur, S. (2021). Identifying and analyzing water demand profile; including the impact of COVID-19 and the month of Ramadan, for selected developments in Dubai, United Arab Emirates. *Water Supply, 21*(3). http://iwaponline.com/ws/article-pdf/21/3/1144/887190/ws021031144.pdf

Sharjah Electricity, Water and Gas Authority (SEWGA). (2020). Statistical book. https://www.sewa.gov.ae/uploads/statspdfar/The%20Annual%20Statistical%20Book%202020%20REV.%202.pdf

The Economic Commission for Western Asia (ESCWA). (2020). The impact of COVID-19 on water-scarce Arab region. https://www.unescwa.org/publications/impact-covid-19-water-scarce-arab-region
The Organisation for Economic Co-operation and Development (OECD). (2020). COVID-19 crisis response in MENA countries. https://www.oecd.org/coronavirus/policy-responses/covid-19-crisis-response-in-mena-countries-4b366396/
The United Nations. (2020). Policy brief: The impact of COVID-19 on the Arab region an opportunity to build back better. https://unsdg.un.org/sites/default/files/2020-07/sg_policy_brief_covid-19_and_arab_states_english_version_july_2020.pdf
The University of Manchester. (2020). Coronavirus lockdown caused dramatic changes in water consumption, research finds. https://www.manchester.ac.uk/discover/news/coronavirus-lockdown-caused-dramatic-changes-in-water-consumption/

CHAPTER 5

Macroeconomic Expectations Facing COVID19: A Sectoral Analysis

Sarfaraz Ali Shah Syed

1 Introduction

The COVID-19 pandemic has caused an unprecedented global crisis, affecting every aspect of human life. The pandemic has resulted in a significant loss of life and has disrupted social, economic, and political systems across the world. The global economy has been severely affected by the pandemic, with businesses forced to shut down, supply chains disrupted, and millions of people losing their jobs. The economic impact of the pandemic is expected to be felt for years to come.

One of the most significant impacts of the pandemic has been on economic expectations in different sectors. Economic expectations are a critical driver of economic behaviour and decision-making. The COVID-19 pandemic has created an environment of uncertainty, making it difficult for businesses and individuals to plan for the future. The pandemic

S. A. S. Syed (✉)
Department of Accounting, Economics, and Finance, Cardiff School of Management, Cardiff Metropolitan University, Cardiff, UK
e-mail: ssyed@cardiffmet.ac.uk

A. Mishrif (ed.), *Economic Effects of the Pandemic*, The Political Economy of the Middle East,
https://doi.org/10.1007/978-981-97-4367-4_5

has also led to changes in consumer behaviour, with people reducing their spending on non-essential items and focusing more on essentials.

The pandemic has affected different sectors of the economy differently, with some sectors experiencing significant growth while others have been severely affected. For instance, the healthcare sector has experienced a surge in demand due to the pandemic, while the tourism and hospitality sectors have been severely impacted due to travel restrictions and reduced demand. Understanding the effect of the pandemic on economic expectations in different sectors is essential for policymakers and businesses to make informed decisions. The COVID-19 pandemic has provided an opportunity to examine the resilience of different sectors of the economy and identify areas that need support to recover from the impact of the pandemic. This article aims to explore the effect of COVID-19 on macroeconomic expectations across different economic sectors. The chapter will provide a sectoral analysis of the pandemic's impact on the global economy and offer insights into the challenges that different sectors are facing. The analysis will focus on various sectors, including manufacturing, services, agriculture, tourism, and the energy sector.

The COVID-19 pandemic has wreaked havoc on the global economy, disrupting all sectors to varying extents. As economists, it is critical to evaluate the impact of the pandemic on sector-wise macroeconomic expectations, in order to inform policy decisions and facilitate a sustainable recovery. In this chapter, we will delve into six critical sectors: Construction, Consumer, Finance, Industry, Retail, and Services. These sectors are vital components of the economy, and their performance is crucial for overall economic growth and stability. We will analyse the challenges faced by each sector during the pandemic, such as changes in consumer behaviour, supply chain disruptions, and government policies aimed at mitigating the pandemic's impact.

Firstly, we will focus on the Construction sector, which has experienced mixed fortunes during the pandemic. While some projects have been stalled due to restrictions on movement and a shortage of labour, others have continued as an essential service. The sector has also faced supply chain disruptions due to the closure of manufacturing plants and shipping bottlenecks. However, the sector's prospects for recovery remain positive, as governments around the world invest in infrastructure projects to boost economic activity.

Next, we will explore the impact of the pandemic on the Consumer sector, which has seen a drastic shift in consumer behaviour. Lockdowns and social distancing measures have resulted in a sharp decline in discretionary spending, especially in the tourism and hospitality industries. The shift to online shopping has also accelerated, with retailers increasingly adopting digital strategies to remain competitive. However, the sector's outlook remains uncertain as consumer confidence and employment levels are still in flux.

The Finance sector has also experienced significant disruption during the pandemic, as low-interest rates and increased uncertainty have hit profitability. Many banks and financial institutions have also faced the challenge of managing a remote workforce, while also dealing with the economic fallout of the pandemic. However, the sector's outlook remains cautiously optimistic, as governments and central banks have rolled out stimulus packages to bolster economic recovery.

The industry sector, which is a significant driver of economic growth, has been hit hard by the pandemic due to supply chain disruptions and reduced demand. The manufacturing sector, in particular, has been affected by factory closures and a shortage of raw materials. The sector's recovery is contingent on the speed of vaccine distribution and government support for revitalizing the industry.

The Retail sector has also seen significant disruption due to the pandemic, with many brick-and-mortar stores closing or struggling to remain afloat. The shift towards e-commerce has been accelerated, with consumers increasingly turning to online shopping for their needs. The sector's prospects for recovery are dependent on the ability of retailers to adapt to changing consumer behaviour and the reopening of physical stores.

Finally, we will examine the impact of the pandemic on the Services sector, which has been heavily impacted by restrictions on movement and social distancing measures. The sector encompasses a wide range of businesses, from healthcare to hospitality, and has experienced varying levels of disruption. While some services have been able to adapt to remote work and online delivery, others, such as tourism and entertainment, have been severely impacted. The sector's recovery is highly dependent on the effectiveness of government policies and the distribution of vaccines.

In a word, the impact of COVID-19 on sector-wise macroeconomic expectations has been significant and varied across sectors. It is crucial for policymakers to consider the unique challenges faced by each sector and implement targeted measures to facilitate a sustainable recovery. By analysing the sectors of Construction, Consumer, Finance, Industry,

Retail, and Services, we hope to provide valuable insights into the macroeconomic implications of the pandemic and inform decision-makers on the most effective strategies to promote economic resilience and growth. Ultimately, our goal is to contribute to a better understanding of the pandemic's impact on the economy and inform policies that can facilitate a sustainable and inclusive recovery for all sectors of the economy.

1.1 European Perspective

As the pandemic swept across the world, it affected different regions and countries to varying degrees. However, in recent European history and the history of the European Union, it has caused the largest and most abrupt contraction in economic activity. The pandemic's impact on economies varied significantly across sectors and within economies themselves. While the travel and tourism industry initially bore the brunt of the impact, other sectors such as manufacturing, construction, and finance were also affected due to disruptions in supply chains.

Monthly business surveys in European Union member countries have provided valuable information on the different impacts of the pandemic across all macroeconomic sectors. Output initially fell sharply in countries such as France, Italy, and Spain due to economy-wide confinement for extended periods. In contrast, some countries, particularly in Northern Europe, employed targeted measures in regions and sectors and relied more extensively on the effective test, trace, and isolate mechanisms to control the spread of the virus.

Although the European Union remains one of the major victims of the virus in terms of human fatalities, the pandemic also significantly impacted the economies. The literature on the subject is now rich, and the impact of the pandemic on economies is still under observation. Most studies point towards an adverse response from the economies towards the COVID-19 shock. However, some studies, including Syed (2022), found asymmetries in the response to decreases in the number of COVID-19 deaths. Furthermore, studies have also recorded quick recovery and stronger come-back in various economies. These observations raise questions about the reliability of any conclusions based on these studies.

One possible answer could be the aggregation bias, as most studies have based their findings on panel analyses, which could conceal important information due to differences in the economies in terms of the impact of COVID-19 and the reaction and responses adopted by the economies facing the pandemic. Studying the impact of COVID-19 from two important angles could provide important evidence: (1) studying countries separately where the impact of the pandemic and the response thereof are different and (2) bifurcating the economies by sectors to differentiate the severely hit sectors from the mitigating and recovery leaders.

However, little work has been done at disaggregated levels, as reported by Syed (2022). Studying the impact of COVID-19 in a segregated manner is necessary, given that the pandemic has affected different sectors differently, and the losses in some sectors have been mitigated by the gains made in others. Service sectors, which require close proximity between consumers and producers or between large groups of consumers, including hospitality services, leisure activities, and cross-border travel, were hard hit across all economies. The manufacturing sector and most other market-based services also tumbled, although the extent of the decline varied. These sectors' decline was typically larger in France and Italy compared to Northern Europe.

Therefore, this study attempts to analyse the sectoral impact of the pandemic. Partly because of the nature of containment measures, the contact-intensive services sector has suffered disproportionately. Abrupt demand shifts and disruptions in global supply and value chains have also affected sectors differently. While the prospects for a quick and strong recovery are good, they differ across sectors. The pandemic may significantly accelerate existing changes in digitization, remote working and education, the green transition, and changes in global value chains. However, understanding the degree of response of different sectors and the force behind these responses is key to designing appropriate policy responses to ensure the sustainability and inclusiveness of these transitions.

We contribute to the existing literature from three aspects:

i. This study is different from other investigations as we are studying the impact of COVID-19 on the expectations of the EU economic agents, and not directly on the economic outcomes. This focus on expectations is motivated by the idea that expectations play a crucial role in shaping economic decisions and outcomes. The pandemic has created significant uncertainty and has led to changes in expectations about the future, which in turn may have affected economic behaviour and outcomes.

ii. We investigate the reaction of not the economies but of the expectations in different economic sectors towards the ups and downs in the number of fatalities. In this regard, we also test the impact by bifurcating the rise and fall in COVID-19 fatalities. This may also lead to further exploring the prevalence and duration of the potential negative and positive biases in the stock markets facing big news. This approach provides a more nuanced understanding of the differential impact of the pandemic across economic sectors and sheds light on the mechanisms through which the pandemic affected the economy.

iii. We disaggregate the EU member countries into quartiles on the basis of the magnitude of fatalities. This allows us to examine how the impact of the pandemic varied across countries with different levels of fatalities. It also enables us to explore the potential spillover effects of the pandemic from more severely affected countries to less affected ones.

Our results are in accord with the existing literature on the pandemic and its effects on equity prices. We find that the response of overall economies and of the different economic sectors was sudden, brutal and consistent with the economic theory—adverse to the outbreak and to the spread of the pandemic news. However, we find that countries with smaller numbers of fatalities also reacted in a similar manner to the highly affected countries. This finding leads us to the extension of this work to the analysis of spillover effects within the EU.

The remainder of this paper is organized as follows: In Sect. 2, we review some of the prominent studies on the subject. Section 3 presents data and testing strategy. In Sect. 4, we record and discuss the results, while Sect. 5 concludes. Overall, this study aims to contribute to a better understanding of the sectoral impact of the pandemic in the EU and to inform policy responses to ensure the sustainability and inclusiveness of the ongoing transitions in the economy.

2 Brief Literature Review

2.1 General

There is a long-standing tradition in literature in macroeconomics assessing the impact of shocks on macroeconomic expectations. With the COVID-19 pandemic, the first half of the year 2020 witnessed the emergence and exponential multiplication of studies focusing on the impact of the pandemic and mobility restrictions, but also on monetary policy announcements and decisions on macroeconomic expectations. A first review of this literature can be found in Brodeur et al. (2021).

This new strand of literature relies on the broader and recent literature in macroeconomics that uses online surveys of households or consumers and experiments to document consumer expectations' formation and response to information, especially about monetary policy announcements (Kamdar et al., 2018). Within the context of the COVID-19 pandemic, a series of worth-mentioning studies seek to assess the influence of the provision of health COVID-19-related facts along with policy announcements on the evolution of concerns and expectations formation (Binder, 2020; Coibion et al., 2020d; Dietrich et al., 2022; Fetzer et al., 2021; Syed, 2022).

Most of these studies focus on the U.S. economy and appeared as early as in March and April 2020. For instance, Fetzer et al. (2020) find that U.S. consumers with cognitive limitations who were surveyed online in early March, tend to be more anxious about the economy in the context of the pandemic than their peers. Such results are consistent with Binder (2020) who surveyed online over 500 U.S. consumers in early March as well and find that many consumers associate bad times with high inflation on the one hand and that those with greater concerns about coronavirus have higher inflation expectations and more pessimistic unemployment expectations than those who express less concern, on the other. In the same vein, Coibion et al. (2020a) using a large-scale survey of U.S. households study the causal influence of the differential timing of local lockdowns due to COVID-19 in the US on macroeconomic expectations, among others at the local level. The authors find that lockdowns have noticeable effects on households' expectations, contrary to COVID-19 infections. Households who live in counties that went into lockdown have more pessimistic unemployment expectations in both the short and medium runs but more optimistic inflation expectations than their peers.

Outside the U.S. context, a few studies are available. In March 2020 (Bu et al., 2020) surveyed graduated students based in Wuhan, China and compared those who were quarantined to the others. The authors find that quarantined graduated students based in Wuhan, China were more likely to have more pessimistic beliefs about the economy, lower risk tolerance and lower trust in others than those who were not quarantined.

In Europe, country-level studies have recently emerged, but a knowledge gap remains. For instance (Valente de Almeida et al., 2020), developed an online panel survey of households in Portugal, following the work of Binder (2020). With regards to expectations, the authors show that individuals who reported being concerned are more likely to expect high to very high current or future negative financial impacts, especially in the short run. Both Binder (2020) and (Coibion et al., 2020c) conduct an information experiment on surveyed U.S. households that consists in randomly providing them with policy announcements or decisions. Binder (2020) interestingly finds that, after exposing them to information about the Fed's policy announcement, the same surveyed US consumers adjust their answers becoming more optimistic about unemployment and revising inflation expectations downward. However, Coibion et al. (2020c), find little evidence that even large policy decisions or announcements have much of an effect on households' beliefs.

Such findings have strong policy implications that are in line with Briscese et al. (2020) who suggest that local authorities and national governments should prioritize communication to manage people's expectations and with Chang and Velasco (2020), who explain that the optimality of (monetary and fiscal) policies rely on these people's expectations. They also document the literature that focuses on the inattention of individual actors to policy actions and announcements.

2.2 *Macroeconomic Expectations*

Several studies have investigated the impact of the COVID-19 pandemic on macroeconomic expectations across different sectors of the economy. Baker et al. (2020) analysed consumer expectations and found that they were significantly affected by the pandemic. However, the study was limited to the US and did not explore the impact of the pandemic on other sectors of the economy.

Fernández-Villaverde and Jones (2020) analysed the impact of the pandemic on macroeconomic indicators and found that the pandemic has had a significant impact on output, employment, and inflation. The study provided valuable insights into the overall impact of the pandemic on the economy but did not focus specifically on the sector-wise impact of macroeconomic expectations.

Coibion et al. (2020b) investigated the costs of the pandemic and found that the pandemic has led to significant declines in consumer spending and increased uncertainty about the future. However, the study did not explore the impact of the pandemic on different sectors of the economy. Kozhan and Thakor (2020) analysed the impact of the pandemic on equity markets and found that the pandemic has led to significant declines in stock prices. However, the study was limited to the financial sector and did not explore the impact of the pandemic on other sectors of the economy. Several studies have investigated the impact of the pandemic on specific sectors of the economy.

Altig et al. (2020) analysed the impact of the pandemic on the service sector in the US and found that the sector has been severely affected due to social distancing measures and reduced consumer demand. However, the study was limited to the US and did not explore the impact of the pandemic on other countries or regions. Brinca et al. (2020) examined the impact of the pandemic on the manufacturing sector in Europe and found that the sector has experienced a sharp decline in output due to supply chain disruptions and reduced demand. The study provided valuable insights into the impact of the pandemic on the manufacturing sector but did not explore the impact of the pandemic on other sectors of the economy. The impact of the pandemic on the retail sector has also been studied in several empirical studies.

McKibbin and Fernando (2020) found that the pandemic has led to significant declines in retail sales globally, with some countries experiencing declines of up to 90%. However, the study was limited to retail sales and did not explore the impact of the pandemic on other sectors of the economy. Deaton and Jain (2020) found that the pandemic has led to changes in consumer behaviour, with consumers shifting their spending patterns towards essential goods and online shopping. The study provided valuable insights into the impact of the pandemic on consumer behaviour but did not explore the impact of the pandemic on other sectors of the economy. Several studies have also examined the impact of COVID-19 on the financial sector.

Avdjiev et al. (2020) investigated the impact of the pandemic on global financial markets and found that the pandemic has led to significant declines in stock prices and increased volatility in financial markets. The study provided valuable insights into the impact of the pandemic on financial markets but did not explore the impact of the pandemic on other sectors of the economy. Cerutti et al. (2020) examined the impact of the pandemic on the banking sector and found that banks are likely to face increased credit risk and liquidity challenges due to the pandemic.

Furthermore, Czernich et al. (2020) find that social distancing measures implemented to reduce the spread of the virus have led to a decline in consumer demand for goods and services, resulting in significant economic losses. The authors also report that the negative effects of COVID-19 on the global economy are likely to be long-lasting, with potentially severe consequences for employment and poverty rates. While the above studies provide important insights into the macroeconomic impact of COVID-19, they do not specifically explore the sectoral impact of the pandemic on the economies. Therefore, there is a need for further research to better understand the impact of COVID-19 on different sectors of the economy, including service, industry, finance, and retail sales. Understanding these sectoral impacts is essential to developing effective policy responses to mitigate the negative economic effects of the pandemic.

To address this research gap, our study aims to investigate the sectoral impact of COVID-19 on macroeconomic expectations. Specifically, we analyse how the outbreak of the pandemic has affected macroeconomic expectations in different sectors of the economy. To achieve this goal, we extend the existing literature on consumer expectations and fluctuation in macroeconomic indicators to other sectors, including service, industry, finance, and retail sales. We also construct factors for three possible and mutually exclusive events (MEEs) of increase, decrease, and no change in COVID-19 infections/fatalities and estimate a latent factor model using GMM techniques. Moreover, we use an MMR model to study the relationship between the change in fatalities caused by COVID-19 and the expectations of economic agents across different macroeconomic sectors in the European Union.

Our study has several contributions to the existing literature. First, it extends the existing literature on the impact of COVID-19 on macroeconomic expectations beyond consumer expectations and fluctuation in macroeconomic indicators to other sectors. Second, it provides insights into the behaviour of economic agents across different macroeconomic sectors in response to changes in COVID-19 infections/fatalities. Third, our study analyses the relationship between the change in fatalities caused by COVID-19 and the expectations of economic agents across different macroeconomic sectors.

This analysis helps to identify the factors that influence the expectations of economic agents in response to the pandemic. In summary, the COVID-19 pandemic has had a significant impact on the global economy, with potentially severe consequences for employment and poverty rates. While several studies have explored the macroeconomic impact of the pandemic, there is a need for further research to better understand the sectoral impact of the pandemic on the economy. Our study aims to contribute to this research gap by investigating the sectoral impact of COVID-19 on macroeconomic expectations in different sectors of the economy.

This study aims to combine this new stream of literature with another recent one that aims to adopt a comprehensive perspective in the study of the COVID-19 shock on different economic sectors. Such an approach argues that expectations vary across agents and countries (Bachmann et al., 2015; Claus & Nguyen, 2020; Dräger et al., 2016; Ehrmann et al., 2015; Malmendier & Nagel, 2016). Most studies find that expectations vary across sectors across economies with different sizes and forms in systematic ways.

We contribute to this literature by providing the first evidence of how the recent COVID-19 period altered the economic expectations of economic agents in the European Union.

3 Data and Empirical Strategy

3.1 *Data*

3.1.1 COVID19 Fatalities

We use monthly data on COVID-19 fatalities because the data on macroeconomic expectations is available only on a monthly and quarterly basis. Our sample consists of all 27 countries in the EU, and we cover the complete period of the COVID-19 pandemic so far January 2020–September 2022. Table 1 exhibits descriptive statistics of COVID-19 fatalities in the European Union, categorized by country, quartile, and overall sample. The results underscore a significant divergence in the pandemic's impact across the region. We acknowledge that some may challenge these findings based on population-weighted deaths in each country, which we have also computed.

However, we caution against relying solely on such metrics, as they may not accurately reflect the true extent of the pandemic's impact. It is worth noting that countries with a high number of fatalities, even with larger populations, experienced a widespread impact across all sectors of their economies. As such, we contend that the absolute number of fatalities shown in Table 1 provides a more robust measure of the incidence and impact of COVID-19 in these countries.

However, as shown in Table 1, our analysis indicated a high level of skewness, with sample countries facing COVID-19 to varying degrees. Therefore, we divided the sample into four quartiles based on the number of fatalities experienced by each country. Quartile 1 comprised countries with the highest death rates, while Quartile 4 included those with the lowest death rates among the sample countries. These findings have significant implications for policymakers and investors seeking to better understand sectoral expectations and inform decision-making during the pandemic.

3.1.2 *Expectations*

In a similar vein as (Syed, 2021), we obtained data on sectoral expectations from the BCS survey. Launched in November 1961 for industry and later extended to include consumers in 1972, this survey has been regularly expanded to include new member states. Conducted monthly, the survey covers six areas: Construction, Consumer, Industry, Financial Services, Retail Trade, and Services. Sample sizes for each sector were provided in the BCS guide for 2020 and ranged from 24,000 for Construction to 44,470 for Investment.

The sample sizes varied by country in proportion to population size, which was particularly relevant for the European Union, consisting of 27 Member States. Our analysis revealed significantly high standard deviations in certain sectors, a finding which we attribute to potential aggregation bias. Notably, Table 1 computed for the complete sample of the European Union showed that not all countries had faced the same degree of fatalities due to COVID-19, and this difference may have been

Table 1 Country-wise COVID-19 fatalities in descriptive statistics

EU-27	*Mean*	*Median*	*Max.*	*Min.*	*Std. Dev.*	*Skew.*	*Kurtosis*	*Sum*
Austria	648.06	357.00	3402	0.00	795.11	1.93	6.53	20,738
Belgium	1021.03	630.00	6889	0.00	1465.40	2.75	10.56	32,673
Bulgaria	1178.56	419.00	4454	0.00	1304.56	0.91	2.53	37,714
Cyprus	36.88	29.50	123	0.00	33.36	0.78	2.72	1180
Czechia	1284.06	277.50	6082	0.00	1744.28	1.34	3.59	41,090
Germany	4685.88	3152.50	23,874	0.00	5233.38	2.03	7.41	149,948
Denmark	222.31	111.00	1089	0.00	274.93	1.75	5.35	7114
Estonia	83.78	40.00	313	0.00	92.89	1.00	2.77	2681
Greece	1034.72	746.50	2710	0.00	891.77	0.45	1.86	33,111
Spain	3565.13	2411.00	16,079	0.00	3590.77	1.76	6.01	114,084
Finland	186.91	95.00	795	2.00	223.41	1.49	4.26	5981
France	4878.69	3194.50	20,823	0.00	4932.72	1.54	5.00	156,118
Croatia	528.19	265.50	2134	0.00	591.92	1.14	3.18	16,902
Hungary	1484.47	403.50	6803	0.00	1906.68	1.30	3.65	47,503
Ireland	248.19	180.00	1161	29.00	293.91	2.15	6.75	7942
Italy	5532.94	3541.50	18,583	0.00	5471.38	0.99	2.73	177,054
Lithuania	291.25	130.00	1181	0.00	334.41	1.13	3.33	9320
Luxembourg	35.28	19.50	174	0.00	43.92	2.02	6.60	1129
Latvia	187.19	99.50	926	0.00	220.40	1.45	5.02	5990
Malta	25.19	17.00	82	0.00	26.69	0.89	2.39	806
Netherlands	727.66	302.50	3771	0.00	882.61	1.75	5.85	23,285
Poland	3673.09	748.50	14,457	0.00	4551.06	1.02	2.68	117,539
Portugal	782.00	401.50	5576	31.00	1181.11	2.80	10.72	25,024

(continued)

Table 1 (continued)

EU-27	*Mean*	*Median*	*Max.*	*Min.*	*Std. Dev.*	*Skew.*	*Kurtosis*	*Sum*
Romania	2094.25	1275.50	10,710	0.00	2447.82	2.03	7.19	67,016
Sweden	632.03	405.00	2864	0.00	722.01	1.58	4.70	20,225
Slovenia	213.16	95.00	1262	0.00	310.32	2.17	7.09	6821
Slovak Republic	639.22	195.00	2547	0.00	851.88	1.25	3.18	20,455
Quartile 01	25,914.44	17,917.50	73,668	0.00	22,322.29	0.82	2.38	829,262
Quartile 02	6028.03	3904.00	18,592	0.00	5462.96	0.83	2.48	192,897
Quartile 03	3209.25	2111.50	11,302	0.00	3015.84	1.07	3.49	102,696
Quartile 04	768.38	560.00	2280	0.00	665.05	0.62	2.25	24,588
The EU	605,482.91	727,835	1,146,524	0.00	400,964.55	−0.18	−1.49	19,980,936

Author's Calculation

Source Thomson Reuters and European BCS data

translated into subsequent sectoral expectations. The sample size across countries is based on the population size of the respective country.[1]

We present some descriptive statistics in Table 2, where one can observe significantly high standard deviations in some sectors. One reason for such dispersion could possibly be the aggregation bias. As the numbers in Table 1 are computed for the complete sample of the European Union, where all the countries have not faced the same degree of fatalities due to the pandemic and this difference has been translated into the consequent sectoral expectations. Based on the output in Table 2, the Construction sector has a mean confidence level of −1.08, indicating low confidence. However, the median confidence level of 2.90 indicates that there is still some optimism in the sector. The minimum confidence level of −19.20 suggests that there is a significant level of pessimism in the sector. The mean expectation for inflation in this sector is 16.05, which is higher than the overall average inflation rate in the economy. The low confidence levels and high inflation expectations may indicate concerns about the future of the Construction sector.

In the Consumer sector, the mean confidence level is −13.79, which is considerably lower than the other sectors, indicating that there is a high level of pessimism in this sector. The mean expectation for inflation in this sector is 30.39, which is much higher than the average inflation rate. Additionally, the mean expectation for unemployment is 30.41, which is also higher than the overall unemployment rate. These results suggest that consumers have a negative outlook on the economy, and their expectations of inflation and unemployment are concerning.

In the Finance sector, the mean confidence level is 8.56, indicating a moderate level of optimism. However, the mean expectation for inflation is 8.78, which is lower than the overall average. The mean expectation for unemployment is 1.74, which is also lower than the overall rate. The

[1] EUROPEAN Union currently consists of 27 Member States: Bulgaria (BE), Croatia (HR), Czech Republic (CZ), Denmark (DK), Hungary (HU), Poland (PL), Romania (RO), Sweden (SE), Belgium (BE), Germany (DE), Estonia (EE), Ireland (IE), Greece (EL), Spain (ES), France (FR), Italy (IT), Cyprus (CY), Latvia (LV), Lithuania (LT), Luxembourg (LU), Malta (MT), Netherlands (NL), Austria (AT), Portugal (PT), Slovenia (SI), Slovakia (SK) and Finland (FI).

Besides many others this approach has been applied by Claus and Nguyen (2020), Dai and Singleton (2000), Ali and Syed (2012), Craine and Martin (2008), and Diebold et al. (2006).

Table 2 Descriptive statistics

Sector	*Variables*	*Mean*	*Median*	*Max*	*Min*	*Std. Dev*	*Skew*	*Kurtosis*
Building	Confidence	−1.08	2.90	7.90	−19.20	8.28	−0.76	2.29
	Inflation	16.05	15.40	53.40	−14.30	21.67	0.12	1.61
	Unemployment	3.80	6.25	13.60	−19.40	8.26	−1.02	3.44
Consumer	Confidence	−13.79	−13.80	−2.10	−27.20	6.95	−0.30	2.10
	Inflation	30.39	22.05	63.20	8.70	18.17	0.43	1.57
	Unemployment	30.41	29.95	62.80	13.40	11.52	0.71	3.14
Finance	Confidence	8.56	11.20	32.60	−53.90	20.22	−1.63	5.66
	Inflation	8.78	12.40	33.90	−65.70	20.13	−1.88	7.46
	Unemployment	1.74	6.25	16.80	−33.30	12.26	−1.00	3.47
Industry	Confidence	−0.11	3.35	14.20	−34.20	12.32	−1.06	3.49
	Inflation	23.98	26.85	59.30	−9.30	21.96	−0.01	1.62
	Unemployment	1.65	6.65	18.00	−29.50	12.34	−0.72	2.56
Retail	Confidence	−4.96	−2.95	8.00	−34.10	10.06	−1.22	4.42
	Inflation	23.89	15.50	57.30	−8.30	21.29	0.31	1.62
	Unemployment	−2.47	−1.30	5.70	−27.60	7.15	−1.64	6.23
Services	Confidence	0.22	8.45	21.40	−48.30	18.96	−1.09	3.49
	Inflation	10.13	10.25	30.50	−13.80	12.66	0.00	1.90
	Unemployment	4.22	7.75	18.10	−32.90	11.74	−1.19	4.40

Confidence (Confidence in the overall macroeconomic environment); Inflation (Price trends over the next 12 months); Unemployment (Unemployment expectations over the next 12 months)
Author's Calculation
Source Thomson Reuters and European BCS data

Finance sector may be more optimistic due to its ability to manage risk and leverage opportunities.

The industry sector has a mean confidence level of −0.11, indicating slight negative sentiment. The mean expectation for inflation is 23.98, which is higher than the overall average, and the mean expectation for unemployment is 1.65, which is lower than the overall rate. The higher inflation expectation in the industry sector may be due to the higher cost of raw materials and other inputs that may increase prices.

In the Retail sector, the mean confidence level is −4.96, indicating negative sentiment. The mean expectation for inflation is 23.89, which is higher than the overall average, and the mean expectation for unemployment is −2.47, which is lower than the overall rate. The lower expectation of unemployment in the Retail sector may be due to its ability to create jobs and contribute to economic growth.

The Services sector has a mean confidence level of 0.22, indicating slightly positive sentiment. The mean expectation of inflation is 10.13, which is lower than the overall average, and the mean expectation of unemployment is 4.22, which is higher than the overall rate. The Services sector may be more optimistic due to its ability to adapt to changing circumstances and provide innovative solutions to customers.

Regarding the COVID-19 variables, the mean number of cases is 48,161,103, with a median of 31,844,830 and a maximum of 164 million. The mean number of deaths is 588,575.4, with a median of 709,361.5 and a minimum of 0. The skewness and kurtosis values suggest that both variables are positively skewed and have a more peaked distribution than a normal distribution. The high number of COVID-19 cases and deaths may negatively impact the economy, especially in sectors that rely on face-to-face interactions or travel.

3.2 *Empirical Strategy*

3.2.1 *Multivariate Multiple Regression Model—(MMR)*

We start with a multivariate regression where multiple explanatory variables are used to explain the response of one dependent variable (see Eq. 1).

$$y_i = \alpha_0 + \beta_1 x_{i1} + \beta_2 x_{i2} + \ldots + \beta_n x_{in} + \varepsilon \qquad (1)$$

$$= \beta_0 + \sum_{j=1}^{n} \beta_j x_{ij} + \varepsilon_i$$

Along similar lines, one can develop a multivariate multiple system as follows:

$$y_{i1} = \alpha_{01} + \beta_{11}x_{i1} + \beta_{21}x_{i2} + \ldots + \beta_{n1}x_{in} + \varepsilon_{i1}$$
$$y_{i2} = \alpha_{02} + \beta_{12}x_{i2} + \beta_{22}x_{i2} + \ldots + \beta_{n2}x_{in} + \varepsilon_{i2}$$
$$\vdots$$
$$y_{ik} = \alpha_{0k} + \beta_{1k}x_{i1} + \beta_{2k}x_{i2} + \ldots + \beta_{nk}x_{in} + \varepsilon_{ik}$$

The aforementioned equations get the matrix notation.

$$\begin{pmatrix} y_{11} & y_{12} & \cdots & y_{1k} \\ y_{21} & y_{22} & \cdots & y_{2k} \\ \vdots & \vdots & \ddots & \vdots \\ y_{n1} & y_{n2} & \cdots & y_{nk} \end{pmatrix} = \begin{pmatrix} 1 & x_{11} \\ 1 & x_{21} \\ 1 & \vdots \\ 1 & x_{n1} \end{pmatrix} \begin{pmatrix} \beta_0 \\ \beta_1 \\ \vdots \\ \beta_k \end{pmatrix} + \begin{pmatrix} \varepsilon_1 \\ \varepsilon_2 \\ \vdots \\ \varepsilon_n \end{pmatrix}$$

where y has a $(n \times 1)$ dimension matrix, x is $[n(n+1)]$, β is $(r+1)$, and ϵ is $(1 \times m)$.

3.2.2 *Factor Model*

In this section, we proceed with a linear simultaneous setup to develop our estimation strategy as follows:

$$\underset{(n\times 1)}{y_t} = \underset{(n\times 1)}{\alpha} \mathrm{COV}_t^{\mathrm{rise}} + \underset{(n\times 1)}{\beta} \mathrm{COV}_t^{\mathrm{fall}} + \sum_k \underset{(n\times 1)}{\gamma_k} f_{k,t} \tag{2}$$

Equation (2) separates the rising infection days from those where we record a decrease in the infection rate, keeping the non-COVID-19 factors apart. By construction, both the negative and positive infection growths are mutually exclusive processes with unit variance. In what follows, we classify observations into three possible sub-periods based on the infection rate variations. Here α, β, and γ are the factor loadings, where α captures the change in sectoral expectation on the three macroeconomics indicators due to one standard deviation unexpected rise in COVID-19 fatalities.

It is worth noting here that when the number of moment functions surfeits the number of unknown parameters the model is over-identified, and it is usually not possible to set the sample average of these moment functions exactly equal to zero. We follow the solution proposed by Hansen (1982), to set a linear combination of the sample average of the moment functions equal to zero, with the dimension of the linear combination equal to the number of unknown parameters (Imbens, 1997). For simplicity we are not presenting the complete derivation of our model and the strategy, however, this could be seen in Syed (2022).

4 Results

4.1 Aggregated Sample

Conventional wisdom reveals that an adverse macroeconomic shock should lead to negative economic expectations. This statement has to be established by looking not only into the overall macroeconomic environment, but a disaggregated analysis of different sectors would bring important evidence. Table 3 records the results of our first simple analysis done for the complete sample, which includes all 27, member nations of the European Union.

The MMR results show the coefficients for the predictors of six different sectors, namely Construction, Consumer, Finance, Industry, Retail, and Services. The predictors are Confidence Indicator (COF), Inflation Expectations (INF), and Unemployment Expectations (UNM).

For COF, a negative coefficient for the Construction and Retail sectors suggests that a higher confidence level is associated with lower order book limitations and business activity sales development, respectively. On the other hand, for the Consumer and Finance sectors, a negative coefficient for COF indicates that a high confidence level is associated with a better financial situation over the next 12 months. A significant relationship is observed between COF and the Industry and Services sectors.

For INF, a positive coefficient for all sectors implies that higher inflation expectations are associated with higher scores on the corresponding confidence indicators. This suggests that businesses in all sectors expect higher inflation in the near future.

Table 3 Multivariate multiple regression results (MMR)

	Building	*Consumer*	*Finance*	*Industry*	*Retail*	*Services*
COF	−0.13	−1.40**	0.81*	0.02	−0.53**	−0.05
	(0.15)	(0.12)	(0.36)	(0.22)	(0.18)	(0.34)
INF	1.61**	3.10**	0.83*	2.47**	2.42**	0.98**
	(0.39)	(0.32)	(0.37)	(0.39)	(0.39)	(0.23)
UNM	0.34*	3.04**	0.15	0.20	−0.27*	0.37*
	(0.15)	(0.21)	(0.22)	(0.22)	(0.13)	(0.22)

Notes (1) COF stands for confidence indicator. For Building Sector it includes following questions: (i) Evolution of your current overall order books, (ii) Main factors currently limiting your building activity. It is calculated as simple mean of the responses received for these two questions. For the Consumer Sector, it is calculated using mean of the responses received for the following four questions: (i) Financial situation over last 12 months, (ii) Financial situation over next 12 months, (iii) General economic situation over next 12 months, and (iv) Major purchases over next 12 months. For the Financial Sector, it is calculated using mean of the responses received for the following four questions: (i) Financial situation over last 12 months, (ii) Financial situation over next 12 months, (iii) General economic situation over next 12 months, and (iv) Major purchases over next 12 months. For the Industry, it is calculated using mean of the responses received for the following four questions: (i) Assessment of order-book levels (ii) Assessment of stocks of finished products, and (iii) Production expectations for the months ahead. For the Retail Sector, it is calculated using mean of the responses received for the following four questions: (i) Business activity (sales) development over the past 3 months, (ii) Volume of stock currently hold, and (iii) Orders expectations over the next 3 months. For the Services Sector, it is calculated using mean of the responses received for the following four questions: (i) Business situation development over the past 3 months, (ii) Evolution of the demand over the past 3 months, and (iii) Expectation of the demand over the next 3 months
(2) INF stands for inflation expectations over the next three months
(3) UNM stands for the unemployment expectations over the next three months
Source Business and Consumer Survey, European Commission. Thomson Reuters

For UNM, a positive coefficient for the Consumer and Services sectors suggests that higher unemployment expectations are associated with a lower financial situation and business situation development, respectively. A positive coefficient for the Construction sector indicates that higher unemployment expectations are associated with more limiting factors for building activity. A negative coefficient for the Retail sector suggests that higher unemployment expectations are associated with higher orders expectations over the next three months. No significant relationship is observed between UNM and the Finance and Industry sectors.

In terms of linking the sectors to the overall economy, the results suggest that inflation expectations have a significant influence on the confidence levels of businesses in all sectors. Higher inflation expectations may lead to higher costs for businesses, which may affect their overall performance. Additionally, higher unemployment expectations have a negative impact on the financial and business situation of businesses in the Consumer and Services sectors. This implies that the overall economy's health and employment outlook can significantly affect specific sectors.

We record wise-spread negativity across all the sectors except the Retail Sector. The results indicate mistrust in the future economic environment by different segments of the economies. We also find that the economic agents expect a surge in inflation facing the COVID-19 shock. Similar adverse expectations have been recorded in terms of the employment situation as well.

One can observe that overall confidence has tumbled in all sectors due to COVID-19. While the results for the construction sector and Industry remain inconclusive, we find strongly negative expectations in the consumer and retail sectors. This explains the consequences of extended confinements, travel restrictions and closure of shopping malls and sale outlets. The financial sector proved resilient and has shown promise during the pandemic which could greatly be attributed to the increased digitalization and notable use of IT-based products in this sector prior to the shock.

Fears of high and unstable inflation could be observed in Table 3, where all the sectors recorded an expected positively proportionate change in inflation in the face of COVID-19 intensity. Particularly the larger sizes of coefficients in the Consumer, Industry and Retail Trade sectors are reflective of the intense and immediate response of these sectors on the back of lockdowns, confinements, and travel restrictions.

Along similar lines, unemployment expectations follow the trend in fatalities due to COVID-19. All the sectors, except for the Retail Trade sector show the dependence of labour market dynamics on the situation created by the pandemic. While there could be several reasons behind the inverse reaction from the Retail sector, one may also attribute it to the increased use of platform markets and the increased tendency of sale purchases at online outlets.

Though we record an obvious following in the behaviour of economic agents in different macroeconomic sectors, these results are for the EU, where different economies faced the pandemic to different degrees. Therefore, in the next section, we disaggregate our sample into quartiles based on COVID-19 fatalities.

4.2 *Disaggregated Sample*

As mentioned earlier, this section reveals the results for our sample in quartiles for Construction, Consumer, Industry, Retail, and Service sectors. Table 4 compiles the results of our MMR for the disaggregated sample on the sectoral expectations about three important macroeconomic indicators: Overall Confidence in the Macroeconomic Environment, Inflation, and Unemployment. Here we record that while the first quartile faced the most fatalities in number, the response of different economic sectors remains similar across different economies.

The table presents the results of an analysis of expectations of inflation and unemployment for different macroeconomic sectors, broken down by quartiles of confidence. The data suggests that there is a relationship between confidence and inflation expectations, as well as between confidence and unemployment expectations.

Across all macroeconomic sectors, as confidence increases from the 1st quartile to the 4th quartile, inflation expectations also increase significantly. The highest quartile, which represents the most confident groups, has the highest inflation expectations. On the other hand, unemployment expectations are relatively stable across quartiles, although there is a slight increase in expectations for the most confident groups.

Looking at the different sectors, the industry and retail sectors have the highest inflation expectations across all quartiles of confidence, while the consumer and services sectors have the lowest. For unemployment expectations, the consumer sector has the highest expectations in the 2nd and 3rd quartiles, while the industry sector has the highest expectations in the

Table 4 MMR results for quartiles

Sub-Groups	*Expectations*	*Macroeconomic sectors*				
	Indicators	*Building*	*Consumer*	*Industry*	*Retail*	*Services*
1st Quartile	Confidence	−4.18**	−9.45**	−2.89**	−3.84**	−3.82*
		(0.88)	(0.77)	(1.21)	(1.15)	(2.09)
	Inflation	13.12**	20.12**	16.46**	19.78**	8.03**
		(2.39)	(1.41)	(2.40)	(2.40)	(1.69)
	Unemployment	0.41	19.51**	−0.72	−0.91	0.77
		(0.88)	(1.69)	(1.17)	(0.77)	(1.08)
2nd Quartile	Confidence	−4.38**	−15.21**	−3.15**	0.67	2.18
		(1.20)	(1.00)	(1.08)	(1.15)	(2.49)
	Inflation	15.99**	21.75**	14.39**	16.21**	6.05**
		(2.61)	(1.74)	(2.21)	(2.43)	(1.67)
	Unemployment	3.35**	24.31**	1.62	2.62**	3.18**
		(1.35)	(2.53)	(1.03)	(0.77)	(1.45)
3rd Quartile	Confidence	−4.30**	-9.19**	1.72	0.50	3.33
		(1.85)	(1.16)	(1.73)	(1.79)	(3.50)
	Inflation	21.70**	32.62**	21.78**	26.09**	11.92**
		(3.93)	(2.30)	(3.31)	(3.61)	(2.33)
	Unemployment	4.40**	17.67**	8.81**	1.80	5.02**
		(2.11)	(2.21)	(2.18)	(1.34)	(2.04)

(continued)

Table 4 (continued)

Sub-Groups	*Expectations*	*Macroeconomic sectors*				
	Indicators	*Building*	*Consumer*	*Industry*	*Retail*	*Services*
4th Quartile	Confidence	−0.59	−16.85**	−2.96	−2.75	−0.06
		(1.93)	(1.45)	(2.54)	(2.06)	(3.52)
	Inflation	31.87**	33.12**	27.96**	35.14**	11.94**
		(5.39)	(3.38)	(4.35)	(3.96)	(2.81)
	Unemployment	8.15**	26.69**	5.62**	−2.79*	5.72**
		(2.16)	(3.31)	(2.68)	(1.52)	(2.00)

(1) 1st Quartile includes: Italy, France, Germany, Poland, Spain, Romania, and Hungary. 2nd Quartile includes: Czech Republic, Bulgaria, Greece, Belgium, Portugal, and the Netherlands. 3rd Quartile includes: Austria, Slovakia, Sweden, Croatia, Lithuania, Ireland, and Denmark. 4th Quartile consists of: Slovenia, Latvia, Finland, Estonia, Cyprus, Luxembourg, and Malta

(2) Confidence (Confidence in overall macroeconomic environment); Inflation (Price trends over next 12 months); Unemployment (Unemployment expectations over next 12 months)

(3) Level of significance: **5%, *10%

(4) Standard errors in parentheses

4th quartile. Overall, the findings suggest that higher confidence is associated with higher inflation expectations, particularly in the industry and retail sectors. However, the relationship between confidence and unemployment expectations is less clear, with some variation across different macroeconomic sectors.

Quartile 01 is composed of highly COVID-19-affected countries. These countries have an interesting commonality in that these are some of the highly populous countries of the EU, and at the same time, these are the relatively stronger and larger economies of the EU. In Table 4, we record our findings, and one may observe that the expectations in all the macroeconomic sectors about the overall confidence in the macroeconomic environment are strongly affected by the consequences of the pandemic. We find an obvious inverse relationship between the way economic agents revise their expectations in the face of evolution in the COVID-19 fatalities. Although we are establishing here the nexus between macroeconomic expectations and the sectoral macroeconomic dynamics, the results have already been validated by the widespread economic downtrend in all these economies. In this regard, inflation expectations also are not an exception, and we find that in all sectors it was expected that rising COVID-19 fatalities may finally result in higher inflation and vice versa. For the expectations regarding Unemployment, our results are mostly inconclusive except in the consumer sector which shares a consistent behaviour of adverse impact of the pandemic on employment conditions in this sector.

Quartile 02 shows a strong resemblance in the way the economic agents revise their expectations facing COVID-19. The results are quite similar in this group of countries to Quartile 01; however, we record strong and significant worries in the job markets in this quartile.

Results in Quartile 03 are also in line with the first two quartiles. However, one may observe that the inflation and unemployment expectations are highly significant and strong in this quartile. One reason for this could be the fact that despite being smaller economies in terms of fatalities and while this group includes mostly the relatively weaker EU economies, the proportionate fatalities in these economies remained very high to their population sizes. This may have resulted in a deep and sharp increase of pessimism and reaction in all sectors of these economies.

Quartile 04 consists of countries with lesser fatalities in total compared to quartile 01, however, when weighted by population, these countries recorded significant numbers. In terms of Overall Confidence, the results for most sectors remain inconclusive, yet Industry followed the trend like the other quartiles. All the sectors show strong and significant expectations of high inflation due to the rise in COVID-19 deaths. Unemployment expectations also remain high and consistent, except in the retail sector. These outcomes lead us to the need of looking into the spillovers across economies and at the same time it reveals the need of studying the response during at least two different scenarios: rising COVID-19 cases and when there is a decrease in COVID-19 fatalities. In this context, the next sub-section briefly describes our results from the factor model.

4.3 *Factor-Based Results for the Aggregated Sample*

In this subsection, we report and discuss our factor model results. Though these results should be interpreted with caution, knowing the size of the time series. As we bifurcate the COVID-19 fatalities time series into rises and falls, this further reduces the number of events. However, as we have already compiled comprehensive results in the previous sections, one may be confident of not being misled by the inconsistencies, if any.

Table 5 presents the outcomes of our factor model, which seeks to identify the factors underlying the revisions of macroeconomic expectations across six critical sectors—Construction, Consumer, Finance, Industry, Retail, and Services—during the COVID-19 pandemic. The results confirm the findings of our previous sections, indicating that the pandemic has had a significant impact on macroeconomic expectations across all sectors.

However, two crucial observations emerge from our analysis. Firstly, we observe that economic agents revise their expectations negatively in response to changes in fatalities, with pessimism persisting even during the days when fatalities are decreasing. This suggests that economic agents are cautious in revising their expectations and tend to be more pessimistic in their outlook, even when the situation appears to be improving.

Secondly, our findings suggest a widespread sense of high expected inflation across all sectors during both the increasing and decreasing fatalities days. This is noteworthy as it is not in line with the standard economic theory, which suggests that inflation expectations should be lower during times of economic crisis, as demand falls and supply chain disruptions occur. The high expected inflation may reflect the uncertainty caused by the pandemic and the unprecedented nature of the crisis.

Table 5 Factor based estimation results

	Building		*Consumer*		*Finance*		*Industry*		*Retail*		*Services*	
	COVID-19 Fatalities											
	↑	↓	↑	↓	↑	↓	↑	↓	↑	↓	↑	↓
COF	−9.11**	1.01**	−2.22**	3.14**	−4.42***	7.12**	2.38**	−2.87**	−16.31**	−1.00**	−1.01**	−3.65**
INF	2.21*	−1.07**	9.11**	-3.11*	−2.13**	−3.17**	−11.39**	−2.71**	−11.29*	−4.78**	−12.32*	−3.87*
UNM	11.25*	−6.73*	13.21*	−7.23**	3.97*	−6.13*	9.33**	5.21**	13.12*	3.19*	11.12*	4.94*

(1) COF stands for confidence indicator. For Building Sector it includes following questions: (i) Evolution of your current overall order books, (ii) Main factors currently limiting your building activity. It is calculated as simple mean of the responses received for these two questions. For the Consumer Sector, it is calculated using mean of the responses received for the following four questions: (i) Financial situation over last 12 months, (ii) Financial situation over next 12 months, (iii) General economic situation over next 12 months, and (iv) Major purchases over next 12 months. For the Financial Sector, it is calculated using mean of the responses received for the following four questions: (i) Financial situation over last 12 months, (ii) Financial situation over next 12 months, (iii) General economic situation over next 12 months, and (iv) Major purchases over next 12 months. For the Industry, it is calculated using mean of the responses received for the following four questions: (i) Assessment of order-book levels (ii) Assessment of stocks of finished products, and (iii) Production expectations for the months ahead. For the Retail Sector, it is calculated using mean of the responses received for the following four questions: (i) Business activity (sales) development over the past 3 months, (ii) Volume of stock currently hold, and (iii) Orders expectations over the next 3 months. For the Services Sector, it is calculated using mean of the responses received for the following four questions: (i) Business situation development over the past 3 months, (ii) Evolution of the demand over the past 3 months, and (iii) Expectation of the demand over the next 3 months

(2) INF stands for inflation expectations over the next three months

(3) UNM stands for the unemployment expectations over the next three months

Source Business and Consumer Survey, European Commission. Thomson Reuters

Overall, the results of our factor model indicate that the COVID-19 pandemic has had a significant impact on macroeconomic expectations across all sectors. Economic agents tend to revise their expectations negatively, and there is a widespread sense of high expected inflation across sectors. These findings underscore the need for policymakers to adopt a cautious and proactive approach to managing the economic fallout of the pandemic, with targeted measures aimed at restoring confidence and promoting economic resilience.

5 Conclusion

Anticipating the response of economic agents to exogenous economic shocks is a critical step towards designing effective policies and solutions. The ability to accurately predict how different sectors of an economy will respond to such shocks is especially important, as it can inform policy decisions and help mitigate the negative impacts of such events. However, as this study has shown, the response of economic agents to shocks can vary significantly across sectors and countries. In particular, the results of this study suggest that there are rigidities in the adjustment of expectations and the presence of asymmetric inconsistencies in the responses of economic agents towards the pandemic shock.

One notable finding is that countries that were less affected by the pandemic also responded in a pessimistic manner, despite having fewer fatalities and disruptions than other countries. This suggests that there may be psychological biases or other factors driving negativity in expectations, even in the absence of significant external factors.

The study also highlights the presence of asymmetries in the behaviour of economic agents across the entire sample, which could be attributed to factors such as uncertainty due to macroeconomic fluctuations or post-crisis precariousness. These asymmetries could potentially contribute to further economic instability and make it difficult to predict and manage the impacts of future shocks.

In conclusion, the chapter emphasizes the importance of anticipating and understanding the response of economic agents to exogenous shocks, and the need for policymakers to develop policies and solutions that take into account the complexity and variability of these responses. This could include measures to address psychological biases, reduce uncertainty, and promote economic stability and resilience in the face of future shocks.

5.1 Practical Implications

The practical implications of this study are significant for policymakers, businesses, and researchers alike. By examining the impact of the COVID-19 pandemic on macroeconomic expectations across various sectors, this research offers actionable insights for navigating future crises. Policymakers can use the findings to design targeted measures that address sector-specific pessimism and stimulate economic recovery. Businesses, on the other hand, can refine their strategies based on a better understanding of how different sectors respond to varying levels of COVID-19 infections and fatalities. This knowledge can aid in crafting adaptive business models, optimizing resource allocation, and managing risk exposure more effectively.

Moreover, the study's focus on the European Union provides valuable information for regional economic planning and coordination. Understanding the relationship between fatalities and economic expectations can guide policymakers in devising coordinated responses to mitigate negative expectations and foster a more resilient economic environment.

The observation that even countries with dissimilar fatality rates exhibit similar behavioral patterns underscores the need for nuanced strategies that account for shared psychological and economic responses across borders. This insight can influence international collaborations and cooperation during global crises, aiding in the development of common strategies to counteract economic downturns.

In essence, this study's practical implications extend to guiding policy formulation, enhancing business resilience, promoting regional collaboration, and fostering a more comprehensive understanding of how societies and economies respond to disruptive events, ultimately contributing to more effective crisis management and sustainable recovery efforts.

References

Ali, S., & Syed, S. (2012). Does greater economic openness grasp the elements of inflation 'surprise'? New evidence using panel data techniques. *International Economics, 130*, 3358.

Altig, D., Baker, S. R., Barrero, J. M., Bloom, N., Bunn, P., Chen, S., Davis, S. J., Leather, J., Meyer, B., Mihaylov, E., Mizen, P., Parker, N., Renault, T., Smietanka, P., & Thwaites, G. (2020). *The economic effects of the pandemic on the service sector: A snapshot*. SSRN.

Avdjiev, S., Gambacorta, L., Goldberg, L. S., & Schia, S. (2020). The impact of the COVID-19 pandemic on international banking. *BIS Bulletin, 3*, 17.

Bachmann, R., Berg, T. O., & Sims, E. R. (2015). Inflation expectations and readiness to spend: Cross-sectional evidence. *American Economic Journal: Economic Policy, 7*(1), 135.

Baker, S. R., Farrokhnia, R. A., Meyer, S., Pagel, M., & Yannelis, C. (2020). How does household spending respond to an epidemic? Consumption during the 2020 COVID-19 pandemic. *The Review of Asset Pricing Studies, 10*(4), 834862.

Binder, C. (2020). Coronavirus fears and macroeconomic expectations. *Review of Economics and Statistics, 102*(4), 721730.

Brinca, P., Duarte, J. B., & Faria-e Castro, M. (2020). *Pandemics depress the economy, public health interventions do not: Evidence from the 1918 flu* (NBER Working Paper (26934)).

Briscese, G., Lacetera, N., Macis, M., & Tonin, M. (2020). *Compliance with COVID-19 social-distancing measures in Italy: The role of expectations and duration* (Vol. 27). National Bureau of Economic Research.

Brodeur, A., Gray, D., Islam, A., & Bhuiyan, S. (2021). A literature review of the economics of COVID-19. *Journal of Economic Surveys, 35*(4), 10071044.

Bu, D., Hanspal, T., Liao, Y., & Liu, Y. (2020). Economic preferences during a global crisis: Evidence from Wuhan. *SSRN Electronic Journal, 10*.

Cerutti, E., Claessens, S., & McGuire, P. (2020). COVID-19 and non-performing loans: Lessons from past crises. *Journal of Financial Stability, 49*, 117.

Chang, R., & Velasco, A. (2020). *Economic policy incentives to preserve lives and livelihoods* (Tech. Rep.). National Bureau of Economic Research.

Claus, E., & Nguyen, V. H. (2020). Monetary policy shocks from the consumer perspective. *Journal of Monetary Economics, 114*, 159173.

Coibion, O., Gorodnichenko, Y., & Weber, M. (2020a). *The cost of the COVID-19 crisis: Lock-downs, macroeconomic expectations, and consumer spending* (Tech. Rep.). National Bureau of Economic Research.

Coibion, O., Gorodnichenko, Y., & Weber, M. (2020b). *The costs of the COVID-19 crisis: Lock-downs, macroeconomic expectations, and consumer spending* (NBER Working Paper (27141)).

Coibion, O., Gorodnichenko, Y., & Weber, M. (2020c). *Does policy communication during COVID work?* (Tech. Rep.). National Bureau of Economic Research.

Coibion, O., Gorodnichenko, Y., & Weber, M. (2020d). *Labor markets during the COVID-19 crisis: A preliminary view* (Tech. Rep.). National Bureau of Economic Research.

Craine, R., & Martin, V. L. (2008). International monetary policy surprise spillovers. *Journal of International Economics, 75*(1), 180196.

Czernich, N., Falck, O., Feld, L. P., Köhler, E. A., & Woessmann, L. (2020). The economic impact of COVID-19 on households and firms: A survey. *ifo Schnelldienst, 73*(8), 0326.

Dai, Q., & Singleton, K. J. (2000). Specification analysis of affine term structure models. *The Journal of Finance, 55*(5), 19431978.

Deaton, B. J., & Jain, S. (2020). *COVID-19 and the demand for online food shopping services: Empirical evidence from Italy*. SSRN.

Diebold, F. X., Rudebusch, G. D., & Aruoba, S. B. (2006). The macroeconomy and the yield curve: A dynamic latent factor approach. *Journal of Econometrics, 131*(1–2), 309338.

Dietrich, A. M., Kuester, K., Müller, G. J., & Schoenle, R. (2022). News and uncertainty about COVID-19: Survey evidence and short-run economic impact. *Journal of Monetary Economics*.

Dräger, L., Lamla, M. J., & Pfajfar, D. (2016). Are survey expectations theory-consistent? The role of central bank communication and news. *European Economic Review, 85*, 84111.

Ehrmann, M., Pfajfar, D., & Santoro, E. (2015). *Consumers' attitudes and their inflation expectations*.

Fernández-Villaverde, J., & Jones, C. I. (2020). *Macroeconomic volatility during the COVID-19 pandemic* (NBER Working Paper (27418)).

Hansen, L. P. (1982). Large Sample Properties of Generalized Method of Moments Estimators. *Econometrica: Journal of the Econometric Society*, 10291054.

Imbens, G. W. (1997). One-step estimators for over-identified generalized method of moments models. *The Review of Economic Studies, 64*(3), 359383.

Kamdar, R., et al. (2018). *The inattentive consumer: Sentiment and expectations*. Manuscript. https://rupalkamdar.github.io/pdfs/InattentiveConsumer.pdf

Kozhan, R., & Thakor, A. V. (2020). COVID-19 and financial markets: A long-term view. *Journal of Financial Stability, 50*, 100076.

Malmendier, U., & Nagel, S. (2016). Learning from inflation experiences. *The Quarterly Journal of Economics, 131*(1), 5387.

McKibbin, W. J., & Fernando, R. (2020). *Global macroeconomic scenarios of the COVID-19 pandemic* (NBER Working Paper (26939)).

Syed, S. A. S. (2021). Heterogeneous consumers in the Euro-Area, facing homogeneous monetary policy: Tale of two large economies. *The Journal of Economic Asymmetries, 24*, e00214.

Syed, S. A. S. (2022). Stock market in the age of COVID19: Mere acclimatization or Stockholm syndrome. *The Journal of Economic Asymmetries, 25*, e00245.

Valente de Almeida, S., Costa, E., Lopes, F. V., Santos, J. V., & Pita Barros, P. (2020). Concerns and adjustments: How the Portuguese population met COVID-19. *PLoS ONE, 15*(10), e0240500.

CHAPTER 6

Is There a Trade-off Between Inflation and Unemployment Rate in Time of a Pandemic? The Case of Malaysia

Lim Thye Goh

1 Introduction

Phillips (1958), after whom the Phillips Curve was named, examined annual wage inflation and unemployment rates in the United Kingdom from 1860 to 1957 and concluded that there was a strong inverse relationship between inflation and unemployment. The Phillips Curve is based on the idea that rising inflation lowers unemployment and vice versa. As a result, the intuition behind the Phillips Curve is simple: if the economy is operating at less than full capacity, an increase in aggregate demand is likely to result in lower unemployment and higher inflation. Because central banks around the world are entrusted by their respective

L. T. Goh (✉)
Department of Economics and Applied Statistics, University of Malaya, Kuala Lumpur, Malaysia
e-mail: ltgoh@um.edu.my

A. Mishrif (ed.), *Economic Effects of the Pandemic*, The Political Economy of the Middle East,
https://doi.org/10.1007/978-981-97-4367-4_6

governments to oversee monetary policy and implement specific macroeconomic strategies such as inflation targeting and low unemployment, the Phillips Curve is an important factor to consider when developing effective macroeconomic policies.

In response to the economic distress caused by the COVID-19 pandemic, Malaysia implemented a number of economic stimulus packages. For example, the first Malaysian Ringgit (RM) 20 billion people-centric Economic Stimulus Package, which aimed to protect the welfare and well-being of Malaysian citizens by boosting household spending, was announced in February 2020. The PRIHATIN Economic Stimulus Package, amounting to RM230 billion, was announced in March 2020. The latest stimulus package was the National People's Well-Being and Economic Recovery Package (Pemulih), which was announced in June 2021. Even though the effects of the fiscal stimulus packages were quite compelling, GDP only recovered from a contraction rate of 17.1% in the second quarter of 2020 to a reduced contraction rate of 2.7% and 3.4% in the third and fourth quarters of 2020. On the other hand, the inflation level improved from a negative rate of 2.3% to a positive 2.0%, but the recorded unemployment rate has remained persistent and well above 4.6% (DOSM, 2021). Thus, questioning the validity of the Phillips Curve in Malaysia, especially during the pandemic.

According to the Gross Domestic Product calculation, the GDP is the monetary value of all finished goods and services produced within a country during a specific period. As a result, it is logical to argue that an increase in GDP could be due to high inflation rather than an increase in the volume of goods and services produced, which would not affect employment. Phillips (1958), on the other hand, argued that inflation and unemployment are trade-offs, with inflation expected to reduce unemployment and vice versa. As a result, if an increase in GDP level was caused by price escalation (inflation), it would have reduced the unemployment rate, as depicted by the Phillips curve concept. As a result, the observed persistence of the unemployment rate may imply that Malaysia's unemployment rate has not been sensitive to changes in the inflation rate, as predicted by the Phillips Curve, or that the relationship between the unemployment rate and inflation is asymmetric (Forbes et al., 2020).

Given that policymakers are still looking for the best way to revitalize the domestic economy and reduce unemployment, the correlation between inflation and unemployment, as demonstrated by the Phillips Curve, is critical for policymakers to draught effective macroeconomic policies. As a result, this research would add to the growing body of literature on the existence of a trade-off between inflation and unemployment in Malaysia and the existence of the Phillips Curve during the COVID-19 pandemic. Furthermore, the use of the nonlinear autoregressive distributed lag (NARDL) model proposed by Shin et al. (2014) to investigate potential long-run asymmetries in the inflation unemployment rate nexus may be able to explain the persistence of Malaysia's unemployment rate. The rest of this paper is organized as follows. The section that follows provides context for the study, followed by a review of previous related literature. Section 3 describes the methodology and data that were used in this study. Section 4 summarizes and discusses the empirical findings. Section 5 also includes policy implications as well as concluding remarks.

1.1 Background

The COVID-19 pandemic was first identified in 2019, and by February 2022, there had been more than 393 million confirmed cases, with more than 5.73 million deaths attributed to COVID-19. More than 2.9 million cases had been confirmed in Malaysia as of February 6, 2022, making it the third highest in the ASEAN region. The Malaysian government, like other national governments around the world, has imposed a series of restrictions (movement control orders [MCO]) to slow the spread of the virus. While the implementation of MCOs may have slowed the COVID-19 transmission rate, the economic distress caused by the pandemic has been severe and long-lasting.

According to a report published by the Department of Statistics of Malaysia (DOSM, 2021), Malaysia's economy contracted by 17.1%, 2.7%, and 3.4% in the second, third, and fourth quarters of 2020, respectively. The overall contraction of Malaysia's GDP in 2020 was found to be 5.6%, which was higher than the Ministry of Finance's initial estimate of 4.5% (DOSM, 2021). Furthermore, with the onset of the COVID-19 pandemic, Malaysia's unemployment rate rose to its highest level since the 2008 Global Financial Crisis, rising from 3.9% in March 2020 to 5% in April 2020, a month after the first MCO was implemented. Unemployment later peaked at 5.3% in May 2020, and while the rate fell to 4.3% in October 2021, it remained significantly higher than the 3.3% rate recorded in December 2019. As a result, the economy has been nose-diving, with escalating effects on the country's Gross Domestic Product (GDP) level and unemployment rate.

1.1.1 *Theoretical Background—Phillips Curve*

Phillips (1958) examined annual wage inflation and unemployment rates in the United Kingdom from 1860 to 1957 and concluded that there was a strong inverse relationship between inflation and unemployment. The traditional Phillips Curve, as shown in Eq. (1), shows that the rate of money wages (gW) rises with the trend rate of growth of money wages (gW^T), but falls with the function of the unemployment rate $f(U)$. As a result, it suggests that money wages are inversely related to unemployment.

$$gW = gW^T - f(U) \tag{1}$$

Thus, higher growth in money wages is expected to stimulate market demand for goods and services, resulting in inflation (demand-pull inflation). As a result, inflation is expected to increase job opportunities, lowering the unemployment rate.

1.1.2 *The Relationship Between Inflation and the Unemployment Rate of Malaysia*

Figure 1 indicates that Malaysia's inflation rate fluctuated over time, while its unemployment rate was relatively persistent. In addition, Fig. 1 captures three crucial crises since the 1920 Great Depression, namely, the Asian Financial Crisis (1997–1998), the Global Financial Crisis (2007–2008) and the current COVID-19 pandemic from 2019. Surprisingly, the inverse correlation between inflation and unemployment was apparent during the Asian Financial and Global Financial crises but not during the COVID-19 pandemic. Following the Asian Financial Crisis, the unemployment rate fell from 3.53 to 3.48%, while inflation rose from 1.42% in 2001 to 1.81% in 2002. However, unemployment rose to 3.61% in 2003 as the inflation rate fell further to 1.09%. During the Global Financial Crisis, a similar trend was observed: the drop in inflation from 5.44% in 2008 to 0.58% in 2009 was accompanied by an increase in unemployment from 3.34% in 2008 to 3.69% in 2009.

On the other hand, unlike the previous two crises, although the recession caused by the COVID-19 pandemic is expected to be the deepest

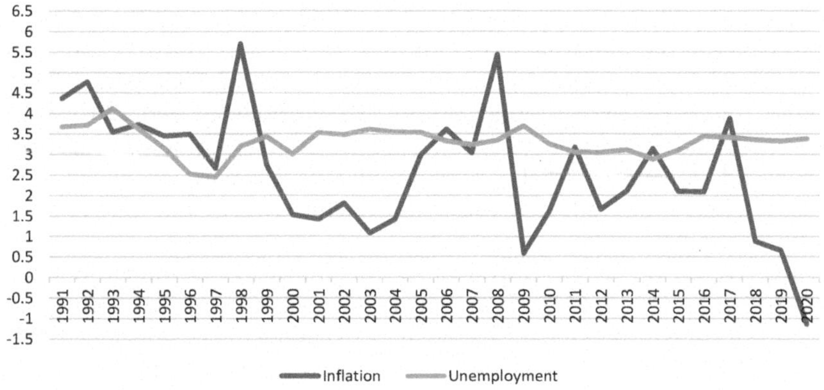

Fig. 1 Malaysia's inflation and unemployment rates (%) from 1991 to 2020 (*Source* Author's own construction)

since the Second World War (World Bank, 2020), unemployment has remained relatively stable in response to changes in the inflation rate. In particular, the significant decrease in inflation from 0.66% in 2019 to a deficit of 1.14% in 2020 was accompanied by only a marginal increase in unemployment from 3.32% in 2019 to 3.38% in 2020. The above indicates that the adjustment in the response of the unemployment rate to the inflation rate has been minimal, calling the Phillips Curve's validity into question during the COVID-19 crisis.

2 Literature Review

This section focuses on empirical evidence from related literature that investigates the relationship between inflation and the unemployment rate.

Using Vector Error Correction Model (VECM) analysis to test for the existence of the Phillips Curve in Malaysia on data ranging from 1973 to 2004, Furouka (2007) concluded that Malaysia's inflation and unemployment rates had a long-run and trade-off relationship. As a result, the Phillips Curve is present in Malaysia. Furthermore, Tang and Lean (2007) confirmed the existence of a Phillips Curve trade-off in Malaysia in both the short and long run, using data from 1970 to 2005. Furuoka and Munir (2009), on the other hand, used panel data analysis on a data set spanning 1982 to 2004 to examine the relationship between unemployment and inflation rates in five ASEAN countries (i.e., Malaysia, Singapore, Indonesia, Thailand, and the Philippines). They found no evidence to support a trade-off relationship between unemployment and inflation rates in the ASEAN countries studied. Similarly, Kaur and Zaharudin (2016) discovered that changes in the level of GDP (Okun's law) affected Malaysia's unemployment rate but not the country's inflation rate.

Iwasaki et al. (2021) investigated the impact of asymmetric wage adjustment costs on the natural unemployment rate in four advanced countries using a nonlinear New Keynesian model. They concluded that wage adjustment costs were highly asymmetric in Japan, the Eurozone, and the United Kingdom, but not in the United States. Thus, the existence of Phillips Curves between wage inflation and the unemployment gap in Japan, the Eurozone, and the United Kingdom is suggested. Al-zeaud and Al-hosban (2015) discovered a negative but nonlinear relationship between unemployment and inflation in the Jordanian economy from 1976 to 2013. Similarly, Alimi and Chakroun (2021) found that a 1% increase in interest rates caused prices to fall by only 0.02%, while the unemployment rate rose by 0.2% in Tunisia. As a result, the inverse relationship between Tunisia's inflation and unemployment rates is confirmed. Finally, Nar (2021) examined the causal relationship between Turkey's inflation and unemployment rate using time series data from 1980 to 2019. He discovered evidence of cointegration and causality relationships between inflation and unemployment in Turkey, indicating that the Phillips Curve was valid.

In contrast, Folawewo and Adeboje (2017) concluded that inflation was positively related to the Economic Community of West African States' unemployment rate (ECOWAS). Coincidentally, Serrano (2018) used the ARMA model on a data set from 1990 to 2016 and concluded that inflation was positively related to Ecuador's unemployment rate. As a result, the Phillips Curve was found to be invalid in the Ecuadorian economy. Liargovas and Psychalis (2020) found that the unemployment rate of Greece was less dependent on inflation as compared in the past. Similarly, Caldentey et al. (2020) concluded that the evidence for a Phillips Curve in Latin America was relatively weak, and that the cause of inflation was frequently cost-push rather than demand-pull. Finally, Luengo-Prado et al. (2018) found that disaggregated inflation rates became less responsive to the aggregate unemployment rate around 2009–2010, using sectoral data at a medium level of aggregation. Furthermore, the slopes of the disaggregated Phillips Curves were reduced in industries such as housing and services.

The preceding discussions provide some insight into the effect of inflation on the unemployment rate in the respective studies. However, despite the fact that the topic has been discussed on a regular basis since 1958, the debate over how much the inflation rate explains a country's unemployment rate continues. Furthermore, the reported results have been inconsistent. Furouka (2007) and Tang and Lean (2007), for example, concluded that Malaysia's inflation and unemployment rates had a long-run and trade-off relationship, but Furuoka and Munir (2009) demonstrated otherwise. Furthermore, the unemployment rate in Malaysia has remained stable despite fluctuations in the inflation rate. As a result, it is possible that the relationship between inflation and the unemployment rate is not symmetrical and is not consistent with theory. As a result, the purpose of this study was to fill a gap in the existing literature by revisiting the relationship between inflation and unemployment rates and investigating the potential asymmetric impact of inflation on Malaysia's unemployment rate. Furthermore, this study aimed to investigate the existence of the Phillips Curve during the COVID-19 pandemic in Malaysia.

3 Methodology

Two estimation techniques were used in this analysis to achieve the study's objectives. To begin, the autoregressive distributed lag cointegration (ARDL) method was used to capture both the long-run and short-run cointegration of Malaysia's inflation and unemployment rates. Second, the nonlinear autoregressive distributed lag cointegration (NARDL) method was used to investigate long-run and short-run asymmetries in Malaysia's inflation and unemployment rates.

3.1 Autoregressive Distributed Lag (ARDL) Technique

Our study focused on the bivariate relationship between unemployment and the inflation rate of Malaysia. The empirical model of the Autoregressive Distributed Lag (ARDL) bounds testing approach, which was developed by Pesaran et al. (2001), is as follows:

$$UEM = f(CPI) \quad (2)$$

UEM refers to the unemployment rate, HC indicates the human capital index, and CPI refers to the inflation rate. Whereas the ARDL cointegration bounds testing model is detailed below:

$$\Delta UEM_t = c + \beta_1 UEM_{t-1} + \beta_2 CPI_{t-1} + \sum_{i=1}^{p} \alpha_{1i} \Delta UEM_{t-i} + \sum_{i=1}^{p} \alpha_{2i} \Delta CPI_{t-i} + \varepsilon_i \quad (3)$$

The Akaike Information Criterion (AIC) and the Schwarz Bayesian Criterion (SBC) procedures were used to choose the optimum lag from the above ARDL model. $\beta_1 and \beta_2$ the vectors of the long-run parameters to be estimated, and all the variables were defined as previously mentioned. Whereas $\sum_{i=1}^{p} \sum_{j}^{k} \alpha_{ji}$ examined the short-run effects of the explanatory factors on the unemployment rate (*UEM*).

The ARDL analysis was implemented using the following steps. First, as suggested by Pesaran et al. (2001), an ARDL model does not allow *I(2)* variables. The presence of *I(2)* variables invalidates the computed F-statistics for the cointegration test. As a result, the Augmented Dickey-Fuller (ADF) and Philips-Perron (PP) unit root tests were used in this study to confirm that all of the variables were either *I(0)* or *I(1)*. In addition, to confirm the results of the ADF and PP unit root tests, the Kwiatkowski–Phillips–Schmidt–Shin (KPSS) test was used. However, Perron (1997) argued that when the stationarity alternative is valid and a structural break is ignored, the power to reject a unit root decrease. As a result, the procedure developed by Zivot and Andrews (1992) to test the null of the unit root against the break-stationarity alternative was included in this study.

Moreover, Perron (1997) claims that the capacity to reject a unit root decline should the stationarity alternative is valid and a structural break is ignored. As a result, the approach devised by Zivot and Andrews (1992) is included in this study to evaluate the null of the unit root versus the break-stationarity alternative. Second, the error correction model was run in conjunction with the ARDL model to determine the optimal lags for the ARDL model. Third, as suggested by Pesaran et al. (2001), the ARDL cointegration bounds test was used to identify the presence of cointegrating variables. Finally, the obtained F-statistic value was compared to the critical values provided by Pesaran et al. (2001) for sample sizes greater than 100 observations or to the critical values provided by Narayan (2005) otherwise. Following that, the long-run model was estimated using the ARDL model with the following constraints:

$$\varphi CPI = \frac{\beta_2}{1-\beta_1} \tag{4}$$

The short-run Error-Correction Model (ECM) was computed after the long-run relationship was determined, where

$$ECT_{t-1} = UEM_{t-1} - \frac{\beta_2}{1-\beta_1} CPI_{t-1} \tag{5}$$

Finally, serial correlation and the stability diagnostic tests were used to assess the estimation's robustness.

3.2 *Nonlinear Autoregressive Distributed Lag (NARDL) Technique*

The second empirical model of this study, as proposed by Shin et al. (2014), outlined the influence of the inflation rate on Malaysia's unemployment rate using the asymmetric cointegration approach. The nonlinear autoregressive distributed lag cointegration (NARDL) technique was used in this study to capture both the long-run and short-run asymmetries between Malaysia's inflation and unemployment rates.

$$UEM_t = \alpha_0 + \alpha_1 CPI_t^+ + \alpha_2 CPI_t^- + \varepsilon_t \tag{6}$$

where, α_{0}, α_{1} and α_{2} are cointegrating vectors or vectors of long-run parameters to be estimated, respectively. $CPI_t^+ and CPI_t^-$ on the other hand, are partial sums of positive and negative changes in the CPI.

$$CPI_t^+ = \sum_{i=1}^{t} \Delta CPI_t^+ = \sum_{i=1}^{t} \max(\Delta OP_i, 0) \tag{7}$$

and

$$CPI_t^- = \sum_{i=1}^{t} \Delta CPI_t^- = \sum_{i=1}^{t} \max(\Delta OP_i, 0) \quad (8)$$

where

$$CPI_t = CPI_0 + CPI_t^+ + CPI_t^- \quad (9)$$

The long-run correlations between the unemployment rate and inflation rate are α_1 and α_2, respectively, based on the formulation mentioned above. α_1 represents the long-run link between unemployment and inflation rate increases, whereas α_2 represents the long-run association between unemployment and inflation rate decreases. The current value of the inflation rate (CPI_t) variable is given by the sum of its original value and the positive and negative partial sums by default, as indicated in Eq. (9).

According to Shin et al. (2014), the long-run Eq. (5) in an autoregressive distributed lag (ARDL) model is as follows:

$$\Delta UEM_t = \beta_0 + \beta_1 UEM_{t-1} + \beta_2 CPI_{t-1}^+ + \beta_3 CPI_{t-1}^- + \sum_{i=1}^{p} \varphi_i \Delta UEM_{t-i} + \sum_{i=0}^{q} (\theta_i^+ CPI_{t-i}^+ + \theta_i^- CPI_{t-i}^-) + \mu_t \quad (10)$$

All the variables were defined as above, with p as the lag order. The long-run parameters in Eq. (6)'s long-run parameters, i.e., $-\frac{\beta_2}{\beta_1} = \alpha_1$ and $-\frac{\beta_3}{\beta_1} = \alpha_2$ were derived from Eq. (10). Besides, $\sum_{i=0}^{q} \theta_i^+$ estimated the effects of inflation rate rises on unemployment, while $\sum_{i=0}^{q} \theta_i^-$ estimated the effects of inflation rate decrease on unemployment in the short run.

Following the preceding steps, the nonlinear ARDL analysis was carried out. First, the unit root tests (ADF, PP, and KPSS) will be performed to ensure that all variables are either *I(0)* or *I(1)*. Second, to estimate Eq. (10), the traditional Ordinary Least Squares (OLS) estimation method was used. Third, the NARDL model was used to run the nonlinear error correction model, which found the optimal lags using a two-step least squares estimation. Fourth, the bound testing approach described by Pesaran et al. (2001) and Shin et al. (2001) was used to determine the presence of cointegrating variables under the NARDL model (2014). The Wald test was then run to see any asymmetry in the long-run impact of inflation on Malaysia's unemployment rate. Finally, the estimation's robustness was tested using serial correlation and stability diagnostic tests.

3.3 Data

This study's analysis focused on monthly data from 2011 to 2021. Data on unemployment and inflation rates were obtained from the Malaysian Department of Statistics (DOSM). This study sought to investigate the impact of inflation on unemployment beginning in 2011 and continuing through the COVID-19 pandemic (from 2019). As a result, this study concentrated on three different sample models and two variables that proxied the inflation rate, namely, the consumer price index (CPI) and the producer price index (PPI). Three sample time frames were used, with data ranging from 2011 to 2021, 2011 to 2018, and 2019 to 2021. The three sample time frames selected highlighted three critical economic stages in Malaysia, namely, after the Global Financial Crisis (from 2011 to 2021), after the Global Financial Crisis to before the COVID-19 pandemic (2011 to 2018), and finally, during the COVID-19 pandemic (2011 to 2018). (2019 to 2021). Because of the scarcity of data, the time frame used to represent the COVID-19 pandemic was based on the year the coronavirus was discovered. Table 1 presents the dataset's descriptive statistics.

4 Empirical Results

This study applied several unit root tests to assess the order of integration of the underlying variables. Traditional unit root tests ADF, PP, KPSS and the structural break unit root test suggested by Zivot and Andrews (1992). As shown in Tables 2 and 3, the ADF, PP, KPSS, and Zivot and Andrews (1992) unit root test confirmed that all of the series were integrated at either order 0 (*I(0)*) or order 1 (*I(1)*). Thus, the absence of *I(2)* variables allowed the legitimate use of the ARDL and NARDL model estimation procedures, as Pesaran et al. (2001) proposed.

Table 1 Descriptive statistics

	Mean	*Std. Dev.*	*Min*	*Max*	*Observations*
Time Frame 1 (Jan 2011–April 2021)					
UEMPR	3.3793	0.5378	2.7000	5.3000	124
UEMNR	0.4941	0.1078	0.3470	0.8261	124
INF (CPI)	2.0024	1.8589	−3.5000	6.7000	124
INF (PPI)	0.3976	6.1703	−10.6000	14.8000	124
Time Frame (Jan 2011–April 2018)					
UEMPR	3.1927	0.2244	2.7000	3.5000	96
UEMNR	0.4526	0.0545	0.3470	0.5250	96
INF (CPI)	2.5833	1.3606	−0.4000	6.7000	96
INF (PPI)	0.8323	6.6773	−10.6000	14.8000	96
Time Frame 3 (Jan 2019–April 2021)					
UEMPR	4.0189	0.7697	3.2000	5.3000	28
UEMNR	0.6363	0.1520	0.5117	0.8261	28
INF (CPI)	0.0107	1.9785	−3.5000	5.5000	28
INF (PPI)	−1.0929	0.7697	−5.8000	10.6000	28

Note UEMPR represents the unemployment rate, UEMNR represents the number of unemployed (in millions), CPI represents inflation, proxied by changes in the Consumer Price Index, whereas INF(PPI) represents inflation, proxied by changes in the Production Price Index
Source Author's own construction

4.1 ARDL Model Estimations

Table 4 shows that the existence of long-run cointegration was tested using bounds testing F-statistics, as proposed by Shin et al. (2014), which can be compared to Pesaran et al. (2001) critical values for observations greater than 100 and Narayan (2005) critical values otherwise. When the calculated F-statistics were greater than the upper bound critical value, it indicated cointegration. To compare the impact of inflation more effectively on Malaysia's unemployment rate across the three economic stages, the sample models were divided into three (3) distinct time frames. Models 1 and 2 were designed to investigate the impact of inflation on the unemployment rate following the 2008 Global Financial Crisis; Models 3 and 4 represented the time period following the 2008 Global Financial Crisis to before the 2019 COVID-19 pandemic; and Models 5 and 6 were designed to investigate the relationship between inflation and unemployment rates during the 2019 COVID-19 pandemic. The findings presented in Table 4 highlight some important yet intriguing findings: (1) Given that the coefficients obtained for Models 1 to 4 were lower than the

Table 2 ADF, PP and KPSS unit root test results

Variable	*Level*			*First difference*		
	ADF	*PP*	*KPSS*	*ADF*	*PP*	*KPSS*
	t-statistics	t-statistics	t-statistics	t-statistics	t-statistics	t-statistics
Time Frame 1 (Jan 2011–April 2021)						
UEMPR	−2.8067	−2.8141	0.1626**	−12.0347***	−12.9540***	0.0633
UEMNR	−2.4725	−2.5400	0.1519**	−10.8364***	−11.2630***	0.0546
CPI	−3.5644**	−3.0617	0.1415*	−8.7503***	−8.4373***	0.0714
Time Frame 2 (Jan 2011–April 2018)						
UEMPR	−2.9221	−5.9588***	0.1299*	−11.5938***	−19.0874***	0.0672
UEMNR	−2.7656	−5.2350***	0.0909	−15.9990***	−17.0667***	0.0624
CPI	−3.2940*	−3.3630*	0.0640	−8.3751***	−9.9472***	0.0630
Time Frame 3 (Jan 2019–April 2021)						
UEMPR	0.6911	0.5194	0.0902	−4.2669***	−2.6536**	0.0868
UEMNR	0.9719	0.6675	0.0905	−4.2202***	−2.5593**	0.0888
CPI	−1.5136	−0.9770	0.1174	−1.8683*	−1.9166*	0.1795**

Notes UEMPR represents unemployment rate, UEMNR stands for the number of unemployed (millions), CPI represents inflation, proxied by changes in the Consumer Price Index. The null hypothesis of the ADF and PP tests is unit root, and the null hypothesis of the Kwiatkowski–Phillips–Schmidt–Shin (KPSS) test is stationarity. The constant and trend terms are included in the test equations, and the SIC is used to determine the appropriate lag order. The significance levels of 1%, 5%, and 10% are indicated by the symbols ***, **, and *

Source Author's own construction

Table 3 Result of unit root test with structural break (Zivot and Andrews one-break test)

Variables	*t-statistics*	*Break year*	*Results*
Time Frame 1 (Jan 2011–April 2021)			
UEMPR	−6.9816***	2020M02	I(0)
UEMNR	−14.8583***	2020M04	I(1)
CPI	−4.3892*	2017M12	I(0)
Time Frame 2 (Jan 2011–April 2018)			
UEMPR	−4.2070*	2015M05	I(0)
UEMNR	−4.6062**	2014M11	I(0)
CPI	−9.2840***	2014 M04	I(1)
Time Frame 3 (Jan 2019–April 2021)			
UEMPR	−13.9000***	2020M03	I(0)
UEMNR	−7.1249***	2020M04	I(0)
CPI	−4.2010*	2021M03	I(1)
Augmented Dickey-Fuller test statistic			
1%	−4.949133		
5%	−4.443649		
10%	−4.193627		

Note UEMPR represents the unemployment rate, UEMNR represents the number of unemployed (in millions), CPI represents inflation, proxied by changes in the Consumer Price Index. ***, ** and * denote the significance at 1%, 5% and 10% levels
Source Author's own construction

upper bound critical values, there was no trade-off between inflation and unemployment in Malaysia in the long run following the Global Financial Crisis and (2) The F-statistics for Models 5 and 6 were rejected at the 10% significance level, indicating a long-run relationship between inflation and unemployment during the COVID-19 pandemic. The results of Models 1 to 4 were unsurprising, as many countries around the world had experienced the same phenomenon. Jerome Powell, Chairman of the Federal Reserve, stated in 2019 that the relationship between unemployment and inflation had collapsed (Bahn & Clemen, 2019). Interestingly, the significance of the results of Models 5 and 6 may have suggested that the COVID-19 pandemic has given the Phillips Curve a new lease on life.

Table 5 summarizes the explanatory variable's short-run and long-run coefficients. Table 5 shows that inflation was inversely and significantly related to Malaysia's unemployment rate in the short run for all the

Table 4 Cointegration Bound tests (ARDL model)

Data range	*Jan 2011 to Apr 2021*		*Jan 2011 to Dec 2018*		*Jan 2019 to Apr 2021*	
Dependent variables	*UEMPR*	*UEMNR*	*UEMPR*	*UEMNR*	*UEMPR*	*UEMNR*
	Model 1	Model 2	Model 3	Model 4	Model 5	Model 6
ARDL Bound test	1.2700	1.6527	1.2594	1.4563	3.9329*	3.8308*
Pesaran et al. (2001)						
Diagnostic checks						
Serial (1) – Lag2	0.2248	0.7680	0.6254	1.4630	2.3801	2.8438
	(0.8937)	(0.6811)	(0.7315)	(0.4812)	(0.3042)	(0.2413)
Serial (2) – Lag 4	6.8075	5.9987	1.9951	1.5499	6.0267	5.9918
	(0.1464)	(0.1992)	(0.7367)	(0.8178)	(0.1972)	(0.1998)
	Pesaran et al. (2001) ($K = 1$, $n = 123$)		Narayan (2005) ($K = 1$, $n = 92$)		Narayan (2005)	
	Lower Bound	Upper Bound	Lower Bound	Upper Bound	Lower Bound	Upper Bound
1%	5.1570	5.9170	5.1570	5.9170	6.0270	6.7600
5%	3.7400	4.3030	3.7400	4.3030	4.0900	4.6630
10%	3.1130	3.6100	3.1130	3.6100	3.3030	3.7970

Note The test statistics of the cointegration tests are compared to the critical values published by Pesaran et al. (2001) for samples with more than 100 observations and to Narayan (2005) for samples with fewer than 100 observations. *P* values are the figures in parenthesis. The Breusch-Godfrey LM test statistics for no serial correction test are Serial (1) and Serial (2). *, **, and *** imply significance at 10%, 5%, and 1% levels of significance, respectively

Source Author's own construction

sampled models. In contrast, only Models 5 and 6 revealed a long-run trade-off relationship between inflation and unemployment (during the COVID-19 pandemic). According to the coefficient obtained for Model 5, a 1% increase in the inflation rate would result in a 0.1276% decrease in Malaysia's unemployment. Despite the fact that the coefficient obtained for Model 6 was lower than the one obtained for Model 5, the trade-off relationship was consistent. Given that higher inflation resulted in a lower unemployment rate, the Phillips Curve appeared to be valid in the Malaysian economy during the COVID-19 pandemic.

4.2 NARDL Model Analysis

Section 4.1 emphasises that, while inflation was significantly related to the unemployment rate during the COVID-19 pandemic period, it did not explain Malaysia's persistent unemployment rate. As a result, we argued that the relationship between inflation and unemployment may not be symmetrical, implying that the response of the unemployment rate to increases in the inflation rate may not be the same as its response to decreases in the inflation rate. As a result, the nonlinear autoregressive distributed lag cointegration (NARDL) approach was used to capture both the long-run and short-run asymmetries in Malaysia's inflation and unemployment rates. Similarly, to the ARDL setup, the existence of long-run cointegration in the NARDL framework can be tested using bounds testing F-statistics, as suggested by Shin et al. (2014). The results in Table 6 show that the calculated F-statistics for Models 5 and 6 were significant at the 10% and 5% significance levels, respectively. As a result, the long-run impact of inflation on Malaysia's unemployment rate is asymmetric.

Model 20 in Table 7 highlights that a 1% increase in the inflation rate resulted in a 0.1236% decrease in the unemployment rate (negative correlation). In comparison, a 1% decrease in the inflation rate led to a 0.3096% increase in the unemployment rate (negative correlation). A similar trend was observed for Model 6, where a 1% increase in the inflation rate led to a 0.0208% decrease in the unemployment rate compared to a 0.0510% increase due to the 1% inflation rate reduction. This, therefore, suggested that the unemployment rate responded more significantly to inflation rate reductions than inflation rate increases during the COVID-19 pandemic. Besides, the significant differences between the negative and positive impacts of the inflation rate on the unemployment rate can also be

Table 5 ARDL (estimates the influence of inflation on the unemployment rate)

Data range	*Jan 2011 to Apr 2021*		*Jan 2011 to Dec 2018*		*Jan 2019 to Apr 2021*	
Dependent variables	*UEMPR*	*UEMNR*	*UEMPR*	*UEMNR*	*UEMPR*	*UEMNR*
	Model 1	Model 2	Model 3	Model 4	Model 5	Model 6
I. Long Run Coefficients						
Intercept	4.5105***	1.1394	3.2605***	0.5971***	3.3096***	0.5477***
	(0.0001)	(0.3669)	(0.0001)	(0.0004)	(0.0001)	(0.0001)
CPI	−0.4359	−0.2038	−0.0113	−0.0364	−0.5696***	−0.0772***
	(1.1618)	(0.5864)	(0.8995)	(0.4412)	(0.0049)	(0.0051)
II. Short Run Coefficients						
Intercept	−4.99E-06	1.64E-06	−0.0121	−0.0014	0.0487	0.0091
	(0.9998)	(0.9995)	(0.4433)	(0.5746)	(0.3376)	(0.1671)
ΔCPI	−0.0950***	−0.0133***	−0.0558**	−0.0081***	−0.1793***	−0.0276***
	(0.0001)	(0.0001)	(0.0014)	(0.0008)	(0.0001)	(0.0001)
ECT_{t-1}	−0.0433*	−0.0120*	−0.2470***	−0.0444	0.0714	0.0818
	(0.0744)	(0.0797)	(0.0005)	(0.1238)	(0.2617)	(0.1846)

Note UEMPR represents unemployment rate, UEMNR stands for the number of unemployed (millions), CPI represents inflation, proxied by changes in the Consumer Price Index. *P* values are the figures in parenthesis. The maximum lag length was set at four. The Akaike Information Criterion (AIC) was used to determine the best lag structure for the ARDL model. The significance levels of 1%, 5%, and 10% are indicated by ***, **, and *, respectively

Source Author's own construction

Table 6 Cointegration Bound tests (NARDL model)

Data range	*Jan 2011 to Apr 2021*		*Jan 2011 to Dec 2018*		*Jan 2019 to Apr 2021*	
Dependent variables	*UEMPR*	*UEMNR*	*UEMPR*	*UEMNR*	*UEMPR*	*UEMNR*
	Model 1	Model 2	Model 3	Model 4	Model 5	Model 6
ARDL Bound test Pesaran et al. (2001)	3.1513	3.1690	3.0746	3.1690	3.8733*	6.1410**
Diagnostic checks						
Serial (1) – Lag2	0.4230	0.0542	1.3730	0.2418	2.8097	1.5234
	(0.8094)	(0.8158)	(0.5033)	(0.8861)	(0.2454)	(0.5000)
Serial (2) – Lag 4	6.4548	1.1365	1.4287	1.1365	8.1300*	1.5927
	(0.1677)	(0.8884)	(0.8392)	(0.8884)	(0.0869)	(0.8131)
	Pesaran et al. (2001) ($K = 1$, $n = 123$)		Narayan (2005) ($K = 1$, $n = 92$)		Narayan (2005)	
	Lower Bound	Upper Bound	Lower Bound	Upper Bound	Lower Bound	Upper Bound
1%	4.3580	5.3930	4.3580	5.3930	5.1550	6.2650
5%	3.2350	4.0530	3.2350	4.0530	3.5380	4.4280
10%	2.7130	3.4530	2.7130	3.4530	2.9150	3.6950

Note The test statistics of the cointegration tests are compared to the critical values published by Pesaran et al. (2001) for samples with more than 100 observations and to Narayan (2005) for samples with fewer than 100 observations. *P* values are the figures in parenthesis. The Breusch-Godfrey LM test statistics for no serial correction test are Serial (1) and Serial (2). *, **, and *** imply significance at 10%, 5%, and 1% levels of significance, respectively

Source Author's own construction

observed in Figs. 2 and 3, where the NARDL multiplier graph shows that the long-run impact of inflation rate reductions was more significant than the positive changes. In addition, the passing-through impact of the inflation rate on the unemployment rate was not as complete as postulated by the Phillips Curve, as a 1% increase in the inflation rate was associated with only 0.1236, and 0.0208% decreases in the unemployment rate and the numbers of unemployed, respectively. The incomplete passing-through impact could have been due to the unfavourable economic climate caused by Malaysia's prolonged implementation of its Movement Control Orders (MCO).

On the contrary, as presented in Table 6, the short-run coefficients suggested that reductions in inflation would result in a higher unemployment rate. On the other hand, inflationary increases had no effect on the unemployment rate in the short term. Therefore, the inverse association between inflation reductions and an increased unemployment rate could be due to falling prices, leading to falling revenue, thus, forcing employers to cut pay and lay off workers. Figures 4 and 5 present the CUSUM stability test diagrams, whereas the Bruesch-Godfrey serial correlation LM statistics for autocorrelation were performed to justify the adequacy of the model specification. The unfolding results in Tables 4 and 6 confirmed the absence of autocorrelation (except LM order 4 of Model 5 in Table 5). In addition, Figs. 4 and 5 indicate no structural instability in the residuals.

4.3 Robustness Checks

To confirm the analysis's robustness and that the inflation rate captured by changes in the consumer price index (CPI) was the correct indicator for Malaysia's unemployment rate. This study also considered the impact of inflation, as measured by changes in the producer price index (PPI), and the estimates are presented in Tables 8 and 9. In addition, Table 8 displays the long-run cointegration and Bruesch-Godfrey serial correlation LM test results. Table 5 shows the short-run and long-run coefficients of the explanatory variable.

The results in Table 9 were consistent with the estimation results obtained by the unemployment rate – inflation rate nexus (changes in CPI). In the long run, the unemployment rate, and the inflation rate, as proxied by changes in the producer price index, were significant for Models 5 and 6. In the short run, however, significant results were obtained for Models 1, 2, 5, and 6.

Table 7 NARDL estimates of the impact of inflation on the unemployment rate

Data range	*Jan 2011 to Apr 2021*		*Jan 2011 to Dec 2018*		*Jan 2019 to Apr 2021*	
Dependent variables	*UEMPR*	*UEMNR*	*UEMPR*	*UEMNR*	*UEMPR*	*UEMNR*
	Model 1	Model 2	Model 3	Model 4	Model 5	Model 6
I. Long Run Coefficients						
Intercept	2.9711***	0.3931***	3.1881***	0.4175***	3.3755***	0.5384***
	(0.0001)	(0.0001)	(0.0001)	(0.0001)	(0.0001)	(0.0001)
CPI_POS	−0.3124**	−0.0572*	−0.0498	−0.0063	−0.1276***	−0.0208***
	(0.0432)	(0.0715)	(0.4791)	(0.5924)	(0.0005)	(0.0040)
CPI_NEG	−0.3311**	−0.0627**	−0.0645	−0.0112	−0.3096***	−0.0510***
	(0.0252)	(0.0401)	(0.3601)	(0.3368)	(0.0001)	(0.0001)
II. Short Run Coefficients						
Intercept	−0.01854	−0.0021	−0.0434*	−0.0050	0.0277	0.0006
	(0.3619)	(0.4565)	(0.0884)	(0.1700)	(0.3951)	(0.8714)
ΔCPI_POS	−0.04223	−0.0055	−0.0572*	−0.0061	0.0137	0.0010
	(0.1217)	(0.1368)	(0.0806)	(0.1632)	(0.6716)	(0.8307)
ΔCPI_NEG	−0.1324***	−0.0185***	−0.0568**	−0.0073**	−0.3303***	−0.0493***
	(0.0001)	(0.0001)	(0.0199)	(0.0243)	(0.0001)	(0.0001)
ECT_{t-1}	−0.0697**	−0.0544**	−0.2419***	−0.1856***	−0.5208***	−0.4044**
	(0.0157)	(0.0134)	(0.0009)	(0.0004)	(0.0085)	(0.0255)

Note UEMPR represents unemployment rate, UEMNR stands for the number of unemployed (millions), CPI represents inflation, proxied by changes in the Consumer Price Index. *P* values are the figures in parenthesis. The maximum lag length was set at four. The Akaike Information Criterion (AIC) was used to determine the best lag structure for the ARDL model. The significance levels of 1%, 5%, and 10% are indicated by ***, **, and *, respectively

Source Author's own construction

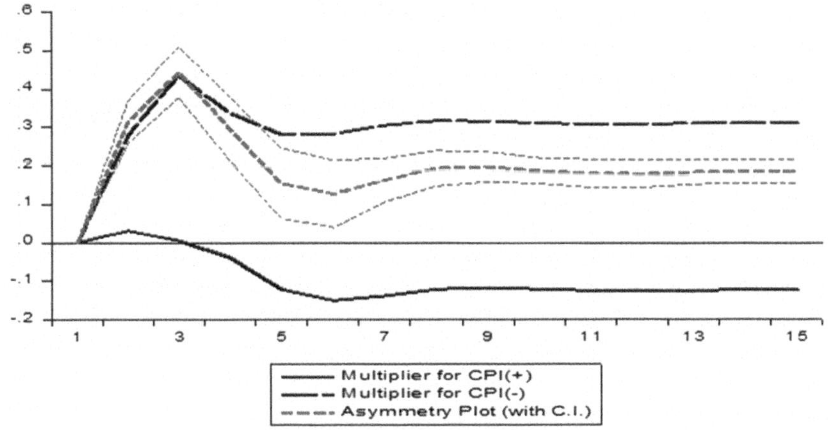

Fig. 2 NARDL multiplier (dependent variable: UEMPR) (*Source* Author's own construction)

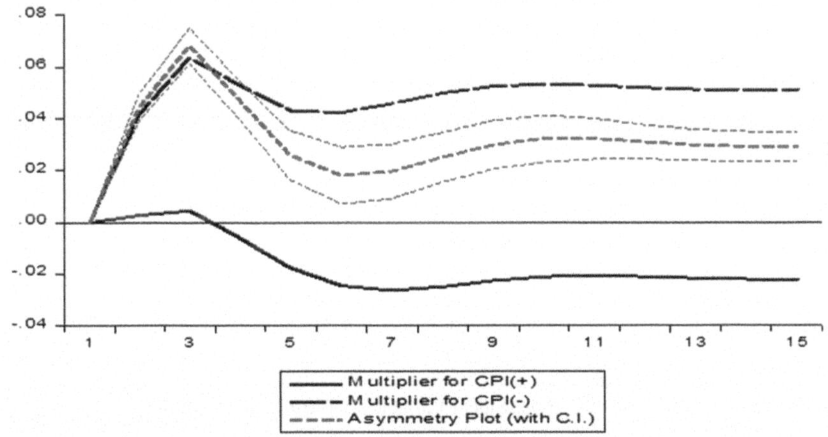

Fig. 3 NARDL multiplier (dependent variable: UEMNR) (*Source* Author's own construction

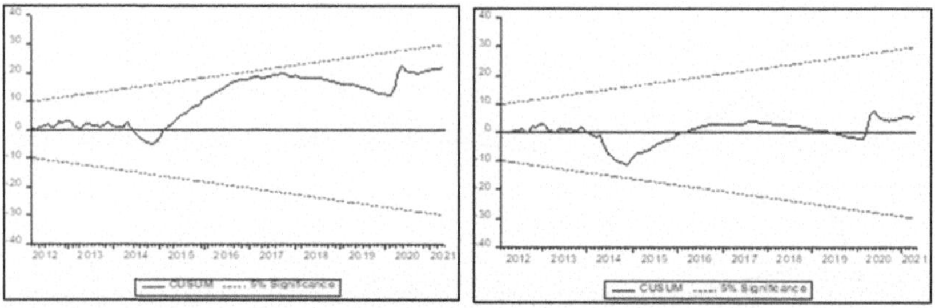

i. Sample period – 2011-2021 (Dependent Variable – UEMPR and UEMNR)

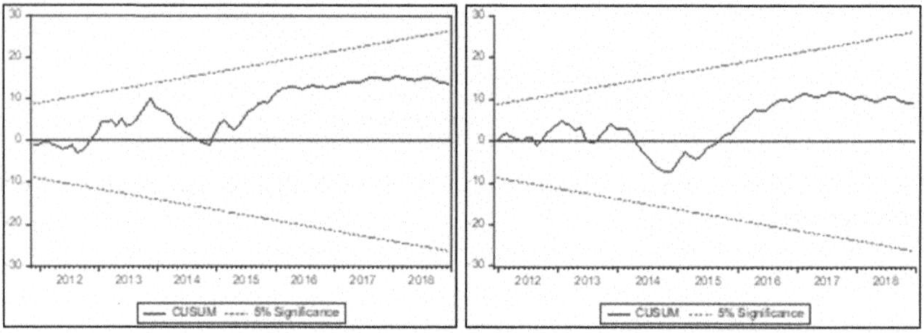

ii. Sample period – 2011-2018 (Dependent Variable – UEMPR and UEMNR)

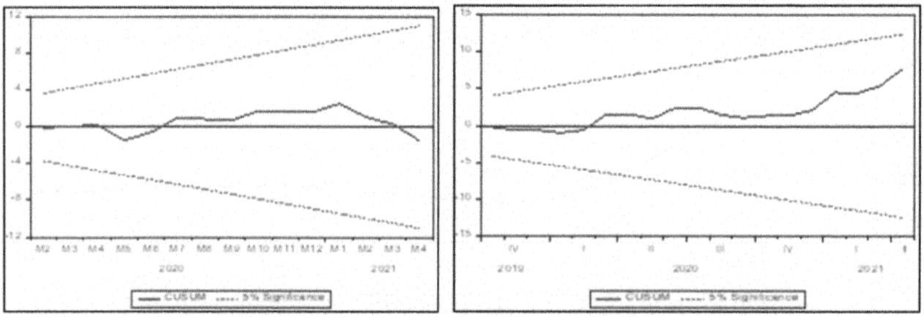

iii. Sample period – 2019-2021 (Dependent Variable – UEMPR and UEMNR)

Fig. 4 CUSUM diagrams—ARDL model (*Source* Author's own construction)

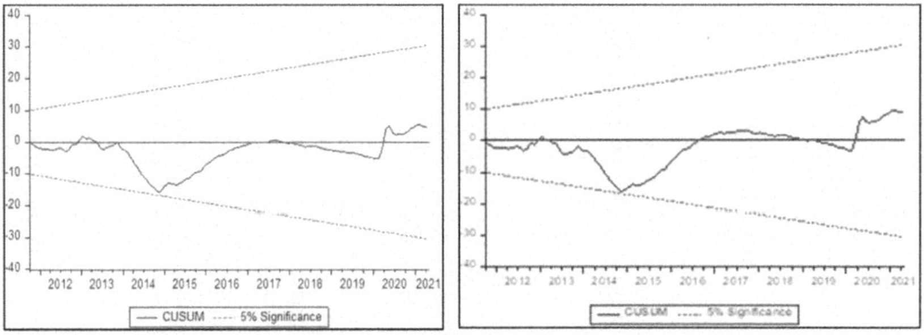

i. Sample period – 2011-2021 (Dependent Variable – UEMPR and UEMNR)

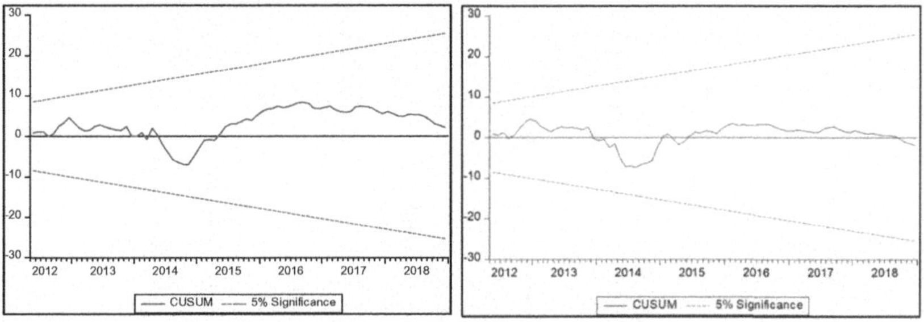

ii. Sample period – 2011-2018 (Dependent Variable – UEMPR and UEMNR)

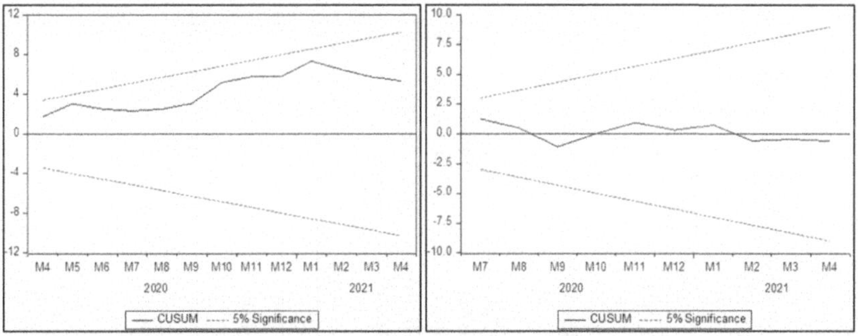

iii. Sample period – 2019-2021 (Dependent Variable – UEMPR and UEMNR)

Fig. 5 CUSUM diagrams—NARDL model (*Source* Author's own construction)

Table 8 Robustness check—ARDL estimates of the impact of inflation on the Unemployment Rate – Inflation Proxied by the Producer Price Index (PPI)

Data range	*Jan 2011 to Apr 2021*		*Jan 2011 to Dec 2018*		*Jan 2019 to Apr 2021*	
Dependent variables	*UEMPR*	*UEMNR*	*UEMPR*	*UEMNR*	*UEMPR*	*UEMNR*
	Model 1	Model 2	Model 3	Model 4	Model 5	Model 6
ARDL Bound test Pesaran et al. (2001)	0.8646	1.3864	1.9911	3.3081	6.8313***	9.1532***
Diagnostic checks						
Serial (1) – Lag2	0.7730 (0.6794)	0.3009 (0.8603)	1.5509 (0.4605)	1.9307 (0.3808)	0.7658 (0.6819)	0.1556 (0.9252)
Serial (2) – Lag 4	3.9963 (0.4065)	3.0190 (0.5546)	2.6730 (0.6140)	3.0695 (0.5463)	2.5705 (0.6321)	2.4434 (0.6548)
	Pesaran et al. (2001) ($K = 1$, $n = 123$)		Narayan (2005) ($K = 1$, $n = 92$)		Narayan (2005) ($K = 1$, $n = 23$)	
	Lower Bound	Upper Bound	Lower Bound	Upper Bound	Lower Bound	Upper Bound
1%	5.1570	5.9170	5.1570	5.9170	6.0270	6.7600
5%	3.7400	4.3030	3.7400	4.3030	4.0900	4.6630
10%	3.1130	3.6100	3.1130	3.6100	3.3030	3.7970

Note The test statistics of the cointegration tests are compared to the critical values published by Pesaran et al. (2001) for samples with more than 100 observations and to Narayan (2005) for samples with fewer than 100 observations. *P* values are the figures in parenthesis. The Breusch-Godfrey LM test statistics for no serial correction test are Serial (1) and Serial (2). *, **, and *** imply significance at 10%, 5%, and 1% levels of significance, respectively

Source Author's own construction

Table 9 Robustness check—ARDL estimates of the impact of inflation on Unemployment Rate – Inflation Proxied by Producer Price Index (PPI)

Data range	*Jan 2011 to Apr 2021*		*Jan 2011 to Dec 2018*		*Jan 2019 to Apr 2021*	
Dependent variables	*UEMPR*	*UEMNR*	*UEMPR*	*UEMNR*	*UEMPR*	*UEMNR*
	Model 1	Model 2	Model 3	Model 4	Model 5	Model 6
I. Long Run Coefficients						
Intercept	3.8986***	0.1222	3.2741***	0.5233***	1.0411	0.1856
	(0.0012)	(0.9168)	(0.0001)	(0.0001)	(0.4713)	(0.2828)
PPI	−0.1905	0.0790	−0.0408	−0.0172	−0.9563**	−0.1363**
	(0.5574)	(0.7573)	(0.3274)	(0.2595)	(0.0477)	(0.0155)
II. Short Run Coefficients						
Intercept	7.72E-07	0.0056*	−0.0098	0.0825***	0.0775	0.0039
	(1.0000)	(0.0626)	(0.5593)	(0.0005)	(0.1502)	(0.9062)
ΔPPI	−0.0304***	−0.0049***	−0.0146	−0.00167	−0.0807***	−0.0126***
	(0.0020)	(0.0003)	(0.1397)	(0.1865)	(0.0029)	(0.0022)
ECT_{t-1}	−0.0212	−0.0076	−0.1423***	−0.0305***	0.0094	0.0031
	(0.1343)	(0.1236)	(0.0032)	(0.0005)	(0.5921)	(0.7337)

Note UEMPR represents unemployment rate, UEMNR stands for the number of unemployed (millions), PPI represents inflation, proxied by changes in the Producer Price Index. P values are the figures in parenthesis. The maximum lag length was set at four. The Akaike Information Criterion (AIC) was used to determine the best lag structure for the ARDL model. The significance levels of 1%, 5%, and 10% are indicated by ***, **, and *, respectively

Source Author's own construction

4.4 *Discussion*

This section presents the main implications of the results obtained from the empirical analysis and robustness checking carried out in this study.

The study's findings are not surprising, as many economists have previously noted that the trade-off between unemployment and inflation has weakened in recent years (Albuquerque & Baumann, 2017; Hong et al., 2018). However, from the results summarised in Tables 4 and 6, inflation failed to explain Malaysia's unemployment rate for two of the monthly data sets, namely, from 2011 to 2021 and 2011 to 2018, suggesting that the Phillips Curve did not exist in Malaysia during those periods. In contrast, inflation was significantly cointegrated with Malaysia's unemployment rate for the monthly data set from 2019 to 2021, indicating that the COVID-19 pandemic has given a new lifeline to the Phillips Curve. Additionally, during the COVID-19 pandemic, inflation was asymmetrically correlated with Malaysia's unemployment rate, indicating that the unemployment rate reacted differently to increases and reductions in the inflation rate. More specifically, as shown in Table 2, Figs. 2 and 3, 1% increase in the inflation rate tended to decrease Malaysia's unemployment rate by 0.1276% (Model 5) or 0.0208% (Model 6). In contrast, a 1% decrease in the inflation rate increased the unemployment rate by 0.3096% (Model 5) or 0.0510% (Model 6), respectively. This finding suggested that the unemployment rate was more sensitive to inflation decreases rather than increases. As a result, providing a good piece of evidence to explain Malaysia's persistent unemployment rate.

The robustness checks revealed that there was no long run cointegration between the unemployment rate and the inflation rate in Malaysia for the sample data from 2011 to 2021 and 2011 to 2018. (Models 1 to 4). Hence, the empirical results were aligned with Furuoka and Munir (2009) and Kaur and Zaharudin (2016)'s findings that Malaysia's unemployment rate was insensitive to changes in the country's inflation rate. However, on the other hand, when proxied by the producer price index (PPI), inflation was also significantly cointegrated with Malaysia's unemployment rate during the COVID-19 pandemic, thus indicating that the COVID-19 pandemic has given a new lifeline to the Phillips Curve.

4.5 *Comparing the Findings from Malaysia to Sultanate of Oman*

The Sultanate of Oman implemented a series of measures to contain the COVID-19 pandemic, including travel restrictions, partial lockdowns, suspension of prayers at mosques, closure of schools and commercial establishments (except essential services), and restrictions on employee attendance at workplaces, in response to the economic distress caused by the pandemic. Furthermore, the government implemented a number of fiscal measures to help the economy, including the suspension of municipal taxes, government fees, and rent payments for businesses in industrial zones. Port and air freight charges were reduced, and loan servicing for development bank and SME support fund borrowers was delayed. Tax-related measures, such as the elimination of fines and penalties for late disclosures, were also implemented. Oman's central bank implemented policy measures to support and provide liquidity to the financial sector, including lowering interest rates by 0.05 basis points to 2.28% in January 2020, 0.13 basis points to 2.15% in March 2020, and finally to 0.5% in May 2020, Central Bank of Oman—GDB (2020).

Due to the pandemic, the Sultanate of Oman's unemployment rate for 2020 increased to 2.94% from 1.85% in 2019, while inflation was −0.90%, a 1.04% decrease from 2019. Thus, from a theoretical standpoint, the Sultanate of Oman has a Phillips Curve, in which inflation and unemployment rates are inversely related. However, in terms of percentage changes, a 0.9% decrease in the inflation rate has resulted in an increase in the unemployment rate of 1.09 percentage point, implying that the adjustment is not symmetrical. In June 2023, the Sultanate of Oman unemployment rate increased to 3.70%, up from 3.60% previously reported in May 2023 (CEICdata.com., 2023). Similar to the empirical findings obtained for Malaysia, policymakers in the Sultanate of Oman should consider how changes in inflation affect unemployment asymmetrically in order to combat the escalating unemployment rate more effectively.

5 Conclusion

Given that Malaysia's policymakers are still searching for the best remedy to rejuvenate the domestic economy and reduce the unemployment rate, the correlation between inflation and the unemployment rate would be vital for the policymakers to draft an effective macroeconomic policy to uplift the economy of the country. The ARDL and NARDL models, proposed by Pesaran et al. (2001) and Shin et al. (2014), were used in this paper to investigate the presence of long-run and asymmetric cointegration between the unemployment rate and inflation (as measured by changes in the consumer price index) in Malaysia. The empirical findings revealed four significant findings: (1) Inflation was significantly associated with the unemployment rate in the short run, but the effect was only temporary. (2) In the long run, there was no trade-off between Malaysian inflation and unemployment. (3) During the COVID-19 pandemic (sample period from 2019 to 2021), the inflation rate was significantly related to Malaysia's unemployment rate, indicating that the COVID-19 pandemic gave the Phillips Curve a new lease on life. (4) Inflation was asymmetrically correlated with Malaysia's unemployment rate during the COVID-19 pandemic. More specifically, a decrease in the inflation rate tended to increase the unemployment rate by a larger margin. In contrast, an increase in the inflation rate would result in a lower deviation in the unemployment rate. Therefore, Malaysia's unemployment rate responded more to the negative changes than positive changes in inflation.

As previously stated, the unemployment rate responded more strongly to negative changes in the inflation rate, implying that the rate of adjustment in the unemployment rate was faster when inflation fell. This indicated that the trade-off between unemployment and inflation was not symmetrical, which contradicted Phillips Curve's intuition. Policymakers should, therefore, pay more attention to reducing the unemployment rate by creating new job opportunities or assisting the unemployed to obtain a job. For example, government agencies could offer job placement services to match unemployed people with potential employers. Besides, policymakers should also investigate an improved reward mechanism compared to the existing Apprenticeship Program, which has required long processing times, to encourage companies to create new vacancies for the jobless. Despite the introduction of various incentive programmes aimed at encouraging employers to create jobs, the unemployment rate has remained high. Thus, policymakers should organize a dialogue with potential employers to promote the incentive program and gather information to improve the mechanism further.

In addition, the implications of the findings suggest that fiscal policy (increases in government spending) have failed to reduce the unemployment rate, monetary policy (such as reducing the interest rate) should be considered by policymakers to stimulate the performance of the job market. Accordingly, lowering the interest rate would discourage saving and reduce the cost of investment, thereby encouraging new investment and creating new employment opportunities (Feldmann, 2013). Finally, policymakers should devise effective strategies to attract more foreign direct investment (FDI). According to a report released by the Malaysia Investment Development Authority Board (MIDA), Malaysia recorded a total of RM80.6 billion in approved investments in the manufacturing, services, and primary sectors in the first quarter of 2021, which is expected to create 32,557 job opportunities (MIDA, 2021). Therefore, signifying that increased FDI inflows would create new job opportunities, lowering unemployment.

Funding This work was supported by the RU Geran—Fakulti Program of Universiti Malaya [Grant number: GPF067B-2020].

References

Albuquerque, B., & Baumann, U. (2017). *Will US inflation awake from the dead? The role of slack and non-linearities in the Phillips Curve* (ECB Working Paper 2001). European Central Bank.

Al-zeaud, H., & Al-hosban, S. (2015). Does Phillips Curve really exist? An empirical evidence from Jordan. *European Scientific Journal, ESJ, 11*(10).

Alimi, K., & Chakroun, M. (2021). Wage rigidity impacts on unemployment and inflation persistence in Tunisia: Evidence from an estimated DSGE model. *Journal of the Knowledge Economy*. https://doi.org/10.1007/s13132-021-00751-8

Bahn, K., & Clemen, A. (2019). *The death of the Phillips Curve is the time to lift up new economic indicators*. https://equitablegrowth.org/the-death-of-the-phillips-curve-is-the-time-to-lift-up-new-economic-indicators/. Assessed 20 June 2021.

Caldentey, E., Perry, N., & Vernengo, M. (2020). The return of Keynes and the Phillips curve in Latin America: Evidence from four countries. *Review of Keynesian Economics, 8*(1), 84–101. https://doi.org/10.4337/roke.2020.01.07

CEICdata.com. (2023). *Oman unemployment rate*. Ceicdata.com; CEICdata.com. https://www.ceicdata.com/en/indicator/oman/unemployment-rate#:~:text=Key%20information%20about%20Oman%20Unemployment

Central Bank of Oman—GDB. (2020). Cbo.gov.om. https://cbo.gov.om/Pages/GDB.aspx

DOSM. (2021). *Key statistics of labour force in Malaysia, April 2021.* Department of Statistics Malaysia, Putrajaya. Malaysia. https://www.dosm.gov.my/v1/index.php?r=column/cthemeByCat&cat=124&bul_id=UXQ2VUpIOVRvT3p6T0NHMHk1TGkxUT09&menu_id=Tm8zcnRjdVRNWWlpWjRlbmtlaDk1UT09

Feldmann, H. (2013). Real interest rate and labor market performance around the world. *Southern Economic Journal, 79*(3), 659–679. Retrieved June 24, 2021, from http://www.jstor.org/stable/23809689

Folawewo, A. O., & Adeboje, O. M. (2017). Macroeconomic determinants of unemployment: Empirical evidence from economic community of West African states. *African Development Review, 29*(2), 197–210. https://doi.org/10.1111/1467-8268.12250

Forbes, K. J., Gagnon, J., & Collins, C. G. (2020). *Low inflation bends the Phillips curve around the world* (Peterson Institute for International Economics Working Paper No. 20-6, 2020, MIT Sloan Research Paper No. 6101-20). https://ssrn.com/abstract=3577993. or https://doi.org/10.2139/ssrn.3577993

Furuoka, F., & Munir, Q. (2009). "Phillips Curve" in selected ASEAN countries: New evidence from panel data analysis. *Sunway Academic Journal, 6*, 89–102.

Hong, G. H., Koczan, Z., Lian, W., & Nabar, M. (2018). More slack than meets the eye? Recent wage dynamics in advanced economies. RePEc—Econpapers. https://econpapers.repec.org/paper/imfimfwpa/2018_2f050.htm

Iwasaki, Y., Muto, I., & Shintani, M. (2021). Missing wage inflation? Estimating the natural rate of unemployment in a nonlinear DSGE model. *European Economic Review, 132*(2021). https://doi.org/10.1016/j.euroecorev.2020.103626

Kaur, G., & Zaharudin, N. A. (2016). Impact of macroeconomic policy instruments and external shock on unemployment rate in Malaysia. In *Conference: BE-ci 2016 International Conference on Business and Economics*. https://doi.org/10.15405/epsbs.2016.11.02.8

Liargovas, P., & Psychalis, M. (2020). Phillips curve: The Greek case. *European Review*, Open Access. https://doi.org/10.1017/S1062798720001301

Luengo-Prado, M. J., Rao, N., & Sheremirov, V. (2018). Sectoral inflation and the Phillips curve: What has changed since the Great Recession? *Economics Letters, 172*, 63–68. https://doi.org/10.1016/j.econlet.2018.08.016

MIDA. (2021). *Malaysia records RM80.6 billion approved investments for the first quarter of 2021.* https://www.mida.gov.my/media-release/malaysia-records-rm80-6-billion-approved-investments-for-the-first-quarter-of-2021/. Assessed 20 June 2021.

Nar, M. (2021). Analysis of the Phillips Curve: An assessment of Turkey. *Journal of Asian Finance, Economics and Business, 8*(2), 57–64. https://doi.org/10.13106/jafeb.2021.vol8.no2.0065

Narayan, P. K. (2005). The saving and investment nexus for China: Evidence from cointegration tests. *Applied Economics, 37*(17), 1979–1990. https://doi.org/10.1080/00036840500278103

Perron, P. (1997). Further evidence on breaking trend functions in macroeconomic variables. *Journal of Econometrics, 80*(2), 355–385. https://doi.org/10.1016/s0304-4076(97)00049-3

Pesaran, M. H., Shin, Y., & Smith, R. J. (2001). Bounds testing approaches to the analysis of level relationships. *Journal of Applied Econometrics, 16*, 289–326.

Phillips, A. W. (1958). The relation between unemployment and the rate of change of money wage rates in the United Kingdom, 1861–1957. *Economica, 25*(100), 283–299. https://doi.org/10.1111/j.1468-0335.1958.tb00003.x

Serrano, L. L. A. (2018). Econometric analysis of inflation and its incidence in Ecuadorian unemployment, period 1990–2016. *Espacios, 39*(32).

Shin, Y., Pesaran, M. H., & Smith, R. J. (2001). Bounds testing approaches to the analysis of level relationships. *Journal of Applied Econometrics, 16*, 289–326. https://pure.york.ac.uk/portal/en/publications/bounds-testing-approaches-to-the-analysis-of-level-relationships

Shin, Y., Yu, B., & Greenwood-Nimmo, M. (2014). *Modelling asymmetric cointegration and dynamic multipliers in a nonlinear ARDL framework*. In R. Sickles & W. Horrace (Eds.), *Festschrift in Honor of Peter Schmidt*. Springer.

Tang, C. F., & Lean, H. H. (2007). Is Phillips Curve stable in Malaysia? New empirical evidence. *Malaysian Journal of Economic Studies, 44*(2), 95–105.

World Bank. (2020). *Malaysian economy showing signs of recovery, projected to grow by 6.7 percent in 2021 following a contraction of 5.8 percent in 2020*. https://openknowledge.worldbank.org/bitstream/handle/10986/34929/155096.pdf. Assessed 8 February 2021

Zivot, E., & Andrews, D. W. K. (1992). Further evidence on the great crash, the oil-price shock, and the unit-root hypothesis. *Journal of Business & Economic Statistics, 10*(3), 251. https://doi.org/10.2307/1391541

CHAPTER 7

Green Economic Recovery After COVID-19: Thoughts and Reflection on the GCC Region and Potential Scenarios for Qatar

Ahmed Badran

1 Introduction

The majority of nations in the world announced the finding of the COVID-19 virus after China first revealed its appearance. Many economies have been brought to a total standstill because of the infection rates within nations rising substantially and quickly. The health systems in many nations, including industrialized ones, also broke down in the face of these negative effects, particularly during the initial waves of the virus's spread. As a result, a series of preventive measures began at airports for travelers coming from China first, then the rest of the world. These measures have led to many successive events that have affected the economic situation worldwide.

A. Badran (✉)
Department of International Affairs, Qatar University, Doha, Qatar
e-mail: a.badran@qu.edu.qa

A. Mishrif (ed.), *Economic Effects of the Pandemic*, The Political Economy of the Middle East,
https://doi.org/10.1007/978-981-97-4367-4_7

Because of the pandemic's impact on oil prices and the consequent reduction in worldwide demand, the world economy entered a state of recession. The pandemic-related closures, for instance, have had a severe impact on the world economy. Because of the economic and industrialization cycle discontinuation, international trade has also been affected. Due to the overall disruption of the intercountry human movement, trade and tourism were most commonly damaged in most nations, especially those that rely heavily on tourism. In this context, the International Monetary Fund (IMF) confirmed that there is a decline in the global economic performance of the, by 4.9% in 2020. The IMF also expected that the recovery phase would be slow because of the conditions that occur at the global level (McGaughey & Lawrence, 2020).

Global economic systems, particularly those of the Gulf States and Qatar, were impacted by the COVID-19 pandemic's effects that were felt on a global scale. The world economy's growth rates were slowed by the COVID-19 pandemic, and demand for raw materials, like as petroleum, which is the main source of wealth in the Arab Gulf nations, also decreased significantly. All economic sectors were negatively impacted by the economic downturn brought on by the COVID-19 pandemic, which spurred many nations to create a strategy to recover from its impacts. This chapter's fundamental concern is: How can economic systems recover sustainably from the COVID-19 pandemic? By using the example of the state of Qatar, three potential scenarios for green economic recovery will be analyzed and compared to underline the importance of considering environmental consideration when recovering from the pandemic.

The main contention is that, in contrast to previous global economic crises, the recent COVID-19 pandemic offers an opportunity for economic systems globally to recover in a way that considers environmental concerns while achieving economic growth. In other words, the oil crisis of the 1970s and the financial crisis of 2008–2009 were both immediately followed by a sharp decline in carbon emissions. Sadly, those low emissions levels did not last for very long. Emissions increased throughout the subsequent recovery phase, outpacing earlier reductions. In contrast to this situation, governments now can achieve the goal of building greener and more sustainable economies by taking actions to integrate the green economic tools into the current practices namely in the polluting sectors.

2 Green Economic Recovery After COVID-19: A Theoretical Framework

This chapter is driven by insights from accounts on ecological economics, green growth theory, social and environmental responsibility, resilience theory, and transition management literature. The main contention is that sustainability and economic decision-making should go hand-in-hand. Economic growth should not come at the expense of environmental degradation. In this context, the chapter provides some insights on how a green economic recovery after COVID-19 can align with the endeavors of the GCC countries in general and Qatar in particular to meet its international environmental obligations and reducing their carbon footprint. To this end, the green growth theory empathizes that green energy can provide one of main drivers for economic recovery after COVID-19. The responsibility for achieving the transition towards green energy system should be a shared one between all societal actors including government agencies and energy companies. The recovery of the GCC economies rely in part on the level of its resilience and its ability to absorb the disruption caused by COVID-19. Additionally, the green transition process should manage in a way that faces the challenges and capitalizes on the opportunities available for Qatar and the rest of the GCC countries. Such theoretical underpinnings will be used in the two sections to follow in order to firstly, assess the economic impact of COVID-19 on the economies Qatar and the GCC countries and secondly, to conceptualize green economic recovery.

2.1 The Economic Impact of COVID-19

The world has been badly impacted by the COVID-19 pandemic, which is regarded as one of the most challenging disasters in recent times. Its effects have spread to various facets of the world's economies, social systems, and health. Countries tried to combat this pandemic, but their efforts were unsuccessful since the virus spread quickly and claimed a large number of lives. The world is at a critical crossroads (McGaughey & Lawrence, 2020). An unusual public health catastrophe has once again brought attention to and worsened long-standing social inequities. Working-class individuals from lower socioeconomic groups and minorities are most impacted by the COVID-19 results, which are unevenly distributed across ethnic, class, and gender lines. Because of the protracted lockdown, the economy has suffered the worst decline in 300 years, with unemployment expected to reach levels unseen in decades. All economic activity depends on the duty of producing and maintaining life, yet this task is still undervalued and marginalized, and the costs it carries are unequally distributed, gendered, and racialized. It has also drawn attention to a care crisis that is pervasive.

A glance at the literature on the economic impact of COVID-19 reveals that despite the fact that this recent COVID-19 pandemic has had negative impacts on the world economy some countries have been affected more than others have by the consequences of the spread of this pandemic. Talha's study (2020), which examined the effects of the COVID-19 virus on economic systems generally, provided convincing data. The analysis demonstrated that the COVID-19 pandemic had a detrimental economic impact on both developed and developing nations. The degrees of effect, however, varied. By comparing the differences between what was anticipated prior to the COVID-19 pandemic and what altered later, the analysis discovered that all signals were unfavorable, particularly at the EU level (Talha, 2020).

The Arab Monetary Fund's report on the prospects for the Arab economy, published in 2021, corroborated the findings and observations by showing that the economic repercussions of the COVID-19 pandemic stretched into 2021. The report also stated that the repeated closures to contain the crisis have caused a 6.5% GDP reduction in wealthy nations. About 130 million people—mostly women and children in unstable communities and states—have seen their standard of living decline because of these ramifications, which also include other negative effects. A further finding of the report was that the closure procedures had a greater impact on countries that depended on foreign labor than on other societies. As a result, the global deficit reached $12.7 trillion, which is extremely harmful for developing nations.

By focusing on the Arab Gulf region, it can be noted that the interruption of trade movement between countries and the precautionary measures that were applied in the wake of the spread of the pandemic have led to a decline in global demand for the petroleum and hydrocarbon products. The Gulf countries depend largely on such exports as a major source of the public budget for those countries. Some studies conducted on the impact of the COVID-19 pandemic on the economies of the Gulf countries have clearly indicated the extent to which these economic systems were affected by the spread of the virus and the subsequent measures. In this regard, some scholars have concentrated on figuring out how the COVID-19 virus has affected the Saudi Arabian Kingdom's economy. The researcher specifically looked at how the pandemic will affect the nation's 2030 goal and its capacity to carry out its many pillars, notably the economic one. The analysis concluded that the pandemic had a detrimental impact on the state's public finances, particularly in terms of income and expenditures. As a result, tax payments were put off, and the Saudi government was eager to infuse enormous sums of money to help the nation's economy function. The COVID-19 pandemic has reduced production, which has resulted in a drop in revenues on a macroeconomic level. The number of unemployed people has risen. In addition to the money spent by the state on unemployment benefits to assist those who lacked a reliable source of income, the state also had to shoulder the enormous costs in the health sector. These policies combined cost the state a lot of money (Mansour, 2021).

One of the studies conducted by KPMG found that Qatar's economy ranked highly in terms of avoiding the pandemic's negative consequences while examining the effects of the COVID-19 virus on the country's economy by comparing it to what occurred in other economies across the world. However, in addition to the impact on the tourism sector, which was heavily impacted, oil revenues were among the sectors that saw a large fall internationally and in Qatar. The study also showed that the effects of the pandemic had little impact on domestic economic sectors like retail trade. According to the report, this is due to the state's support of these industries ever since the blockade crisis. The study found that shopping centers were the most adversely affected, whereas the pandemic had a moderate impact on merchants and a minimal influence on the supply chain. The real estate industry is one of the areas of the Qatari economy that has been most impacted by the COVID-19 outbreak (KPMG, 2020).

The United Arab Emirates was the primary subject of several studies that tracked the economic, social, and political impacts of the COVID-19 pandemic. The report emphasized the difficulties that made the effects of the COVID-19 pandemic on the UAE worse, such as the nation's reliance on immigrant labor and its heaviest reliance on oil exports. The survey found that the UAE, which draws many visitors from around the world, experienced a significant impact. The pandemic has caused a decrease in this number. As a result, several things had an impact on the economy of the nation. In response, the state pumped about 27 billion dollars to support sectors, especially the energy sector, and then increased the support to reach 34 billion, which shows the extent of the economic problem faced by the country (Talji, 2020).

Some research has been done on the ways in which workers have been impacted by the spread of the virus in addition to looking at how the pandemic has affected economic systems and economic indicators. Due to the loss of many of these workers' jobs, the COVID-19 pandemic had an impact on the working circumstances of employees in many different economic sectors. Manufacturing and retail are two of the most significant economic sectors that have been impacted by the pandemic. In this regard, the International Labor Organization has established that about 1.25 billion people, or 38% of the global labor force, are employed in industries that have suffered substantially from the crisis, which has had a negative impact on working conditions for those employees. As noted by Amin, many middle- and low-income countries have been affected. There was also a significant impact on the informal sectors, as the two were affected by it due to their lack of access to social protection services or health services. The data of the International Labor Organization indicated that the situation of job losses was clearly linked to the level of the spread of the COVID-19 pandemic, as well as the nature of the measures that were taken to limit its negative effects. Hence, the organization was directed to take measures and policies to ensure the preservation of the livelihoods of employees (Amin, 2020).

At the country level, many countries including the state of Qatar have developed and put in place the required measures and policies in order to minimize the potential negative impacts of the pandemic. Countries around the world have taken measures to encourage the employment process by providing support to the affected economic sectors, as well as paying attention to monetary and fiscal policy. Many governments have also focused on supporting jobs and companies and increasing the level of social protection for all workers and employees in different sectors. In addition, many measures have been implemented that help protect workers, exempt them from taxes and provide them with financial support. It also stressed the need to take care of workers in their workplaces, and to strengthen occupational health and safety procedures. Moreover, various work arrangements have been implemented such as working from home, providing health services and supporting paid leave (Amin, 2020).

In the literature assessing the impact of the pandemic on labor conditions, special attention has been given to certain vulnerable groups of the workforce including migrant labor, women and those who work in the hidden economy. In this context, the Human Rights Council's report focused on the impact of the pandemic on the rights of migrant workers. The report emphasized the willingness of the State of Qatar since the beginning of the pandemic to preserve the rights of all groups and provide care for them without discrimination. In this regard, the state has assigned the Ministry of Administrative Development to cooperate with various competent authorities to take the necessary measures to protect Qatari and non-Qatari workers and preserve their rights. The Qatari government has also developed an urgent policy to respond and effectively implement the decisions to ensure the provision of safety and health requirements within work and housing (Human Rights Council, 2020).

While most studies concentrated on the economies of nations or those with significant economic interests, other studies brought light on a significant portion of society, particularly those engaged in what is known as the "hidden economy" or "non-permanent employment." These employees do not receive any form of social security (Schneider, 2022). According to the study's findings, the COVID-19 pandemic had the greatest economic impact on these categories. Many business owners have let this group of workers go because of preventive measures and closure decisions. They consequently discovered that they were unable to cover their fundamental demands, such as the price of rent or food. The rates of poverty, unemployment, and social destitution have increased because of these effects.

The study carried out by El-Sayed, which highlighted the social and economic consequences of the pandemic on women, is one of the studies that dealt with the impact of the pandemic on the most afflicted groups in society. In this aspect, the study supported the notion that, on an economic and social level, women were among the categories most impacted by the COVID-19 pandemic. The difficulties with poverty and inequality that primarily affect women have been made worse by the COVID-19 virus outbreak. According to this viewpoint, the results of several studies supported the idea that the impacts of the COVID-19 virus on women were evident in the greater suffering that women experienced because of gender inequality in the performance of domestic tasks. The shutdown of nurseries, the suspension of schools and colleges, and distant employment all had an impact on women, who were more negatively impacted than men in this regard because of these changes were (El-Sayed, 2022). Mohamedin noted in a similar vein that the impoverished and illiterate women who provide for their families have been impacted by the interaction of social and economic pressures, further marginalizing this group (Mohamadin, 2020).

The prior analysis of the literature made it evident that many of the studies concentrated on the varied implications of the COVID-19 pandemic on nations, particularly the Arab countries and several Gulf states including Saudi Arabia, Qatar, and the United Arab Emirates. Most of the study done in this field focused on one or two components of the pandemic. As a result, the current study has chosen to concentrate on a crucial topic: how can economic systems recover from COVID-19 while relying on the concept of a green recovery? This subject is crucial and aligns with the national strategies of several Arab Gulf nations, which emphasize achieving sustainability across a range of sectors and reducing reliance on hydrocarbon exports and petroleum derivatives.

2.2 Conceptualizing Green Economy and Green Economic Recovery

In response to COVID-19, the fifty largest economies proposed fiscal spending of USD14.6 trillion for 2020, of which USD1.9 trillion (13.0%) was for long-term economic recovery (O'Callaghan & Murdock, 2021). Despite such huge levels of government spending, the question remains to what extent this public money will help build better, sustainable, and resilient economic systems. The current indicators do not support the assumption that the money to be spent in order to recover from the COVID-19 Pandemic will help build a better sustainable economy. As reported by the International Energy Agency only around 2% of economic bailout money worldwide was going to clean energy (The International Energy Agency, 2021). Furthermore, Nahm et al. have noted "analysis of pandemic economic recovery packages from the 20 largest economies reveals that governments are not spending on emissions cuts despite promises to 'build back better". Only 6% of funds for the pandemic recovery have been set aside for initiatives that will reduce greenhouse gas emissions, such as electrifying automobiles, improving building efficiency, and putting in renewable energy sources (Nahm et al., 2022). Such observations call for a better understanding of what green economy entails and what is needed to achieve green economic recovery from COVID-19 pandemic.

Before we address the idea of a green economic recovery, it is important to note that the phrase "green economy" was initially connected to the global financial crisis of 2008, which had a considerable negative influence on the economic systems of most countries. Reviewing the current economic paradigm that has endured for a long time is the central notion of this approach. This global economic model as a series of zero—sum games describe the link between economic growth and natural resources. As a result, increasing economic development levels will eventually come at the expense of environmental resources that must be depleted in order to accomplish these goals. It is vital to re-evaluate the connection between economic development and environmental resources given the obvious degradation of environmental resources and the advent of transnational environmental issues, such as the problem of climate change and global warming. Finding novel approaches to achieving economic growth that do not harm the environment or deplete its resources is necessary.

The term "environmental sustainability" came into use in this context, emphasizing the need to consider the rights of future generations in the natural resources that are currently available by rationalizing their use and maximizing their economic efficiency through their use in development processes. Applying the tools of the green economy generally and throughout the period of recovery from crises like the COVID-19 crisis is one approach to attain the sustainable development goals from this perspective. In this context, Yazid points out that, recent global economic crises have prompted in-depth assessments of the dominant economic models in an effort to gauge how well-being might be raised for everybody. It is commonly known that economic activities use up a large portion of the biomass present on Earth, leading to several recurrent financial crises (Yazid, 2017). Accordingly, the green economy responds to these crises by reorganizing the economic systems so that its activities center on investing in green sectors in a way that produces sustainable development.

The green economy's ability to provide a balance between social justice, environmental sustainability, and economic growth is one of its most crucial tenets. This equilibrium would offer a solid foundation for addressing any deficiencies that the COVID-19 pandemic may have brought about in the national and local economies. In other words, the green economy relies on the use of renewable natural resources and clean energy, which helps to increase human well-being and lower environmental dangers. In order to achieve sustainable development through establishing environmental balance, the green economy incorporates environmental factors into the instruments and methods utilized to do so

(O'Callaghan et al., 2022). In this way, the green economy aims to ultimately increase the long-term efficiency of the traditional economy. The maximum productivity of resources, particularly water and energy, is increased by green economic activity. Adopting the concept of a green economy also lowers the rising levels of environmental pollution since investments in it are made in resource management that is sustainable and increases environmental productivity.

When viewed from this perspective, the notion of the "green economy" offers us a broad concept that encompasses a variety of economic instruments. With the help of these technologies, the objectives of sustainable development can be supported economically. The ideas extend to a variety of economic areas, such as green transport, green building renovations, green energy efficiency, natural capital, and green R&D (O'Callaghan & Murdock, 2021; O'Callaghan et al., 2022). In order to do this, nations must be committed to changing with the times, emphasize the value of education, and address the skills gap by creating educational initiatives that encourage sustainable growth (Jamal, 2020). The green economy can therefore provide opportunities to alter the course of economic growth so that the global economy becomes a low-carbon economy. Utilizing economic and energy resources as effectively as possible achieves this (Diyar, 2019). In this regard, AL-Arabi noted that the climatic changes brought on by global warming and the diversity of pollutants have compelled a re-evaluation of the global economic model's guidance in the direction of enacting the green economy (Al-Arabi, 2019). This trend has been reinforced by the rise in energy usage and the threats to the ecological balance that this creates.

In light of the previously mentioned discussion, it is generally acceptable to define the term "green recovery" as "a series of economic recovery measures aligned with achieving long-term climate change and sustainability objectives, to move toward a sustainable and economic model for the planet, which is both more resilient and inclusive" (https://www.iberdrola.com/). In this view, a "green recovery" concentrates on ideas and practices that will help the environment and people for a very long period. Ecosystem preservation and climate change mitigation are crucial components of environmental protection, but so are job creation in the clean energy industry, preserving everyone's health and safety alongside emphasizing climate justice.

To achieve a green economic recovery, justice, renewable energy, sustainability, and ecosystem restoration are all essential foundations.

Since they are being affected by the pandemic the most severely, the vulnerable groups need aid. They require food, clothing, and jobs. Justice and equality must be the cornerstones of our shift to a greener economy in order to guarantee that nobody is left behind. In addition, governments need to invest far more extensively in clean energy infrastructure and renewable energy sources while exiting areas that contribute to pollution. Achieving net-zero policy objectives will also be supported by the modernization of public transportation and the construction of energy-efficient residences and buildings. Increased government support for sustainable energy will result in more "future-proof"jobs being created in the new economy. Initiatives in education and training will be essential in this situation. Environmentally, restoring ecosystems, and ensuring that everyone has access to nature are crucial to combating climate change and advancing human wellbeing. Accordingly, unless we also make sure the recovery is not based on an increase in emissions and extraction, the climate problem and the natural emergency will worsen despite the temporary reduction in rising emissions (McGaughey & Lawrence, 2020).

To reach these goals in the wake of an economic crisis including the COVID-19 pandemic, packages of environmental, regulatory, and fiscal reforms should be prepared. The fiscal policies that, among other things, promote the use of renewable energy, efficient energy consumption, nature-based solutions, sustainable transportation, green innovation, and green jobs to boost the economy and the environment.

3 Green Economic Recovery: Potential Scenarios for Qatar

COVID-19 had an impact on the Qatari economy, particularly the tourism industry, as hotel room occupancy fell to 5%. In addition, Qatar's exports fell from 372 million riyals in 2019 to 282 million riyals in 2020. The reduction in gas and petroleum product costs brought on by the suspension of international trade and the shutting down of ports and airports. The Qatari economy was able to weather this crisis, though. On March 15, 2020, the Supreme Committee for Crisis Management was established to assume control of the COVID-19 crisis. Many policies have been created and put into place, such as the one that lowers interest rates while delaying instalment payments. The state provided financial support and incentives amounting to 75 billion Qatari riyals to support all sectors of the state and to be able to pay the salaries of employees to protect the social rights of all members of Qatari society. These policy actions were important but not sufficient to secure a green economic recovery from the COVID-19 crisis. Hence, the purpose of this section of the chapter is to analyze and contrast three different scenarios to maintain the policy initiatives put forth by the Qatari government to ensure a green recovery from the pandemic.

3.1 Scenarios Definition

Three scenarios can be defined when looking at the potential green recovery in Qatar after COVID-19. The first is a Business as Usual (BAU) scenario, which has no emissions reduction objective and does not consider the possibility to develop smart-city and smart-technology concepts (Badran, 2021). This scenario only takes into account the objectives of the Qatar National Vision 2030 in term of natural gas vehicles and concentrated solar power (CSP) plants deployments. The second is a Green Qatar (GQ) scenario in which we limit GHG emissions in the power and private transportation sectors. This corresponds to a stringent 60% emissions reduction in 2050 for the two sectors together compared to BAU levels. This differs strongly from the Qatar National Vision 2030 objectives. The third is a Smart-City (SC) scenario, which assumes a further deployment of smart-city concepts similar to Lusail city. It imposes the same emissions reduction pathway as for the GQ scenario but assumes a new districts standardization to smart-city concepts (e.g., integrated transport and advanced district cooling systems), contributing to a reduction of useful demands and higher efficiency. We consider, in the present simulation, that a third of new useful transport and cooling demands is in smart districts.

The underlying assumption here is that to deal with the COVID-19 challenges from a green economic recovery perspective, the State of Qatar should rely on substituting fossil fuel source with variable renewable ones. Added to this, there is another game changing phenomenon represented by the drive toward smart cities in Qatar. The cities in Qatar are very modern and they are ready to embrace the smart city paradigm and concept. The development of the internet of things, which characterizes smart cities, will translate for the energy system into a development of smart-grid connected; distributed energy resources and this should help tremendously the penetration of variable renewable energy sources.

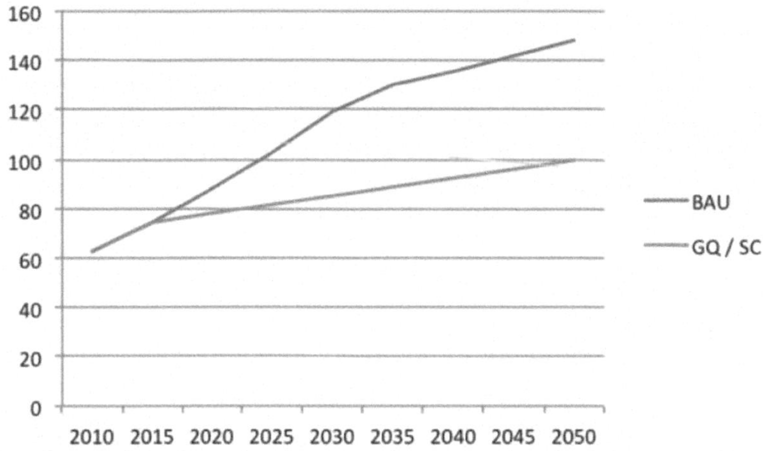

Fig. 1 Emissions pathways for BAU, GQ and SC scenarios (*Source* Babonneau et al., 2023)

Excluding fugitive emissions, the GQ and SC scenarios are equivalent to a reduction of 34% of GHG emissions compared to the BAU scenario, as displayed in Fig. 1.

Note that, for the moment, we do not address abatement issues in all economic sectors as the evolution of non-energy, gas and LNG industries depends mainly on political decisions more than on technological choices. The emissions reduction potentials of these specific sectors are discussed later (Babonneau et al., 2023).

3.2 Results and Discussions

We compare the energy system evolutions of Qatar on two contrasted scenarios, i.e., Business as Usual (BAU) and Green Qatar (GQ) scenarios, and we discuss, in particular, the role of renewable energies in power generation and electric vehicles in the private transportation sector. The evolution of other transportation, industry and gas sectors, as well as the potential impacts of a broader cooperation with Middle East and Asia are discussed separately in the conclusion. Comparison of BAU and GQ scenarios. Simulation results are displayed on Figs. 2, 3 and 4, which show the evolution of emissions, of power generation and of private transport on the period 2010–2050.

First, one observes in Fig. 2 the respective contributions of transport and power sectors in achieving emissions reduction objectives. The private transport appears to be the main contributor. Electric vehicles help strongly from 2025, as can be seen on Fig. 3 with an activity share close to 95% between 2025 and 2050. The remaining emissions in transport are

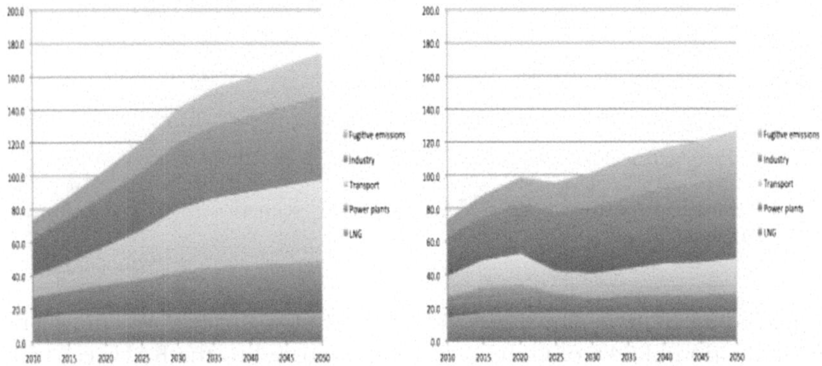

Fig. 2 Evolution of CO_2 emissions in BAU (left) and GQ (right) scenarios (in Mt CO_2) (*Source* Babonneau et al., 2023)

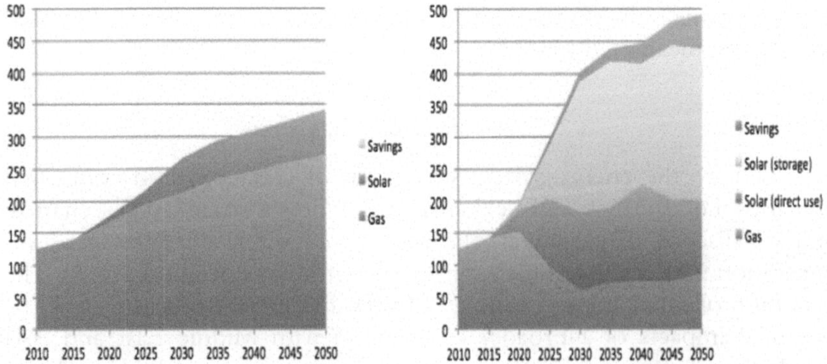

Fig. 3 Evolution of power generation in BAU (left) and GQ (right) scenarios (in PJ) (*Source* Babonneau et al., 2023)

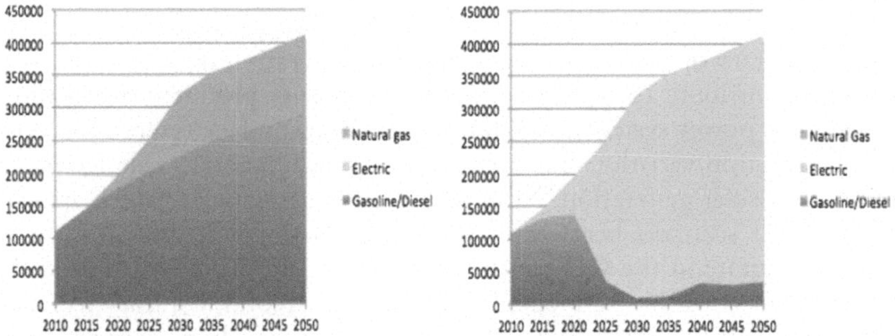

Fig. 4 Evolution of private transportation in BAU (left) and GQ (right) scenarios (in kkm/day) Evolution of private transportation in BAU (left) and GQ (right) scenarios (in kkm/day) (*Source* Babonneau et al., 2023)

mainly linked to other transport activities that are not constrained in the present study. In power generation, CSP plants are privileged technologies for reducing emissions contributing to almost 66% of power generation in 2050. Figure 3 also shows a slight decrease in the use of existing gas power plants. This is due to the very stringent reduction in CO_2 emissions imposed to the power sector. This would certainly be politically difficult to justify.

Regarding electricity demand and production, Fig. 3 shows a significant increase of production in 2050 from 350 PJ in the BAU scenario to 440 PJ (without energy savings) in the GQ scenario, resulting essentially from the new EVs demand in the private transport.

We also notice that in a constrained emissions context, the model exploits the potential of energy savings in residential, commercial and government buildings with investments mainly in insulation and refurbishment for reducing the needs for space cooling. For solar production, we distinguish direct use and stored electricity. The high penetration of EVs combined with Vehicle to Grid (V2G) capability enables the optimization and rationalization of energy uses. In fact, through demand-response (DR) mechanisms, the model al- lows the electricity demand to adapt to implicit pricing signals. This is the case, for EVs charging and the use of EVs batteries to provide temporary storage. DR is thus facilitating the demand/supply balance for electricity by smoothing production and consumption over the different times.

Moreover, we observe that both CSP and EVs technologies are very complementary options, EVs fostering solar generation development. EV batteries contribute to store intermittent electricity production and thus provide the power systems with the necessary secondary reserve to cope with production variations intervening, in a fast time scale, due to intermittency of solar generation. Note that natural gas vehicles, which appear in the BAU scenario because of the Qatar National Vision 2030, no longer penetrate in the GQ scenario. First, they are not compatible with the stringent emissions reduction objective and, second, contrary to EVs, natural gas vehicles cannot provide system services such as secondary reserves needed for power network stability. Also, note that, as the model does not include the carbon capture and sequestration (CCS) technologies to produce hydrogen from natural gas, fuel cell cars cannot be a viable option. Finally, we estimate the systemic discounted extra cost associated to the GQ scenario (compared to the BAU scenario) to be around \$60 billion for the period 2020–2050. This cost corresponds mainly to investments in CSP plants and EVs.

The Smart-City scenario we now focus on the SC scenario, which assumes a strong development of the Qatar energy system to smart-cities and smart-districts. The model does not consider the investment costs related to new smart-districts but instead intends to estimate the avoided cost for the energy system when developing such smart-city concepts. As previously mentioned, we consider that a third of new forthcoming useful demands will be in smart districts. Figure 4 displays the penetration of SC-based mobility on the transportation sector, which is quite significant. As for cooling, it contributes to slightly reducing the electricity demand. As shown on Fig. 4, SC-based development reduces the need for electricity storage compared with the GQ scenario.

The impact on the energy system of a transition toward smart city could take many forms. First, by providing two-way communications between consumers and electricity producers, the smart city will foster demand response and distributed energy resource management. Second, new forms of demand for energy services will materialize in the transport, housing and service sectors that could contribute to lowering the environmental footprint of the energy sector. Third, the smart-grid connection of distributed energy resources and the possibility to provide secondary reserve through grid storage and distributed system service, like e.g., reactive power compensation, will facilitate the penetration of variable renewable energy in the energy system (Fig. 5).

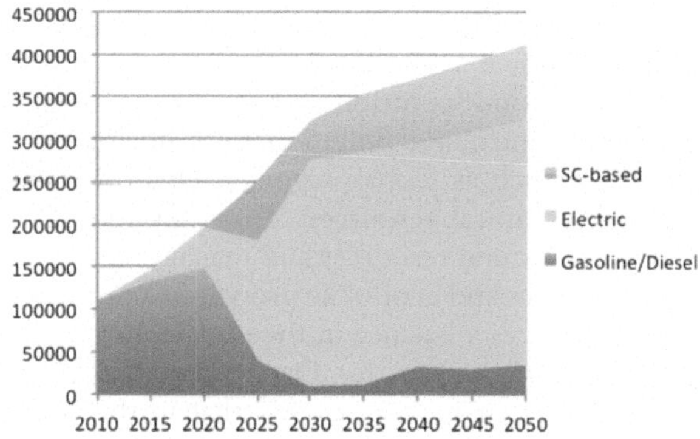

Fig. 5 Impact of SC mobility on the transportation sector (*Source* Babonneau et al., 2023)

We estimate a discounted avoided cost of around $10 billion on the time span 2025–2050, by comparing the systemic costs of the GQ and SC scenarios. This cost includes energy savings due to the use of more efficient smart technologies for transportation and cooling services and investment savings for standard technologies (e.g., EVs). This avoided cost should be compared to the extra development cost of smart-districts in Doha (Babonneau et al., 2021).

4 Conclusions

The purpose of this chapter was to determine how economic systems might rebound from the negative consequences of the COVID-19 crisis. The arguments in this chapter have led to the conclusion that this crisis has had a significant impact on the majority of economic systems worldwide. With the increasing rise in infections, all nations—developed and developing—have suffered, and many health systems have even crumbled. The loss of many workers' jobs was one of the COVID-19 pandemic's most significant adverse consequences on the economy. Due to the COVID-19 virus's global spread, trade between nations has been hampered, and economic growth rates have fallen across the board.

In the transition towards better, greener, and more suitable economic systems, the notion of green economy was regard in this chapter as an alternative to the economy based on development that pollutes the environment, or what is known as the black or fossil economy based on oil. Hence, the green economy contributes to reducing risks at the environmental level and controlling pollution by reducing the destructive environmental effects such as global warming, environmental pollution, and the depletion of natural resources. The adoption of this concept also helps to conserve natural resources and manage waste resulting from industrialization processes and economic growth in a rational manner and in a manner which restores a balance in the ecosystem.

Regarding the future scenarios for Qatar related to the adoption of green recovery tools the chapter concluded that in the context of stringent emissions reduction policies, EVs with their batteries play a key role in the penetration of intermittent solar productions. They facilitate the supply/demand balance for electricity by smoothing production and consumption and they help significantly to the stability of the power distribution systems by providing secondary system reserves. Additionally, to reduce drastically carbon emissions, Qatar is expected to lower the dependence of its domestic consumption to natural gas, an evolution that would liberate further natural gas for LNG export. Furthermore, the systemic discounted extra cost associated to a Green Qatar scenario (compared to the BAU scenario) is estimated to be around $60 billion for the period 2020–2050. This cost corresponds mainly to investments in concentrated solar plants and electric vehicles. Finally, the deployment of new smart transportation and heating concepts might contribute significantly to paving the way to a low economy as they reduce slightly the electricity and mobility demands. The discounted avoided cost of smart-district development is estimated to be around $10 billion in the time span 2025–2050.

These findings have practical implications for policymakers, businesses, and other green energy concerned stakeholders. For policymakers, the findings of this chapter can form the base for formulating and putting in place green recovery strategies in Qatar and GCC countries. These strategies can emphasize the importance of greater investments in green energy technologies and infrastructure. In that sense, Qatar and the GCC countries can achieve green and sustainable economic growth. Businesses can also benefit from the findings of this chapter particularly in relation to investment decisions. The discussion in the chapter made it clear that investing in green and smart technologies and energy systems if the way forward for the GCC countries should they want to meet their international obligations in the area of environment and climate change. That means such businesses have new investment opportunities, which may result in more jobs and better economic conditions for the society as a whole. Other energy stakeholders in Qatar such as KAHRAMAA can play a major role in designing awareness campaigns to prepare the people in the society for the green energy transition. The appropriate regulatory framework that ensures the proper enforcement of green energy transition policies could support such robust green governance system.

To sum up, lower emissions with better climate and environmental benefits for people and the environment are the hallmarks of a greener recovery trajectory. These should be the cornerstones of net-zero emissions policies as they are in line with the 1.5 °C warming goal. Governments now have the chance to "build back better," but doing so takes political will, financial flexibility, and resources, as well as outside assistance from leaders in green finance and technology. As they weigh the need to solve the current climate catastrophe with the need to recover from the economic damage caused by COVID-19, developing countries including Qatar must make delicate, time-bound, and intertemporal decisions.

Bibliography

Al-Arabi, A. (2019). The green economy in Malaysia: Choice or inevitability? *Journal of Strategy and Development, Abdelhamid Bin Badis University Mostaganem, 9*.

Amin, K. (2020). Analytical review of the proposed recommendations in international reports to deal with the economic and financial repercussions of the COVID-19 pandemic. *The Egyptian Journal of Development and Planning, 28*, 31–64.

Babonneau, F., Badran, A., Benlahrech, M., Haurie, A., Schenckery, M., & Vielle, M. (2021). Economic assessment of the development of CO_2 direct reduction technologies in long-term climate strategies of the Gulf countries. *Climatic Change, 165*(3–4), 64. https://doi.org/10.1007/s10584-021-03058-4

Babonneau, F., Badran, A., Haurie, A., Schenckery, M., & Vielle, M. (2023). GCC countries strategic options in a global transition to zero-net emissions. *Environmental Modeling & Assessment*. https://doi.org/10.1007/s10666-023-09904-2

Badran, A. (2021). Developing smart cities: Regulatory and policy implications for the State of Qatar. *International Journal of Public Administration*, 1–14. https://doi.org/10.1080/01900692.2021.2003811

Diyar, A. (2019). The impact of the green economy on growth and sustainable development: A standard study on a group of developed and developing countries. *Journal of Financial, Accounting and Administrative Studies, University of Larbi Ben M'hidi Oum El Bouaghi*, *6*, 11.

El-Sayed, H. (2022). The economic and social repercussions of the COVID-19 pandemic and its impact on women in Egyptian society. *The Arab Journal of Literature and Human Studies, 21*, 295–332.

Human Rights Council. (2020). *Joint questionnaire for mandate holders of the special procedures of the United Nations Human Rights Council*. https://www.ohchr.org/en/calls-for-input/1970/joint-questionnaire-covid-19-and-human-rights

Jamal, I. H. (2020). The economic measures taken by the State of Qatar and their impact in confronting the COVID-19 crisis. *Bayt Almashura Journal, 13*, 125–162.

KPMG. (2020). *The potential impact of the emerging coronavirus on the Qatari economy*. https://assets.kpmg.com/content/dam/kpmg/qa/pdf/2020/4/potential_impact_of_covid-19_on_the_qatar_economy.pdf

Mansour, A. (2021). The effects and economic dimensions of the corona virus (Covid-19) on the public finances in the Kingdom of Saudi Arabia and ways to treat it. *The Scientific Journal of Economics and Trade*, 519–552.

McGaughey, E., & Lawrence, M. (2020). *The green recovery act 2020*. https://uploads-ssl.webflow.com/5e1b5c6919c05c76379535f9/5f0379ca94d438b843b8fdef_The

Mohamadin, S. (2020). Reading in the economic, political and security files: The economic effects and social repercussions of the corona virus pandemic, harmonies of danger and signs of optimism. *Business Administration, 169*, 6–8.

Nahm, J. M., Miller, S. M., & Urpelainen, J. (2022). G20's US$14-trillion economic stimulus reneges on emissions pledges. *Nature, 603*(7899), 28–31.

O'Callaghan, B., & Murdock, E. (2021). *Are we building back better?* The United Nations Environment Programme. https://www.unep.org/resources/publication/are-we-building-back-better-evidence-2020-and-pathways-inclusive-green

O'Callaghan, B., Yau, N., & Hepburn, C. (2022). How stimulating is a green stimulus? The economic attributes of green fiscal spending. *Annual Review of Environment and Resources, 47*(1), 697–723. https://doi.org/10.1146/annurev-environ-112420-020640

Schneider, F. (2022). New COVID-related results for estimating the shadow economy in the global economy in 2021 and 2022. *International Economics and Economic Policy, 19*(2), 299–313. https://doi.org/10.1007/s10368-022-00537-6

Talha, A. (2020). *The economic repercussions of the novel coronavirus on Arab countries*. Arab Monetary Fund.

Talji, I. N. (2020). *The Economic*. Arab Center for Research and Policy Studies.

The International Energy Agency. (2021). *Sustainable recovery tracker key findings*. https://web.archive.org/web/20210724144648/https://www.iea.org/reports/sustainable-recovery-tracker/key-findings

Yazid, T. (2017). The green economy is a sustainable development that combats pollution. *Journal of Financial, Accounting, and Administrative Studies, University of Larbi Ben M'hidi Oum El Bouaghi, 8*.

PART II

The Impact of COVID-19 on Finance and Financial Policies

CHAPTER 8

The Impact of COVID-19 on the Banking Sector in Oman

Abdullaziz M. Al Rahbi

1 Introduction

The outbreak of COVID-19 has endangered the global economy and disordered the financial markets around the globe. Massive undesirable economic shocks in size and scale have shaken the financial soundness of most contact-intense services providers and companies (Elnahass et al., 2021) pointed out that even the financial sector has been affected by the rapid and unforeseen nature of the shock.

The eruption of COVID-19 has also damagingly affected the profitability of banks. It has caused them to lose money due to the failure of their borrowers to service their loans. Over half of US banks reported

The views reported in this chapter are those of the authors and do not represent and should not be reported as those of the Central Bank of Oman.

A. M. Al Rahbi (✉)
Central Bank of Oman, Muscat, Oman
e-mail: Abdullaziz.alrahbi@cbo.gov.om

A. Mishrif (ed.), *Economic Effects of the Pandemic*, The Political Economy of the Middle East,
https://doi.org/10.1007/978-981-97-4367-4_8

a decline in their profits, leading them to set aside billions of dollars as provisions to cover their losses (Schroeder, 2021).

Likewise, the economy of the Sultanate of Oman was hindered by the dual shocks of COVID-19 and historically low oil prices in 2020. The prolonged low oil and gas prices negatively impacted the government's fiscal and external deficits and drove public debt to 69.7% of GDP (Ministry of Finance, Oman, 2021).

Governments worldwide have stepped up their containment efforts to prevent the spread of COVID-19 through social distancing, major lockdowns, and total curfews. In turn, these contamination measures undesirably impacted the economic activities of most firms and households. Firms experienced significant drops in revenue and faced higher costs due to the outbreak (Barua, 2020), which, in turn, will limit their ability to repay their debt. Against this backdrop, banks have seen a strident decline in income and a surge in doubtful loans. This will likely negatively impact banks' profit and solvency (Beck & Keil, 2022).

Several studies have shown that the outbreak of COVID-19 has adverse effects on banks' profitability (e.g., Elnahass et al., 2021). These studies, part of a growing body of research on the pandemic, focus on the disease's different impact on banks' financial performance.

This chapter analyzes the various factors that affect the financial performance of banks. In addition to the interest rate and capital ratios, other factors such as the growth of GDP and the non-performing loan (NPLs) ratio are also considered to determine bank profitability.

In addition, this chapter focuses on the various factors that affect banks' profitability. These include the capital ratios, the non-performing loan ratio, and the loan-to-deposit ratio. The chapter's findings have important implications for regulators and banking institutions during stressful times.

The chapter aims to comprehensively analyze the effects of the COVID-19 pandemic on banks' profitability in the Sultanate of Oman. It also seeks to explore the various factors that affect the financial performance of these establishments and have a more profound understanding of these factors and their latent impact on banks' performance.

1.1 Research Questions and Hypotheses

The outbreak of COVID-19 had a significant impact on the banking sector and the financial markets (Borri & Di Giorgio, 2022). AlShekaili, Ali and, Karim, Asif indicated that 95% of major Omani banks showed a negative growth of 41.4% y.o.y by the end of the second quarter of 2020 as compared to the same period in 2019 (Al Shekaili & Karim, 2020). As per the Central Bank of Oman data, the Net profit of Other Depositary Corporations fell by 39.2% and reached R.O 241.4 million by the end of 2020 as compared to R.O 397.3 million at the end of 2019 (CBO, 2021). Given the massive decline in net profit of Banks operating in Oman during 2020, the chapter aims to answer the following questions:

Q1: Has COVID-19 impacted the financial performance of Banks operating in Oman?
Q2: Is there a significant association between banks' internal factors and their profitability?
Q3: Is there a significant relationship between external factors and the profitability of commercial banks?

The author expects that Omani banks have been affected by the COVID-19 pandemic. Moreover, both internal and external factors are significant determinants of the profitability of banks in Oman. Henceforward, this chapter aims to test and evaluate the following hypotheses:

H1: The impact of the COVID-19 pandemic is negatively related to the financial performance of Chinese and U.S. banks.
H2: Internal factors affect banks' financial performance in Oman.
H3: External factors affect banks' financial performance in Oman.

2 Literature Review

The theoretical framework of this chapter encompasses multiple economic theories and concepts. First, it leans on financial economics, particularly the theories explaining how economic fluctuations affect financial institutions' profitability (Smith, 2010). Here, the countercyclical lending perspective is vital, as it involves banks increasing loan loss provisions during good times and decreasing them during downturns to stabilize the credit cycle (Brown & Johnson, 2015).

Secondly, this study incorporates the elements of monetary policy theory, evaluating the efficacy of monetary easing - including lowering interest rates and reserve requirements, to inject liquidity into the economy during downturns (Taylor, 1993). This relates directly to Keynesian economics, emphasizing that during periods of economic downturn, government intervention can spur economic activity (Keynes, 1936).

The chapter also employs crisis management theories in finance. It assesses the effectiveness of government measures such as liquidity support to banks to ensure financial stability during crises (Bernanke, 2009). This evaluation allows us to understand the practical implications of these theoretical concepts better and provides insights into their effectiveness in real-world scenarios (Fisher & Merton, 1984).

There is a vast literature on the determinants of commercial bank profitability. In 1966, Zoellner and Hester published a chapter that revealed that various factors affect banks' profitability.

2.1 Determinants of Profitability for Commercial Banks

Although Bourke was the first to classify these factors into two main categories, internal and external factors, his chapter showed that there is no comprehensive census on the importance of these factors. In 1992, Molyneux and Thornton replicated Bourke's work on European banks.

The management of banks has the power to control certain internal factors such as the level of extra reserve, investment, and liquidity. However, external factors such as inflation and market share can affect banks' profitability.

2.1.1 Internal Determinants

In 1999, Baka. S and Guru categorized internal bank factors into financial and non-financial statement variables. The former affects the income and balance sheets directly, while the latter has no direct impact on the financial results.

a. **Capital**

The capital adequacy ratio measures the bank management's commitment to providing adequate financing for its operations. In 2004, Frame and White noted that the banking industry is heavily regulated due to its vital role in the economy.

b. **Credit Ratio**

Banks' level of liquidity is related to their net profit and interest rate elasticity. In addition, there is an indirect relationship between the loan-to-deposit ratio and banks' liquidity. According to Bourke, there is strong evidence that liquidity can significantly affect a bank's profitability.

c. **Economies of Scale (Size)**

Bank management has the power to increase or decrease the size of a bank by engaging in mergers and acquisitions. In 1993, Runkle and Boyd noted that the presence of large banks in an efficient environment could lead to higher profitability. In 1985, Smirlock pointed out that a high level of economies of scale can boost a bank's profitability.

2.1.2 External Determinants

a. **Banking Sector Competition**

One of the most critical factors affecting a bank's profitability is its market share. According to Heggested and Mingo in 1976, market share can lead to higher performance. However, it can also decrease the capacity of a bank to control the prices of its products and services. In 1998, Huizinga and Demirg-Kunt noted that regulations aimed at reducing the dominance of a bank's market share could hurt a bank's profitability.

b. **Business Cycle**

Although sound lending practices are required for sustained economic growth, the country's macroeconomic environment can affect the level of lending. In 2012, Allen and colleagues analyzed the returns of financial institutions over the period 1973 to 2003. They found that the country's macroeconomic conditions can also influence the factors that affect a bank's profitability.

2.2 *Profitability Determinants Used in Selected Countries*

2.2.1 *Greece*

Athanasoglou, Delis, and Brissimis conducted a chapter in 2008 to analyze the various factors that affect a bank's profitability in Greece. They found that the industry's structure can influence a bank's profitability. The chapter's authors used a method known as the generalized method of moments to analyze the multiple factors that affect a bank's profitability. They focused on the Greek banking sector's imperfect competitive environment and profit persistence. The chapter's authors found that productivity and capital ratio are significant factors that affect a bank's profitability. However, they found that credit risk can negatively affect a bank's profitability. Greek banks tend to follow a risk-averse strategy, which results in lower profits. The high level of competition in the Greek banking industry had negatively affected the profitability of some banks. In terms of macroeconomic factors, they found that inflation and the business cycle are the most critical factors that affect a financial sector's profitability.

2.2.2 *The Middle East and North Africa*

In 2008, Omran and Naceur analyzed banks' profitability and regulations in 10 Middle East and North Africa (MENA) countries. They used a panel of data collected from 173 banks. They classified the various explanatory variables into two categories.

The first category of bank-specific variables is the net interest margin. The second category is the other factors that affect a bank's profitability, such as the operating expenses ratio and credit risk. They used the country's GDP per capita as a proxy for its economic cycle.

Among economic indications, researchers tend to include the inflation rate since the region witnessed a period of high inflation in the early 2000s. Besides these, other economic indicators, such as the credit extension to the private sector, are also considered to analyze the bank's performance. In 2008, market capitalization increased rapidly following the rise in oil prices. According to Naceur and Omran (2010), a bank's capital ratio is critical to its profitability. The increase in market capitalization is expected to boost a bank's profitability since it allows it to take advantage of the opportunities that come with having more capital.

In their chapter, Naceur and Omran (2010) noted that the increase in reserve ratio could boost a bank's profitability, suggesting that banks are more likely to hold more reserves at their respective central banks.

2.2.3 Gulf Cooperation Council

In 2014, Murthy and Al Muharrami analyzed the factors that affect a bank's profitability in the Gulf Cooperation Council. They used data collected from 37 banks in the region from 1999 to 2012. They used a fixed effect, a random effect, and a pooling ordinary least square method. The two categories of bank-specific variables were classified into the first and second categories. The first considers the factors that affect a bank's profitability, while the second focuses on the industry's characteristics. They tried to link the factors affecting a bank's profitability to the industry's overall features. The third category of bank-specific variables is macroeconomic indicators, which include the country's inflation and GDP per capita. They found that capital and risk-based capital ratios are critical factors that affect a bank's profitability. They noted that banks that finance their activities through equity perform better than those that rely on loans. This means that lower interest margins are likely to occur for them. However, they found that credit risk can negatively affect a bank's ROAA. They also noted that the interest rates on deposits and loans had changed significantly during the years before the financial crisis.

Despite the various factors affecting a bank's profitability, surveying literature confirms that the determinants of banks' performance vary depending on the country. For instance, the chapter results in Greece differed from those in other countries.

3 Empirical Model and Hypotheses

This chapter aims to analyze the impact of various factors on the profitability of Oman's commercial banks. The data collected for this chapter come from bank-specific data, industry-specific, and some economic indicators. A panel data regression model is used to analyze the quarterly results of seven banks for the period 2013Q1–2022Q2.

A bias and consistency model are used to analyze the data. There are also potential omitted variables that can affect the estimates. These include time-invariant and time-variant factors. For instance, time-invariant factors can be bank-specific error components. Conversely, time-variant factors can be variables across time and banks. Using a panel data model is appropriate because it allows us to control the variable biases, which leads to an unbiased estimate. This chapter also uses various statistical techniques to analyze the data. Some of these include fixed effects (FE), random effects (RE), and the pooling ordinary least square model (POLS).

To estimate the profitability of banks in Oman, we need to add a lagged dependent variable. This can be done because the profit tends to be influenced by the previous period's value. Another critical factor that we need to consider is the autocorrelation of macroeconomic and banking indicators (Flamini et al., 2009).

3.1 *Pooled Ordinary Least Square Model (POLS)*

$$ROA_{i,t} = \alpha_0 + \delta ROA_{i,t-1} + \sum_B \beta_1 X^B_{I,t} + \beta_2 X^F_t + \beta_3 X^M_t + \text{covid\_ 19} + \varepsilon_{i,t} \quad (1)$$

where, $ROA_{i,t}$ is the return on average assets of bank i at period t. ${X^B}_t$, ${X^F}_t$ and ${X^M}_t$ are vectors of banksspecific factors, financial sector concentration, and macroeconomic variables, respectively. δ measures the speed of adjustment of mean reversion in which a value close to 0 is associated with a higher speed of adjustment. The variable *covid*19 is a dummy variable that takes a value of 1 during the period of covid-19 first discovered in Oman, i.e. March 2020 until June 2022, and 0 otherwise. $d\varepsilon_{i,t}$ represents regression residuals.

The typical expectations for cross-sectional analysis are considered. Reliability relies on the strong stress of 'strong exogeneity assumption' $E(\varepsilon_{i,t}|\alpha_i X_{i,1} \ldots X_{i,7}) = 0$ *i.e.* the error term $\varepsilon_{i,t}$ is uncorrelated with the independent variable at any point of time and 'random effect assumption' $E(\alpha_i|X_{it}) = 0$ *i.e.* α_i is uncorrelated with the independent variables at any point in time (Wooldridge, 2010). The chapter assumes that unobserved heterogeneity across the banks is captured by α_i the time-variant is captured by $\varepsilon_{i,t}$. The downside of the POLS technique is that it can be biased due to the "random effects assumption". For instance, if the data is collected with a serial correlation, the outcomes might be biased (Greene, 2012; Koutsoyiannis, 1993).

3.2 Fixed Effects Model (FEM)

$$ROA_{i,t} = \alpha_0 + \delta ROA_{i,t-1} + \sum_{B} \beta_1 X_{I,t}^{B} + \beta_2 X_{I,t}^{F} + \beta_3 X_t^{M} + \text{covid\_ } 19 + \varepsilon_{i,t} \quad (2)$$

The fixed effects estimator is used to analyze the bank-specific data. It is consistent with the strict exogeneity assumption and allows the bank-specific effects to be correlated with the regressors. In this method, we use a time-demeaned model. Since the data collected for this time-variant chapter come from bank-specific data, we can recover the effects of the variable by considering the residuals variation of the dependent variable, which cannot explain the independent variable. The FE estimation is consistent but inefficient, unlike the RE, which is both consistent and efficient under strong assumptions (Cameron & Trivedi, 2005).

3.3 Random Effects Model (FEM)

$$\text{ROA}_{i,t} = \alpha_0 + \delta \text{ROA}_{i,t-1} + \sum \beta_1 X_{I,t}^{B} + \beta_2 X_t^{F} + \beta_3 X_t^{M} + \mu_{i,t} \text{ and } \mu_{i,t} = \varphi_i + \varepsilon_{i,t} \quad (3)$$

where $\mu_{i,t}$ consists of φ_i that is the bank-specific error component and $\varepsilon_{i,t}$ which includes cross-sectional errors and time series errors. If the variable of interest is time-invariant, then the RE method is used. The coefficient of the estimator is not powerful enough to explain the results (Stock & Watson, 2012). This can be attributed to (i) the perfect multicollinearity in the dataset used and (ii) there are no differences in the independent variable. To avoid this issue, we use the RE method proposed by Cameron and Trivedi (2005). If the autocorrelation structure is identified, OLS has consequently altered into the Feasible Generalized Least Square (FGLS) method, which results in the RE estimator.

The Hausman test is a statistical method used to estimate the required coefficients; when both the FE and RE methods can estimate values of the coefficients, the main downside of the test is that it is unacceptable if the error term is not Independent and Identically distributed (i.i.d) (Cameron & Trivedi, 2005).

4 Data and Methodology

4.1 Data

The chapter is focused on commercial banks in Oman, excluding Islamic banks. The sample is a balanced panel of data composed of seven banks. The data collected to cover the period from 2013 to 2022 were collected by. These banks represent over 90% of the assets of conventional banks in Oman (CBO, 2022).

The banks that are represented in the chapter are Al Ahli Bank (AHB), Bank Muscat (BM), Sohar International Bank (SIB), Dhofar Bank (DHB), HSBC Oman (HSOM), Oman Arab Bank (OAB), and the National Bank of Oman (NBOB). All of the data collected for this chapter came from Bloomberg Terminal. The macroeconomic indicators were also attained from the Central Bank of Oman's quarterly bulletin.

4.2 Research Variables

4.2.1 Independent Variable

ROA: The return on assets is a measure of the performance of banks. It is used to measure how well a bank manages its assets. According to a 2015 chapter by Petria and colleagues, banks can generate a profit by considering the total assets of their customers.

$$ROI = \frac{After\,Tax\,Income}{Average\,Total\,Assets} \tag{4}$$

4.2.2 Explanatory Variable

a. Bank-specific Determinants

Size: A bank's total assets are typically used to indicate its size. Nevertheless, this is not the case for every bank. Large banks have clerical and bureaucratic issues that can lead to various inefficiencies. In 2008, Athanasoglou and colleagues noted that the relationship between a bank's profitability and size might not be linear.

Capital: Besides generating a profit, capital can also play an essential role in various undesirable scenarios. For instance, it can cushion the effects of deposit withdrawals. A well-capitalized bank could face a capital run, which occurs when a large number of its depositors withdraw their funds at the same time. A well-capitalized bank would have lower borrowing costs than its less capitalized counterparts (Flamini et al., 2009). However, higher capital requirements could also reduce a bank's profit potential. In 2005, Athanasoglou and colleagues found that higher capital requirements can lead to a less profitable bank. Nevertheless, in 1995, Berger and Athanasoglou published a chapter that found a positive relationship between capital and profitability.

$$Capital = \frac{Total\ Equity}{Total\ Assets} \tag{5}$$

NIM: The net interest margin measures the spread between the interest the bank receives from its loans and the interest it pays on its assets. A bank's profitability is a significant funder (BenNaceur & Omran, 2010).

$$NIM = \frac{Net\ Interest\ Income}{Average\ Earning\ Assets} \tag{6}$$

Efficiency: The efficiency ratio is used to measure the competence of a bank by comparing its non-interest expenses to its net revenue. In 2007, Al-Haschimi noted that operational inefficiency is a crucial aspect that affects the bank's profitability in developing economies. However, Bourke (1989) showed that European banks that have better quality management could improve their profitability. He noted that higher efficiency could lead to lower expenses and higher after-tax profits. Management's aptitude to enhance the bank's productivity would help cut non-interest expenses.

$$NIM = \frac{Operating\ Expenses}{Operating\ Income} \tag{7}$$

Risk: A chapter conducted by Ahokpossi in 2013 revealed that using total assets to measure credit risk is a standard method financial institution use to assess their risk. It shows that increasing the loan to total assets can improve the bank's chance of experiencing loan loss. Other studies have also shown that increasing the loan to total assets can increase the risk of experiencing loan default (Ahokpossi, 2013; Angbazo, 1997). Credit scoring is one of the most effective ways financial institutions can mitigate credit risk. This method evaluates the likelihood of a borrower going past their credit card payment.

$$Risk = \frac{Total\ Loans}{Total\ Deposits} \tag{8}$$

b. Banking Sector Determinants

Concentration: Studies on banks' market power have been conducted in the literature. They have shown that a higher market share can lead to more effective interest rate spreads. In 2006, Al Muharrami and colleagues noted that the banking system in Oman is modeled as a monopolistic competition sector. They used the Herfindahl–Hirschman Index to measure market concentration. The Herfindahl–Hirschman Index is a statistical measure that shows the total market share of banks in each banking sector. In 2021, the HHI was at about 2101, making the Omani banking sector falls under the moderately concentrated industry. This is close to the result of a chapter conducted by Rath, Mishra and Al Yahyaei, in 2014. According to the US Department of Justice, a high HHI score of over 1500 is considered moderately high Table 1.

c. Macroeconomic Development Determinants

Growth: To analyze the business cycle's effects on the profitability of financial institutions, the chapter uses economic growth. In 1999, Demirguc-Kunt and Huizinga, noted that the business cycle could positively impact banks' profitability. In 2010, Al Saqri pointed out that the rise in oil prices could positively affect Oman's output growth.

Inflation: The effects of inflation on the profitability of financial institutions will only be realized once they fully anticipate the movement of

Table 1 HHI benchmark for evaluating market concentration

Treatment	*HHI Score*
Competitive sector	HHI < 1500
Moderately concentrated sector	HHI > 1500 < 2500
Highly concentrated sector	HHI > 2500

Source U.S Department of Justice, 2010

inflation. This means that when a bank increases its interest rates based on the expected inflation, it can boost its profitability. Other studies conducted by other researchers, such as Bourke (1989), Molyneux and Thornton (1992), and Demirguc-Kunt and Huizinga (1999), also found that inflation can have a positive effect on the profitability of financial institutions.

In Oman, however, inflation is masked by the country's subsidies. This makes the impact of inflation on the profitability of financial institutions indeterminate.

A summary of the various variables that are used in this chapter is presented in Table 2. They are also shown to measure their expected effect on the profitability of banks operating in Oman.

5 Results and Analysis

5.1 Descriptive Statistics

Table 3 reports the descriptive statistics of all pooled variables in this chapter.

Table 4 reveals that Bank Muscat has the highest ROA mean, followed by OBA, NBO and Ahli Bank. While Bank Muscat has the most increased size of R.O 12,858.3 million, all the rest of the banks are very close regarding their asset size. In terms of NIM, Bank Muscat is leading, followed by NBO. Meanwhile, Sohar International has the highest LDR, with 117.4%, followed by NBO and Bank Muscat. Regarding Capital Ratio, NBO has the highest ratio among the banks in this chapter, followed by Bank Muscat and Bank Dhofar.

The summary statistics of bank-specific variables of each bank are reported in Table 4.

5.2 Model Analysis

Table 5 presents the model result where the coefficients represent the effect of each independent variable on the ROA dependent variable.

The significance coefficient of the lagged ROA indicates that profits in Oman's banking sector persist. This result confirms results stated by Athanasoglou et al. (2008) for Greece, Petria et al. (2015) for Europe and (Flamini et al., 2009) for SSA countries.

Table 2 Variables definition, measure and expected effect of explanatory variables

Variable	*Description*	*Measure*	*Expected effect*
Dependent variable			
ROA	Return on Average Assets	Net Profit/Average assets	N/A
Independent variable			
(A) Bank-Specific Determinants			
1. CAP	Capital Ratio	Total Equity/Total Assets	+
2. RISK	Loan to Deposit Ratio	Total Loans/Total Deposits	–
3. EFFE	Efficiency Ratio	Non-interest expenses/Net Revenues	–
4. NIM	Net Interest Margin	Net Interest/Average Earning Assets	+
5. SIZE	Total Assets	Natural Logarithm of total assets	?
(B) Industry-Specific Determinants			
1. HHI	Herfindahl–Hirschman Index	Natural logarithm of squared percentage share of assets to industry assets of each bank	?
(C) Macroeconomic Determinants			
1. GROWTH	Economic Growth Rate	Natural Logarithm of Nominal quarterly Growth	+
2. INFL		Annualized percentage change in CPI	+

Source Summary of the literature review

Table 3 Descriptive statistics

	ROA	*SIZE*	*NIM*	*RISK*	*INFLATION*	*HHI*	*GROWTH*	*EFFIC*	*CAPITAL*
Mean	1.2	4176	0.7	98.3	0.8	2254	2.0	50.0	14.2
Median	1.3	3181	0.7	103.9	0.9	2228	1.8	46.5	14.0
Maximum	5.1	13,073	1.7	133.0	4.0	2606	38.9	117.1	19.7
Minimum	−0.3	1396	−0.1	47.3	−1.5	2046	−23.9	26.5	8.6
Std. Dev.	0.6	3202	0.2	20.2	1.2	145	14.4	13.0	2.2
Skewness	1.90	1.90	1.00	−0.70	0.40	1.20	0.4	1.5	0.2
Kurtosis	15.90	5.00	7.60	2.60	3.40	3.90	2.70	6.30	3.00
Count	238.0	238	238	238	238	238	238	238	238

Source Author's calculations

Table 4 Summary statistics for individual bank

	ROA	*Size*	*NIM*	*RISK*	*Effic*	*Capital*
BM						
Mean	1.6	11,710.3	1.0	109.3	41.6	14.7
Std. Dev.	0.2	1134.9	0.2	5.6	5.1	1.9
NBO						
Mean	1.3	3583.7	0.8	110.3	41.6	17.3
Std. Dev.	0.4	266.3	0.2	10.0	11.2	1.8
SOH						
Mean	1.0	2956.6	0.6	117.4	45.0	12.7
Std. Dev.	0.3	746.7	0.1	10.7	6.7	2.1
DHOF						
Mean	1.1	3952.4	0.7	109.3	49.3	14.1
Std. Dev.	0.3	495.4	0.1	7.9	10.2	2.1
HSBC						
Mean	0.7	2361.3	0.6	59.8	66.2	13.7
Std. Dev.	0.4	90.0	0.1	4.1	13.8	0.5
AHLI						
Mean	1.3	2229.1	0.6	82.0	51.5	13.5
Std. Dev.	0.3	484.6	0.2	3.7	12.7	1.3
OBA						
Mean	1.4	2440.4	0.7	100.0	50.0	13.3
Std. Dev.	1.0	612.7	0.1	4.9	48.1	12.8

Source Author's calculations

Table 5 Summary regression result of fixed effect

Variable	*Coefficient*	*Std. Error*	*t-Statistic*	*Prob.*
C	4.7316	1.1721	4.0370	0.00*
ROA (−1)	0.3929	0.0528	7.4455	0.00*
CAPITAL	0.0246	0.0130	1.8955	0.06**
NIM	0.1409	0.1040	1.3547	0.18
RISK	−0.0066	0.0027	−2.4318	0.02**
EFFIC	−0.0125	0.0016	−7.8520	0.00*
SIZE_LN	−0.3964	0.1342	−2.9534	0.00*
HHI	0.0000	0.0001	0.0826	0.93
GROWTH	0.0013	0.0031	0.4082	0.68
INFLATION	0.0066	0.0162	0.4075	0.68
ADJUSTED R2: 82.3%		Significant level * 1%, ** 5%, *** 10%		

Source Author's calculations

The capital coefficient is positive and significant, indicating that Omani banks have successfully used their capital to enhance their profitability. The higher the assets a financial institution has financed through equity, the lower the need for interest-bearing loans from the money market. This means that the bank's sensitivity to interest rate movements is higher. This result is consistent with the results of several chapters, such as Sree Rama Murthy and Al-Muharrami (2014), Berger (1995), Flamini et al. (2009), Athanasoglou et al. (2008) and Hesse and Poghosyan (2009).

The risk coefficient of banks in Oman is negative, as expected. However, as the coefficient's magnitude is minimal, the country's banks are taking steps to improve their screening procedures for potential borrowers. The Central Bank of Oman has issued guidelines to strengthen financial institutions' lending practices.

The efficiency ratio of financial institutions in Oman is negative and significant, as expected. This is because the country's central bank has imposed a ceiling on the interest rates banks can charge on personal loans. Another reason why banks in Oman are reluctant to increase their customer's loan rates is due to the competition from other financial institutions. This chapter provides strong evidence supporting the importance of managerial efficiency in the profitability of financial institutions (Athanasoglou et al., 2008; Petria et al., 2015; Hesse & Poghosyan, 2009; Samad, 2015).

The market concentration variable of banks in Oman is insignificant. However, the value of the HHI has been declining significantly over the past few years. This indicates that small banks in Oman have increased their market share. The Structure–Conduct–Performance (SCP) hypothesis also supports the idea that smaller banks have been able to make better investment decisions, which leads us to the negative sign of Size.

Surprisingly, the size coefficient is negative and significant at a 1% level, indicating that banks in Oman are facing challenges in seizing their economies of scale.

Various macroeconomic factors influence the profitability of banks in Oman. For instance, economic growth and inflation have a significant impact on the performance of the country's banks. The link between inflation and banks' profitability is realized when the deposit and lending interest rates have varying sensitivity to inflation. For instance, banks can attract deposits with low-interest rates by implementing prize schemes. On the other hand, they can increase their margins by adjusting their lending rates. This chapter supports the findings of previous research conducted by Sree Rama Murthy and Al-Muharrami (2014), Athanasoglou et al. (2008), and Gelos (2006).

However, the growth coefficient is positive, yet it is not significant, indicating that non-oil economic activities growth is not a major determinant of banks' performance in Oman. This is also attributed to the low economic growth environment the country has been experiencing since the drastic decline in oil prices in the winter of 2014.

Here we come to the most critical variable this chapter is investigating; the COVID-19 pandemic has certainly impacted banks operating in Oman, with the COVID-19 variable being negative and significant. The magnitude of the pandemic's impact on banks' returns on average assets operating in Oman is around 19%.

6 Concluding Remarks and Some Implications for Policymakers

The global economy is expected to be severely affected by the COVID-19 pandemic. This was apparent in banks' performance during the pandemic. The chapter aimed to provide a systemic analysis of the effects of COVID-19 on the profitability of Oman's banks. It also explores the various factors that affect the operations of these institutions.

In this chapter, I investigated and compared the financial performance of major banks operating in Oman. The findings of this chapter can help policymakers develop regulations that will help prevent banks operating in Oman from experiencing excessive fluctuations in their profitability.

- Banks in Oman should have a sufficient capital reserve to cover their potential losses. This reserve can help them manage their loan loss provisions and maintain their profitability.
- To maintain profitability, banks should focus on improving their business strategies and making sound investments. This can help them reduce their overheads and improve their efficiency. The chapter also found that the profitability of banks in Oman is sensitive to the level of non-interest expense.
- As the competition in the financial sector deepens, policymakers in Oman should encourage the country's banks to play by the rules and regulations. They should also adopt more innovative governance practices to improve their operations.

- Energy price fluctuations influence the country's business cycle. Like most sectors in Oman, the banking sector's performance is impacted by the energy market shocks. To that end, policymakers in Oman should speed up their efforts toward enhancing economic diversification.

This chapter aimed to analyze the various factors that affected the profitability of Oman's commercial bank between March 2014 and June 2022. The chapter found that external and bank-specific factors can affect the profitability of banks working in Oman. The chapter showed that, on average, banks in Oman had lost 19% of their profitability during the pandemic.

The bank-specific factors analyzed were capital, efficiency, and net interest margin. The chapter found that the capital ratio and the net interest margin are highly significant. The former is measured by the total equity to total assets ratio, while the latter is by the interest spread to assets ratio.

In contrast, the efficiency of banks is negatively affected by the level of management inefficiency. Despite the various factors that affect banks' profitability, the chapter's model did not find that the size of banks was significant in determining the level of profitability.

The chapter found that the profitability of banks in Oman is positively related to the country's economic growth due to the high oil prices. Higher oil prices are needed to boost the banks' profits and increase revenues. However, volatility in oil prices can affect the operations of financial institutions in the country.

The chapter reveals significant insights into the performance of Oman's banks amid the COVID-19 pandemic and offers actionable strategies for both financial institutions and policymakers. It underscores the need for robust capital reserves, enabling banks to manage potential losses and maintain profitability. Banks can achieve efficiency and reduce overhead by enhancing business strategies and sound investments. Policymakers must foster compliance with rules and regulations while encouraging innovation in governance practices, aligning with the increasingly competitive financial landscape. The chapter's findings also illuminate the sensitivity of Oman's banking sector to energy price fluctuations, necessitating expedited efforts in economic diversification. This analysis between March 2014 and June 2022 emphasizes the role of external and bank-specific factors such as capital, efficiency, and net interest margin in profitability, with particular attention to the effects of high oil prices and their volatility. By implementing these strategic insights, Oman's banking sector can build resilience against future challenges and contribute positively to the country's economic growth, even in the face of global disruptions like the COVID-19 pandemic.

References

Ahokpossi, C. (2013). *Determinants of bank interest margins in sub-Saharan Africa*. IMF Working Paper, WP/13/34. International Monetary Fund.

Al Shekaili, A. S., & Karim, A. M. (2020). Impacts of pandemic coronavirus COVID-19 on banking sector mid-year financial result in Sultanate of Oman. *Solid State Technology, 63*(6). Retrieved from https://www.solidstatetechnology.us/index.php/JSST/article/view/2851

Angbazo, L. (1997). Commercial bank net interest margins, default risk, interest-rate risk, and off-balance sheet banking. *Journal of Banking and Finance, 21*(1), 55–87.

Athanasoglou, P., Brissimis, S., & Delis, M. (2008). Bank-specific, industry-specific and macroeconomic determinants of bank profitability. *Journal of International Financial Markets, Institutions and Money, 18*(2), 121–136.

Barua, S. (2020). Understanding coronanomics: The economic implications of the coronavirus (COVID-19) pandemic. University Library of Munich. Retrieved from https://ideas.repec.org/p/pra/mprapa/99693.html

Beck, T. H. L., & Keil, J. (2022). Have banks caught corona? Effects of COVID on lending in the U.S. *Journal of Corporate Finance, 72*, 102160. https://doi.org/10.1016/j.jcorpfin.2022

Berger, A. N. (1995). The relationship between capital and earnings in banking. *Journal of Money, Credit, and Banking, 27*, 432–456.

Bernanke, B. (2009). *The Federal Reserve's balance sheet: An update*. Speech delivered at the Federal Reserve Board Conference, Washington, DC.

Borri, N., & Di Giorgio, G. (2022). Systemic risk and the COVID challenge in the European banking sector. *Journal of Banking & Finance, 140*, 106073. https://doi.org/10.1016/j.jbankfin.2022

Bourke, P. (1989). Concentration and other determinants of bank profitability in Europe, North America and Australia. *Journal of Banking and Finance, 13*, 65–79.

Brown, A., & Johnson, B. (2015). Countercyclical lending: Theory and practice. *Journal of Banking and Finance, 56*, 103–120.

Cameron, A. C., & Trivedi, P. K. (2005). *Microeconometrics: Methods and applications*. Cambridge University Press.

Central Bank of Oman. *Annual report various issues*. Central Bank of Oman.

Demirguc-Kunt, A., & Huizinga, H. (1999). Determinants of commercial bank interest margins and profitability: Some international evidence. *The World Bank Economic Review, 13*(2), 379–408.

Elnahass, M., Trinh, V. Q., & Li, T. (2021). Global banking stability in the shadow of Covid-19 outbreak. *Journal of International Financial Markets, Institutions and Money, 72*, 101322. https://doi.org/10.1016/j.intfin.2021

Fisher, I., & Merton, R. C. (1984). Crisis management in financial markets. *Financial Analysts Journal, 40*(6), 14–20.

Flamini, V., Schumacher, L., & McDonald, C. (2009). The determinants of commercial bank profitability in sub-Saharan Africa. *IMF Working Chapters, 9*(15), 1.

Gelos, G. R. (2006). *Banking spreads in Latin America*. IMF Working Paper, WP/06/44. International Monetary Fund.

Greene, W. (2012). *Econometric analysis*. Pearson.

Hesse, H., & Poghosyan, T. (2009). *Oil prices and bank profitability: Evidence from major oil-exporting countries in the Middle East and North Africa*. IMF Working Paper, WP/09/220. International Monetary Fund.

Hester, D., & Zoellner, J. (1966). The relation between bank portfolios and earnings: An econometric analysis. *Review of Economics and Statistics, 48*, 372–386.

Keynes, J. M. (1936). *The general theory of employment, interest and money*. Macmillan.

Koutsoyiannis, A. (1993). *Modern microeconomics*. Macmillan.

Ministry of Finance, Oman. (2021). Final دليل قراءة الموازنة [FinalBudget Reading Guide]. Retrieved from https://www.mof.gov.om/downloadnew.aspx?id=wgI8Q. [Accessed July 1, 2024].

Molyneux, P., & Thornton, J. (1992). Determinants of European bank profitability: A note. *Journal of Banking and Finance, 16*, 1173–1178.

Naceur, S., & Omran, M. (2010). The effects of bank regulations, competition, and financial reforms on banks' performance. *SSRN Electronic Journal*.

Petria, N., Capraru, B., & Ihnatov, I. (2015). Determinants of banks' profitability: Evidence from EU 27 banking systems. *Procedia Economics and Finance, 20*, 518–524.

Rath, D., Mishra, R., & Al Yahyaei, Q. (2014). *Concentration and competition in Oman's banking sector implications for financial stability*. Central Bank of Oman.

Samad, A. (2015). Determinants bank profitability: Empirical evidence from Bangladesh commercial banks. *International Journal of Financial Research, 6*(3), 173–179.

Schroeder, P. (2021). U.S. bank profits plunge 70% on coronavirus loss provisioning. Yahoo Finance. Retrieved from https://finance.yahoo.com/news/u-bank-profits-plunge-70-162202728.html [Accessed June 18, 2022].

Smirlock, M. (1985). Evidence on the (non) relationship between concentration and profitability in banking. *Journal of Money, Credit, and Banking, 17*, 69–83.

Smith, J. (2010). *Financial economics: A comprehensive introduction.* XYZ Publishing.

Sree Rama Murthy, Y., & Al-Muharrami, S. (2014). *Financial sector development and the determinants of bank profitability: A GCC panel chapter.*

Stock, J. H., & Watson, M. W. (2012). *Introduction to econometrics* (3rd ed.). Addison-Wesley.

Taylor, J. B. (1993). Discretion versus policy rules in practice. *Carnegie-Rochester Conference Series on Public Policy, 39*, 195–214.

Wooldridge, J. (2010). *Econometric analysis of cross section and panel data* (2nd ed.). MIT Press.

CHAPTER 9

The Positive Impact of Covid-19 on Omani Banks' Practices and Services

Iman Al-Kendi and Mulook Al Zadjali

1 Introduction

Coronavirus disease also referred to as Covid-19, is a contagious illness brought on by a Coronavirus (Ramasamy, 2020). The COVID-19 epidemic and the tactics necessary to contain it placed a tremendous economic burden on the world (Banks et al., 2021). An unparalleled level of systemic economic disruption has been caused by the COVID-19 pandemic. It simultaneously disrupted many markets and quickly spread to both public and private finance (Dunz et al., 2021).

The global economy has stagnated because of COVID-19. As a result, financial institutions had issues with intermediation income, loan performance, and liquidity (Jeris and Nath, 2021; Rizwan et al., 2022). A financialv crisis is not what the Covid-19 crisis is. However, it increases the likelihood of a banking crisis because it paralyzes the economy and seriously affects financial markets. This would amplify the current economic

I. Al-Kendi (✉) · M. Al Zadjali
Central Bank of Oman, Muscat, Oman
e-mail: Iman.AlKendi@cbo.gov.om

A. Mishrif (ed.), *Economic Effects of the Pandemic*, The Political Economy of the Middle East,
https://doi.org/10.1007/978-981-97-4367-4_9

crisis and lengthen the forthcoming recession. The Covid-19 situation is not a financial crisis, but it could be a significant test of the resilience and strength of European banks (Couppey-Soubeyran et al., 2020).

1.1 Oman Banks During Covid-19 Crisis

In Oman, the pandemic was successfully controlled, and the government and the Central Bank of Oman (CBO) took the necessary steps to minimize its economic impact. The Sultanate currently has about 26 banks, including local, foreign, specialized, and Islamic banks (Central Bank of Oman, 2020). Banks were on the front lines of executing financial support measures put forth by the government and the Central Bank of Oman (CBO) while also having to deal with Covid-19 (Macfarlane & Petluri, 2021). To best serve their customers, banks in Oman worked very hard to digitize and convert all of their products and services to digital platforms (Al Shekaili & Karim, 2020). Banks acted immediately to help clients use existing digital and remote channels more effectively, which help stop the spread of COVID-19. Superior customer experience in the context of COVID-19 entails clarity and transparency, support for digital tools that many customers are still unfamiliar with, and new products and services for customers who are in need (Bensley et al., 2020).

In this regard and to evaluate the beneficial effects of services rendered by commercial banks in Oman during the COVID-19 pandemic crisis, the authors undertook a comparative analysis to examine how the epidemic has affected their ability to provide services. The authors differentiated between commercial banks based on their e-services, ease of use, operational services, quick response times, business continuity Plan during the Covid 19 outbreak, and customer support similarities and variances.

This chapter is organized as follows: Sect. 2 briefly presents some previous studies which highlighted and assessed the service resilience of banks around the world during Covid-19. Section 3 presents the methodology that the authors used to prove the main reason behind this chapter. Section 4 analyzes the chapter findings along with the discussion. The conclusion is covered in Sect. 5.

2 Literature Review

As the biggest test for financial systems since the global financial crisis of 2008–2009, the COVID-19 epidemic is wreaking havoc on the worldwide economic and financial landscape (Barua & Barua, 2021). There are few amounts of literature that assess the service resilience of banks around the world during Covid-19.

To examine how COVID-19 affected Islamic banking, three potential risks, including financing concerns, asset impairment, and tightening the profit-sharing structure. Islamic banks are more adaptable to the economic crises brought on by the COVID-19 pandemic than traditional banks (Hasan, 2020). During the epidemic, all Islamic banks in Indonesia implemented corporate social responsibility programs, fulfilling their part in the effort. They have encouraged civic engagement by making a variety of donations to lessen the effects that are already being felt. According to the research by Abbas and Frihatni, the donations made to help people survive during the coronavirus outbreak were evidence of banking social responsibility (Abbas & Frihatni, 2020). Furthermore, the research by Korzeb and Niedzióka aimed to evaluate the COVID-19 pandemic's potential consequences on the commercial banks that operate in Poland's banking industry. 13 commercial banks' diagnostic features were chosen for its deployment. According to the survey, the biggest banks operating in Poland are the ones least vulnerable to the pandemic's effects. The banks that were most at risk from the crisis were selected at the same time (Korzeb & Niedzióka, 2020).

More in more, by concentrating on the distinctions between banks with worse and better capitalization at the beginning of the pandemic, Dursun-de Neef and colleagues examined how European banks responded to the COVID-19 outbreak. The authors show that whereas loans from European banks were dramatically reduced at the start of the pandemic, loans from banks with stronger exposure to the COVID-19 epidemic were, on average, reduced by a significant amount less (Dursun-de Neef, 2021). In the same year, the goal of Obeidat and colleagues' study was to report on the performance of Jordanian banks in 2020 and examine the factors that affect that performance. The performance of all 13 listed Jordanian banks is examined between 2010 and 2020 in terms of return on assets and net interest margin, considering factors like equity capital, bank expenses, size, income diversification, loan loss provisions, lending to the government, and economic growth.

According to the 2020 financial statements, Jordanian banks' profitability (return on assets) fell by nearly 48 percent from 1.43 percent in 2019 to 0.74 percent in 2020 (Obeidat et al., 2021).

Besides, Ghosh and Saima's study aimed to forecast and examine the financial sustainability and resilience of Bangladeshi commercial banks in the face of the COVID-19 pandemic's detrimental consequences. For their study, a sample of 18 publicly traded commercial banks on the Dhaka Stock Exchange has been used. Banks are divided into three groups (each consisting of six banks), namely top resilient, moderate resilient, and low resilient, based on their performance scores under the TOPSIS and HELLWIG procedures. To control the COVID-19 pandemic, it is discovered that EBL and DBBL banks are the most robust banks in Bangladesh, while one bank is the least resilient (Ghosh & Saima, 2021). According to Siska and his colleagues' research, there was a considerable difference between Commercial Conventional Banks' profitability, efficiency, liquidity, and credit risk before and after Covid 19 (Siska et al., 2021).

3 Methodology

3.1 Population

The chapter was built on a sample size of (9) commercial banks that existed in the Omani local market. These banks were targeted for data collection to analyze the Positive Impact of the Covid-19 pandemic on Omani Bank's Practices.

3.2 Comparative Analysis

The methodology of data collection was based on a comparative analysis tool for (9) commercial banks in the Omani market that took certain actions and provided flexy measures during the coronavirus epidemic. A comparative analysis methodology details how data or practices compare to one another and clarifies how they relate. Performing market research not only gives proof to support your conclusions, but it also might present a new perception or angle that is not considered previously (Indeed, 2021).

3.3 Data Analysis

To meet the chapter's objectives, the authors researched the market, magazines, newspapers, banks' websites, and their social platforms to gather information on banks' services provision. Comparative analysis is a well-suited tool for this chapter that can be used for comparing banks' services to one another. This method allows us to better understand the changes made in the banking sector during the epidemic. In the initial step, local banks' websites were searched. The data collected on the sample of (9) local banks were then divided into four main categories: Awareness and support, operational services, technical advancements, and Business Continuity Plan during the outbreak.

4 Findings and Discussion

In this section, the chapter findings or the results obtained from the qualitative approach provide insights into the main operational support and E-services provided by a random number of 9 banks because of the Covid-19 lockdown. The comparison summary of the data collected is highlighted as follows in Table 1.

Table 1 confirms the positive impact of Covid-19 on commercial banks' practices and services. Since the start of the COVID-19 outbreak, banks have found it is critical to creating a Business Continuity Plan (BCP) if they do not have one or revise the current BCP to better serve their employees and customers taking into consideration a healthy working environment. Although not all the banks posted or published their Business Continuity Plans during the time of the covid-19 pandemic, however; every bank spares no effort in developing BCP that fits the coronavirus situation. Additionally, banks are considered one of the important bodies that affect a country's financial system. Hence, keeping smooth daily operations is a must to develop the country's economy and better serve the nation. Moreover, the coronavirus epidemic has accelerated the usage of fintech, E-services, and other technological advancements. Generally, the banks outperformed on both sides, community support, and services provisions during the epidemic.

Table 1 A comparison summary of data collected for nine commercial banks in Oman

Bank Name	*Awareness and Support*	*Operational Service*	*Technical or E-service*	*Business Continuity*
Bank Muscat	Enhanced trust and business relationship with customers through text messages, Bank Muscat mobile banking, and emails to assure safe and healthy workplace for their employees, customers, and stakeholders. They also applied social distance and transparent barrier at different bank Muscat branches	Offered a support to customers affected by COVID-19 epidemic. In fact, the suffered clients may have the choice to defer their loans payments excluding credit card dues for agreed specific time. This facility has started with the coronavirus outburst and suspended on 31st December 2021 (Bank Muscat, n.d.)	• Opened a new page named "Covid-19 help page-Bank Muscat", and easily accessible by the customers through internet banking and bank Muscat mobile banking (Bank Muscat, n.d.) • Maximized E-services provision through the internet banking, and mobile banking	Business Continuity Plan was developed to ensure that bank's services are available to all its customers and stakeholders locally and internationally (The Arabian Stories, 2020)

Bank Name	*Awareness and Support*	*Operational Service*	*Technical or E-service*	*Business Continuity*
National Bank of Oman	• In October 2020, NBO Pledged OMR 1 Million in the fight against the COVID-19 outbreak in Oman (NBO, 2020b) • Raised awareness during the epidemic through cares campaign, including forming key teams to ensure business continuity and extend help to customers with advice, SMS, emails, and social media (NBO, 2020c)	Applied working from home for a number of it staff whereas its services' provisions and daily operations remained largely unaffected (NBO, 2020a)	• In March 2020, NBO was fronting the safe banking as they were ready to assist clients digitally (NBO, 2020d) • Different NBOs Apps were developed to reduce physical attended to banks' branches such as NBO's MarketZone app which is used to serve investors' requirements across the sultanate (NBO, 2020d) • They promote using badeel prepaid cards and made it available for both NBO and Non-NBO customers to go cashless and contactless (NBO, 2020a)	• Developed and tested business Continuity Plans that's aligned to its operating model and regulatory framework • To ensure business services provisions in the event of an emergency or crisis (NBO, 2020c)

(continued)

Table 1 (continued)

Bank Name	*Awareness and Support*	*Operational Service*	*Technical or E-service*	*Business Continuity*
HSBC	• Stay Connected with HSBC around the world • Used Client focused approach more efficiently. They spread awareness through different articles on partnership excellence in fighting COVID-19 published on HSBC's official website (HSBC, 2022a)	During the same period, HSBC Oman and Sohar International have agreed to an (MoU) regarding a potential merger of the two banks (HSBC, 2022b)	• Improved the digital enhancements, helping the customers to have contactless services • Encouraged innovation and transformation • Enlarged the usage of relative applications such as "HSBC net" with 24/7 support to accelerate all local and international payment operations (HSBC, 2022a)	No data

Bank Name	*Awareness and Support*	*Operational Service*	*Technical or E-service*	*Business Continuity*
Bank Dhofar	They spread awareness through their websites and encouraged the clients to stay home for their safety and the community and conduct their operations online (Bank Dhofar, 2022a)	Daily Operations remained unaffected although they offered their staff the option to work remotely from home. Bank Dhofar continued providing its services to customers around the clock through e-banking channels (Times of Oman, 2020)	• Provided 24/7 electronic channels for customers to go cashless • Enhanced the mobile banking App to better serve their customers (Bank Dhofar, 2022b) • Opened a donation window to customers in the bank Dhofar mobile banking App to donate to the Ministry of Health COVID- 19 Account (Bank Dhofar, 2022b) • Advised the customers to conduct their transactions through mobile banking, internet banking, phone banking and call center (Times of Oman, 2020)	Not Available

(continued)

Table 1 (continued)

Bank Name	*Awareness and Support*	*Operational Service*	*Technical or E-service*	*Business Continuity*
Sohar International	Completed the vaccination for employees and their families, then provided social support to the community in which they extended the vaccination to Omani welfare associations, such as: a. Disabled in Sohar b. Oman Cancer Association c. Media and strategic partners (Sohar International Bank, 2021c)	• Continued daily operations while managing the well-being of its employees and overall work environment • Sohar International received the "Managing Health at Work" award and the "Best Employer Brand Award" for care provided to the people (Sohar International Bank, 2021a) • They analyzed the covid-19 changes made worldwide after the lockdown and build the way forward Sohar international must consider being stronger in the market • Strengthened their growth strategy by enhancing their partnership locally and internationally (Sohar International Bank, 2021c)	• Sohar International focused on technological developments to innovate its practices and increase customer satisfaction which falls Consistently with Oman Vision 2040 objectives, which promote digitalization in the sultanate (Sohar International Bank, 2021b) • Part of leading the innovation in the banking sector, Sohar International is planning to be the "Digital Transformation Partner" at New Age Banking Summit in Oman (Sohar International Bank, 2021b)	A healthy working environment and a vaccinated workforce were the main drivers of Sohar international's Business Continuity Plans

Bank Name	*Awareness and Support*	*Operational Service*	*Technical or E-service*	*Business Continuity*
Ahli Bank	• Cared about safety and was following the latest instructions provided by the Ministry of Health, to ensure the safest possible environment for employees, stakeholders, and clients (Ahli Bank, 2022) • Ahli Bank Donated around OMR 1 Million to the fight COVID-19 outbreak and raised awareness during the epidemic (Ahli Bank, 2022)	• During the epidemic, Ahli Bank's Crisis Management Team (CMT) has been involved to study the covid 19 effects and operational preparedness to ensure the continuation of active bank practices to maximize the bank's response to customer needs (Ahli Bank, 2022) • Provided Covid19 national guarantee program that aims to provide financial and economic support for the private sector, amounting to Qatari Rial 75 bln (Ahli Bank, 2022)	• Maximized the benefit of mobile banking and internet banking to protect the well-being of staff and customers • Enlarged corporate branch services through E-channels such as Ahli-net, Ahli B2B (Ahli Bank, 2022)	Developed and tested a business Continuity management manifesto that's aligned with its operating model and regulatory requirements to ensure service continuity in case of unplanned crisis (Ahli Bank, 2022)

(continued)

Table 1 (continued)

Bank Name	*Awareness and Support*	*Operational Service*	*Technical or E-service*	*Business Continuity*
Bank of Baroda	Bank of Baroda announces special COVID-19 package for Active Business correspondents, such as: a. community support of Rs. 10 lakh in case of unfortunate death resulting from COVID-19 b. support of Rs. 60,000 in case of hospitalization c. the amount of Rs. 1000 for hygiene maintenance (Bank of Baroda, 2022a)	Continued to operate and the branches remained open taking into consideration staff safety (Bank of Baroda, 2022b)	Bank's services can be accessed through digital channels (Bank of Baroda, 2022b)	Not Available

Bank Name	*Awareness and Support*	*Operational Service*	*Technical or E-service*	*Business Continuity*
First Abu Dhabi Bank	• Concerned to provide a healthy working environment as they focused on the wellbeing of staff and customers • Followed the latest advice provided by the Ministry of Health regarding Covid-19 precautious measures (First Abu Dhabi Bank, 2022)	• They are in the process of revising the FAB operations taking into consideration people's safety (First Abu Dhabi Bank, 2022) • Implemented support measures for its stakeholders in response to the epidemic. They provided different financial or repayment reliefs among different bank products. Additionally, it provided payment deferral facilities to its customers (First Abu Dhabi Bank, 2020)	Continued to provide the services through its digital channels	Closely monitoring the changes in the market to best serve their customers and provide support as deemed necessary (First Abu Dhabi Bank, 2022). Hence, the continuation of the current business plan or adjustments made to it
Qatar National Bank	Spread awareness on World Mastercard and World Elite travel insurance policies and coverage during the epidemic (Qatar National Bank, 2022)	• Offered Covid-19 National Response Support program for a limited beneficiary (Qatar National Bank, 2022) • Continued to run the daily operations while taking into consideration employee and customer safety	Maximized the usage of mobile banking, internet banking, E-Business, trade portal, and other digital channels (Qatar National Bank, 2022)	Not Available

Source Authors' calculations

5 Conclusion

Banks and other financial firms have already seen major consequences from COVID-19 and are likely to continue to do so (Berger et al., 2021). The Covid-19 crisis has already demonstrated how several policy instruments could be implemented concurrently by various institutions to stabilize the financial system and the economy (Restoy, 2020). Additional aid initiatives are required to ease the financial strain brought on by the COVID-19 explosion, and preparing for the global economic slump has become a challenge for most nations (Korzeb & Niedziółka, 2020). To aid in their recovery from the effects of COVID-19, banks must keep their attention on their customers' requirements.

Going forward, it is of utmost importance that the commercial banks should tackle the expected increase of technological advancements in banking services especially after covid-19, and their continued support to ease the daily operations to best serve their customers.

References

Abbas, A., & Frihatni, A. A. (2020). The social role of Islamic banks in Indonesia during the pandemic of COVID-19. *European Journal of Islamic Finance,* (16).

Ahli Bank. (2022). COVID-19 National Response Guarantee Programme. Retrieved from: https://www.ahlibank.com.qa/covid-19-national-response-guarantee-programme. Retrieved on 1 September 2022.

Al Shekaili, M. A. S., & Karim, A. M. (2020). Impacts of pandemic Coronavirus COVID-19 on banking sector mid-year financial result in sultanate of Oman. *Solid State Technology, 63*(6), 2311–2325.

Bank Dhofar. (2022a). Bank Dhofar participates at MSX roadshow as a strategic sponsor. https://www.bankdhofar.com/en-gb/News.aspx. Retrieved on 1 September 2022.

Bank Dhofar. (2022b). COVID 19 preventive measures. https://www.bankdhofar.com/en-gb/COVID_19_Preventive_Measures.aspx. Retrieved on 1 September 2022.

Bank Muscat. (n.d.) COVID-19 help page. https://www.bankmuscat.com/en/awareness/Pages/update.aspx. Retrieved on 1 September 2022.

Bank of Baroda. (2022a). Bob World Internet (Internet Banking). https://www.bankofbaroda.in/personal-banking/digital-products/instant-banking/internet-banking-baroda-connect. Retrieved on 1 September 2022.

Bank of Baroda. (2022b). COVID 19 Products. https://www.bankofbaroda.in/covid-19-products. Retrieved on 1 September 2022.

Banks, L. M., Davey, C., Shakespeare, T., & Kuper, H. (2021). Disability-inclusive responses to COVID-19: Lessons learnt from research on social protection in low-and middle-income countries. *World Development, 137*, 105178.

Barua, B., & Barua, S. (2021). COVID-19 implications for banks: Evidence from an emerging economy. *SN Business & Economics, 1*(1), 1–28.

Bensley, E., Chheda,S., Schiff, R., Stephens, D., & Zhou, N. (2020). Remaking banking customer experience in response to coronavirus. https://www.mckinsey.com/industries/financial-services/our-insights/remaking-banking-customer-experience-in-response-to-coronaviru. Retrieved on 1 September 2022.

Berger, A. N., Demirgüç-Kunt, A., Moshirian, F., & Saunders, A. (2021). The way forward for banks during the COVID-19 crisis and beyond: Government and central bank responses, threats to the global banking industry. *Journal of Banking & Finance, 133*, 106303.

Central Bank of Oman. (2020). Annual Report 2020. https://cbo.gov.om/sites/assets/Documents/English/Publications/AnnualReports/AnnualReport2020.pdf

Couppey-Soubeyran, J., Perego, E., & Tripier, F. (2020). European banks and the Covid-19 crash test (No. 30). EconPol Policy Brief.

Dunz, N., Essenfelder, A. H., Mazzocchetti, A., Monasterolo, I., & Raberto, M. (2021). Compounding COVID-19 and climate risks: The interplay of banks' lending and government's policy in the shock recovery. *Journal of Banking & Finance*, 106306.

Dursun-de Neef, H. Ö., & Schandlbauer, A. (2021). COVID-19 and lending responses of European banks. *Journal of Banking & Finance, 133*, 106236.

First Abu Dhabi Bank. (2020). FAB implements support measures for its stakeholders in response to COVID-19. https://www.bankfab.com/en-ae/about-fab/group/in-the-media/fab-implements-support-measures-for-its-stakeholders-in-response-to-covid-19. Retrieved on 1 September 2022.

First Abu Dhabi Bank. (2022). Coronavirus Help & Support. https://www.bankfab.com/en-ae/personal/help-and-support/coronavirus/overview. Retrieved on 1 September 2022.

Ghosh, R., & Saima, F. N. (2021). Resilience of commercial banks of Bangladesh to the shocks caused by COVID-19 pandemic: An application of MCDM-based approaches. *Asian Journal of Accounting Research, 6*(3), 281–295.

Hasan, Z. (2020). The impact of Covid-19 on Islamic banking in Indonesia during the pandemic era. *Journal of Entrepreneurship and Business, 8*(2), 19–32.

HSBC. (2022a). Diversification and a strong partnership with HSBC, mitigated the impact of COVID-19 on Khimji Ramdas. Retrieved from: https://www.business.hsbc.co.om/en-gb/insights/innovation-and-transformation/together-with-khimji-ramdas. Retrieved on 1 September 2022.

HSBC. (2022b). HSBC Bank Oman SOAG (HSBC Oman) and Sohar International Bank SAOG (Sohar International) non-binding agreement on potential merger. https://www.business.hsbc.co.om/en-gb/insights/innovation-and-transformation/together-with-khimji-ramdas. Retrieved on 1 September 2022.

Indeed. (2021). What is comparative analysis and how is it used? https://www.indeed.com/career-advice/career-development/comparative-analysis. Retrieved on 1 September 2022.

Jeris, S. S., & Nath, R. D. (2021). US banks in the time of COVID-19: Fresh insights from the wavelet approach. *Eurasian Economic Review, 11*(2), 349–361.

Korzeb, Z., & Niedziółka, P. (2020). Resistance of commercial banks to the crisis caused by the COVID-19 pandemic: the case of Poland. Equilibrium. *Quarterly Journal of Economics and Economic Policy, 15*(2), 205–234.

Macfarlane, K., Petluri, R. Oman banking perspectives 2021. (2021). Innovating, balancing and governing. https://assets.kpmg/content/dam/kpmg/om/pdf-2021/10/oman-banking-perspectives.pdf

NBO. (2020a). Choose your NBO prepaid card. https://www.nbo.om/en/Pages/Personal-Banking/Products/Cards/Prepaid-Cards.aspx?csrt=5641575713724564739. Retrieved on 1 September 2022.

NBO. (2020b). National bank of Oman pledges OMR 1 million in the fight against covid-19 outbreak in Oman. https://www.nbo.om/en/Pages/News/NATIONAL-BANK-OF-OMAN-PLEDGES-OMR-1-MILLION-IN-THE-FIGHT-AGAINST-COVID-19-OUTBREAK-IN-OMAN.aspx?csrt=9069009560177791378. Retrieved on 1 September 2022.

NBO. (2020c). Precautionary measures we're taking against novel coronavirus COVID-19. https://www.nbo.om/en/Pages/COVID-19-Updates.aspx. Retrieved on 1 September 2022.

NBO. (2020d). Spearheading safe banking, national bank of Oman is fully ready to serve customers digitally. https://www.nbo.om/en/Pages/News/SPEARHEADING-SAFE-BANKING,-NATIONAL-BANK-OF-OMAN-IS-FULLY-READY-TO-SERVE-CUSTOMERS-DIGITALLY.aspx?csrt=9069009560177791378. Retrieved on 1 September 2022.

Obeidat, M., Tarawneh, A., Khataibeh, M., & Ghassan, O. M. E. T. (2021). The performance of banks in a developing country: Has Covid-19 made any difference? *Journal of Economics Finance and Accounting, 8*(2), 102–108.

Qatar National Bank. (2022). Travel Insurance Policies during COVID-19. https://www.qnb.com/sites/qnb/qnbqatar/page/en/entravelcovid19.html. Retrieved on 1 September 2022.

Ramasamy, D. (2020). The trend of COVID-19 at Bengaluru: Prediction to continue the better epidemic management. *International Journal of Current Research and Review, 12*(13), 56–60.

Restoy, F. (2020). Central banks and financial stability: A reflection after the Covid-19 outbreak. Financial Stability Institute, Bank for International Settlements.

Rizwan, M. S., Ahmad, G., & Ashraf, D. (2022). Systemic risk, Islamic banks, and the COVID-19 pandemic: An empirical investigation. *Emerging Markets Review*, 100890.

Siska, E., Gamal, A. A. M., Ameen, A., & Amalia, M. M. (2021). Analysis Impact of Covid-19 Outbreak on Performance of Commercial Conventional Banks: Evidence from Indonesia. *International Journal of Social and Management Studies, 2*(6), 8–16.

Sohar International Bank. (2021a). Sohar international bank SAOG financial statements for the year ended 31 December 2021. https://soharinternational.com/media/3408/sohar-international-fs_2021_pending-cbo-approval.pdf. Retrieved on 1 September 2022.

Sohar International Bank. (2021b). Sohar International to be the "Digital Transformation Partner" at New Age Banking Summit Oman. https://www.soharinternational.com/newsroom/2021/september/sohar-international-to-be-the-digital-transformation-partner-at-new-age-banking-summit-oman/. Retrieved on 1 September 2022.

Sohar International Bank. (2021c). Sohar International's COVID-19 vaccination drive extended to welfare associations and strategic partners. https://soharinternational.com/newsroom/2021/august/sohar-international-s-covid-19-vaccination-drive-extended-to-welfare-associations-and-strategic-partners/. Retrieved on 1 September 2022.

The Arabian Stories. (2020). Bank Muscat rolls out measures for safety and wellbeing of customers and staff while ensuring business continuity. https://www.thearabianstories.com/2020/03/24/bank-muscat-rolls-out-measures-for-safety-and-wellbeing-of-customers-and-staff-while-ensuring-business-continuity/. Retrieved on 1 September 2022.

Times of Oman. (2020). Bank Dhofar's digital banking ensures safe banking experience during COVID-19. https://www.bankdhofar.com/en-gb/COVID_19_Preventive_Measures.aspx. Retrieved on 1 September 2022.

CHAPTER 10

The Impact of Applying the GFSM 2014 on Public Sector Assessment during the COVID-19 Pandemic: Applied in Australia and Oman

Mustafa Hamid Salim Abid

1 Introduction

Many specialized international organizations have provided a set of statistical systems that provide homogeneous information for the country's economy. The Government Finance Statistics Manual is the integrated perspective of these systems. The International Monetary Fund issued the Government Finance Statistics (GFS) Manual for the year 1986, but the great development witnessed by the government's financial performance and the complications in evaluating its performance, the Government Finance Statistics emerged in 2001, and developed in 2014. The guide is considered a major development in the standards for preparing and

M. H. S. Abid (✉)
Alzaiem Alazhari University, Khartoum North, Sudan
e-mail: mhalhkeem@hotmail.com

A. Mishrif (ed.), *Economic Effects of the Pandemic*, The Political Economy of the Middle East,
https://doi.org/10.1007/978-981-97-4367-4_10

presenting public financial information. It was linked between specific accounting rules and an analytical framework for financial statistics. This link achieved many advantages, the most important of which are developing an economic, functional, and geographical classification of statistics, which enables the measurement of performance efficiency in public sector institutions. It also improves the quality of planning for the state's macroeconomic policies, enabling the management of state affairs in a period of crisis. The COVID-19 pandemic is considered one of the largest crises that the world has experienced, as all studies proved its significant impact on the public sector in countries of the world.

1.1 Problem of the Chapter

The assessment of the impact of the COVID-19 pandemic on the public sector depends on financial statistics produced by specialized organizations and institutions in countries. These statistics are used in an analytical framework that includes a set of financial and economic indicators that enable the economy to be measured from different aspects.

1.2 Questions of the Chapter

The main question of the chapter is whether it is possible to assess the impact of the COVID-19 pandemic on the public sector using the analytical framework of the GFSM 2014? From which the following sub-questions were derived:

Q1: Is the impact of the COVID-19 pandemic on the public sector assessed using public financial indicators?

Q2: Is the impact of the COVID-19 pandemic on the public sector can be assessed using wealth and debt indicators?

1.3 Importance of the Chapter

The successive crisis in the world and their increasing severity made it necessary to accurately assess the use of the economic resources of countries. The COVID-19 pandemic is the best example of this. During these crises, countries need a system of accounts that achieves financial transparency, so that the performance of public sector institutions can be evaluated. GFSM 2014 provides an analytical framework that enables this. The chapter aimed to achieve the following objectives:

- Using GFSM 2014 in evaluating the efficiency of public sector performance during the COVID-19 pandemic,
- Measuring the impact of COVID-19 on the countries implementing GFSM 2014.
- A case study of global best practices.

1.4 *Hypotheses of the Chapter*

The main hypothesis of the chapter is that the impact of the COVID-19 pandemic on the public sector can be assessed using the analytical framework of the Government Financial Statistics Guide 2014, from which the following sub-hypotheses were derived:

H1: The impact of the COVID-19 pandemic on the public sector can be assessed using public financial indicators.

H2: The impact of the COVID-19 pandemic on the public sector can be assessed using Wealth and debt indicators.

1.5 *Limitation of the Chapter*

The countries to be applied were identified based on their commitment to a high degree of disclosure of financial statistics, and the varying level of maturity in implementing the GFSM 2014. Therefore, the countries of Australia and the Sultanate of Oman were chosen.

The period to evaluate the public sector performance of the Australian government from 2017–2018 to 2020–2021, as well as the public sector performance of the Government of the Sultanate of Oman from 2018 to 2021.

The performance of the public sector was analyzed using six indicators, which were divided into two groups: public finance indicators include; Gross operating balance (GOB), below-the-line transactions, and transfer payments excluding grants, and wealth and debt indicators include; Total debt, net financial value, and change in net worth.

The determinant of the chapter is the level of commitment to applying the GFSM 2014 in the final accounts of the government of the Sultanate of Oman, as financial statistics for revenues and expenditures were available, and they are not classified according to the GFSM 2014, which made the chapter use one indicator, which is the Gross Operating Balance (GOB), to evaluate the performance of the public sector of the Sultanate of Oman.

1.6 Previous studies

Many writers dealt with government finance statistics and their impacts and for this study, the chapter will show some of these studies:

The study of (Wines et al., 2015) aimed to analyze the nature and comparability of budget balance (surplus/deficit) numbers headlined by the Australian Commonwealth Government and the governments of the six Australian States and the two Australian Territories. This is towards implementing the Australian Accounting Standard AASB 1049 for financial reporting for the government and the general government sector at the national, state, and local levels. A case study method is adopted based on an analysis of the values of the general budget balance in the general government sector budget data for each of the nine Australian governments for eight fiscal years from 2004–2005 to 2011–2012.

The findings reveal that none of the nine Australian governments have placed the full balance of the budget on an accrual basis since the implementation of IAS 1049 in 2008. The study focuses on the accounting environment for the Australian general government sector and its significant implications for demystifying the presentation and monitoring of budget values, and information asymmetry problems that can arise. The study highlights how governments have been selective in the manner in which they present important budget aggregates. This has important practical and social implications, as the budget balance number is one of the most important measures used to evaluate a government's fiscal management and responsibility.

The consider of (Pilcher & Gilchrist, 2019), clarified that, in the last two decades of the twentieth century and into the twenty-first century the Australian public sector has experienced crucial change of operations and the processes of regulating its operations. These changes exuding from new public administration which had moreover been embraced in other Western popular governments move the center of public sector organization from the control of inputs to the interest of outputs and results. By the early 1990s, a move to performance administration in the Australian public sector by a deep discussion almost financial terms, a Commitment to great commercial hones from the private sector, and a center on embracing market arrangements if possible.

The presentation of private-sector accrual accounting measures and a general-purpose financial reporting system that has the fundamental objective of releasing responsibility in the public sector. An assist thought was that the appropriation of accrual basis was not able to be a substitution for cash basis since Australia's structure requires the yearly allotment of expenditure. There is a third detailing instrument, Government Finance Statistics (GFS), which gives measurements to help in getting (among other things) a worldwide comparison of the financial execution of the government. Whereas there is a few commonalities among these three frameworks, what has brought about is a divided responsibility scene.

The study (Baum et al., 2020), ensuring that state-owned enterprises (SOEs) are efficient and managed prudently is important for economic and social reasons. The paper presented an analysis of managing fiscal risks in SOEs, by identifying the main driver items that impact the fiscal risks of budget, introducing risk tools to enhance the monitoring of SOEs, and discussing the challenges in developing strategies to mitigate fiscal risks to ensure the SOEs are managed efficiently and prudently. Finally, the paper explained the benefits of fully integrating SOEs into the overall fiscal framework. The main recommendation to Governments is to develop a stronger capacity to monitor and mitigate the risks from SOEs.

The study (Seiferling, 2020), discusses why problems with data quality continue to exist. Case study of public sector debt statistics in the United Kingdom, the purpose of this study is to examine the quality of public sector financial statistics, through debt and debt-to-GDP ratios in budget expansion in size amid the COVID-19 pandemic. The findings of the study suggest the government still does not seem to feel sufficient pressure to provide quality financial statistics based on well-defined methodology, and financial statistics reports have become numerous and complex, thus making it difficult to explain their analysis.

The study of (Silvia et al., 2021), centered on the association between management and accounting with accrual data as an interface. Accounting information, organized on an accrual basis, oversees to give reasonable accounting information for the performance, to make substantiated and transparent choices, as a reference basis for proficient management. The communication between accounting and assess reporting in the public accounting system makes harmony in displaying financial/non-financial information, a key component in public administration. The study comes about uncovering a far reaching and solid intrigued in sound reporting that can make strides transparency all through a performing administration system. The IPSAS project and change to accrual bases pointed to alter mistakes between accounting and assess reporting, and improve great governance, to encourage transparency and comparability.

The ponder of (Zubíková & Smolák, 2022) given a rundown of chosen macroeconomic impacts of the COVID-19 pandemic in the Czech Republic, included an evaluation of certain actualized financial and monetary policies, and utilized information from 2019 to compare the improvement of the financial performance amid the COVID-19 pandemic with the period some time recently the onset of the pandemic, 2020 and 2021 on a month to month or quarterly basis, specific consideration is paid to monetary policy impacts. The study too examined the volume of financial measures taken to moderate COVID-19 pandemic impacts, the prohibitive measures presented to Czech family units and firms as well as labor market improvements from 2019 to 2021, counting evaluation of the total labor efficiency record. The article concludes that, amid the COVID-19 pandemic, macroeconomic measurements in the Czech Republic acted by the set up fractional theories of the Mundell-Fleming demonstrate and by the theory of the altered Phillips bend. Conceivable causes of the critical increment in expansion since September 2021 incorporate 2020 ostensible public and private sector salary development, which appeared speedier development than total labor efficiency, and the exceedingly expansionary fiscal policy that characterized the 2021 pre-election period.

The study of (Syahputra et al., 2022) aimed to identify and analyze the impact of external pressure and environmental uncertainty on the quality of financial reporting. The study results prove that the pressure resulting from the COVID-19 pandemic has an increasing effect on the quality of financial reporting. The effect of the COVID-19 pandemic on countries such as America, Spain, and Italy make the world's economic situation worse. The study indicated external pressure on the quality of public sector financial reporting in the future and the effect of environmental uncertainty of the COVID-19 pandemic on public sector performance.

The chapter note that, The study of (Wines et al., 2015) concentrated on Australian government budget balance numbers the hybrid nature of public sector accrual accounting, The study of (Pilcher & Gilchrist, 2019) dealt with Public Sector Accounting, Accountability and Governance, and the study of (Baum et al., 2020) investigated managing fiscal risks from state-owned enterprises, while the study of (Seiferling, 2020) dealt with apples, oranges and lemons: public sector debt statistics in the twenty-first century, and the study of (Silvia et al., 2021) investigated the link between public management and accounting from the point of view of performance, whereas, the study of (Zubíková & Smolák, 2022) investigated macroeconomic impacts of the Covid-19 pandemic in the Czech republic, and the study of (Syahputra et al., 2022) dealt with explanatory study related to the impact of the COVID-19 pandemic in the implementation of public sector accountability for financial reporting quality from SKPD in North Sumatera Province. The current chapter differs from other studies by investigating the impact of applying the government finance statistics manual on evaluating the public sector during the COVID-19 pandemic. Also, there are differences in spatial limits and time limits.

2 Literature Review

The International Monetary Fund (IMF) issued the Government Finance Statistics (GFS) manual in 1986, which included a new classification of the state's general budget and the amendment of some accounting bases. Then the IMF issued a Financial Statistics manual in 2001 as a result of the great development witnessed by the government's financial performance and the increase in the complexity of financial activities in the country and the evaluation of its performance. It is considered a major development in the field of standards for preparing and presenting public financial information. The accrual basis for recording financial transactions was adopted and the GFSM 2001 was established to bring accountability and transparency into government finances and operations (IMF, About Government Finance Statistics, 2014).

The third edition of the Government Finance Statistics Manual came in 2014 (GFSM, 2014), as a result of the update in System of National Accounts (SNA) 2008, which provides a comprehensive, consistent, and flexible set of macroeconomic accounts for policy development and analysis. It was prepared and issued under the auspices of the United Nations, the European Commission, the Organization for Cooperation and Development, the International Monetary Fund, and the World Bank Group. As well as updated in Balance of Payments and International Investment

Position Manual (BPM6) 2008, it provides balance of payments statistics that must be produced in a systematic and orderly manner, so that it is comprehensive, timely, and highly reliable.

The analytical framework GFSM 2014 represents a quantitative tool that supports the analysis of public finances and facilitates the identification, measurement, monitoring, and evaluation of the impact of the government's economic policies and other activities on the economy.

The chapter concluded that the most important features of GFSM 2014 can be explained in the following:

- Harmonious with other economic statistical systems (SNA, BPM6).
- Provides an adequate framework for the economic analysis of the government's fiscal policy.
- Assists in setting and developing appropriate financial policies for the general government.
- Covers and consolidates all balances and flows.
- It helps in evaluating the performance of the public sector, with the possibility of making local and international comparisons.
- Consolidate financial data at all levels of government, in a way that consolidates data at the international level.
- Ensures the possibility of moving to the accrual accounting system while maintaining the accounting on a cash basis.

2.1 Accounting rules for government finance statistics

The accounting rules related to measuring flows and balances in the GFSM confirm the information disclosure by this system with the accepted standards to generate accounting and economic statistics, The GFSM Government Statistics Manual included seven rules: (IMF, GFSM, 2014, p. 47).

Accounting System Type: The accounting system relies on the theory of double entry in recording operations, and the system made for the state and government institutions a balance sheet "in which the data of assets, liabilities, and the net value of the governmental unit or the sector as a whole are collected" (IMF, GFSM, 2014, p. 47).

Time of Recording Flows: The recording of flows and balances depends on the accrual basis because it shows the entire movement of the process from the moment of its establishment until its completion with all the stages in which it took place (time of revenue generation, use of resources, incurring liabilities, acquiring assets). As for the cash basis, cash flows are restricted when the ownership of cash is transferred from one unit to another. It does not show the obligations that the government unit has to pay or collect (arrears) (IMF, GFSM, 2014, p. 48).

Valuation: Flows and balances are evaluated at current market prices on their recording dates and the date of preparing the balance sheet. Instead of the historical cost, which depends on evaluating the flows and balances based on the date of their recording only, without paying attention to the changes that occurred in successive years. To clarify the changes in the value of flows and balances, a Statement of Other Economic Flows has been added to clarify changes in balance positions due to evaluation at current prices (IMF, GFSM, 2014, p. 55).

Currency—Unit of account: It is the disclosure of all data in one currency only, including all flows and balances expressed in another currency, and this is a prerequisite for building consistent and analytically useful statistics. If the financial assets and liabilities are in the foreign currency, then compiling the GFS in a single currency is required to produce meaningful statistics (IMF, GFSM, 2014, p. 59).

Derived Measures: The derived measures consist of summaries and items of sub-accounts, which are important analytical tools that summarize the values of selected flows and balances, each of which has been individually entered into the government financial statistics system. For example, transactions in assets and liabilities are divided into three sections: transactions in non-financial assets, transactions in financial assets, and transactions in liabilities. These three sections can be considered as total transactions in assets and liabilities or as items of transactions in non-financial assets, transactions in financial assets, and transactions in liabilities (IMF, GFSM, 2014, p. 60).

Netting of Flows and Stock Positions: It is a horizontal analysis of the analytical framework in which the balances at the beginning of the period are linked to the flows that occurred during the period to give the balances at the end of the period. It includes four sections Net worth, non-financial assets, financial assets, and Liabilities (IMF, GFSM, 2014, p. 61).

Consolidation: It is a method of displaying the statistics of a group of units as a single unit. This rule added According to the functional division, the data displayed for a group of units shall be unified, and elimination of the centers of flows and balances between groups of consolidated units, is to avoid double counting (IMF, GFSM, 2014, p. 62).

2.2 *The Government Finance Statistics Analytic Framework*

It is a general framework that includes many categories of flows and balances on a gross or net basis. Figure 1 shows the analytical framework consisting of three financial statements, an opening and closing balance sheet, a statement of operations, and a statement of other economic flows.

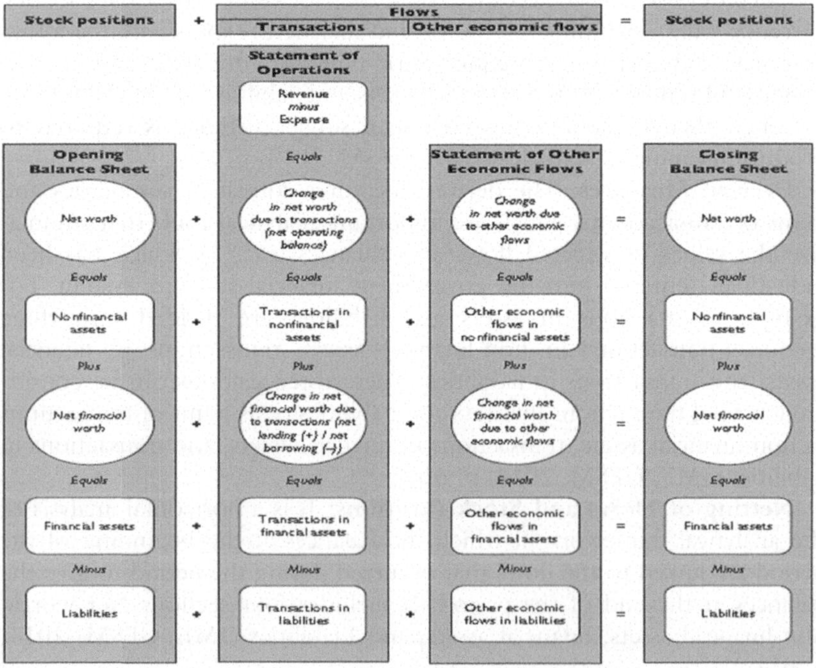

Fig. 1 GFS analytic framework (*Source* International Monetary Fund, Government finance statistics manual 2014, Washington, D.C., 2014, p. 68)

From the above figure, the chapter concluded that the financial statements are classified in the analytical framework: (IMF, GFSM, 2014, p. 65).

- Stock positions: include three types; Assets (non-financial and financial), Liabilities, and Net worth, and they are disclosed in the balance sheet.
- Flows: All changes that occurred in the value of stocks, and flows are calculated on a net and gross basis and disclosed in the statement of operations and other economic flows. Flows are divided into two parts: transactions and other economic flows.
- The GFS analytical framework integrates flows and balances based on the equation

$$S0 + F = S1$$

Noting that:

($S0$) Represents the value of a certain balance at the beginning of the period.

($S1$) Represents the value of a certain balance at the end of the period.

(F) Represents the net worth of the inflows during the period that affected the balance.

2.3 *Fiscal Analysis*

The GFSM 2014 framework is creating fiscal indicators. these indicators produced for the general government and public sectors. Fiscal indicators for the subsectors of the general government and the public sector can also be produced to take account of the decentralized nature of fiscal responsibilities in an economy. Using data from the GFS framework enhances the comparability of data across countries, which is important in establishing robust analytical findings.

2.4 *Fiscal Indicators Available from the GFS Framework*

The GFS framework produces fiscal indicators from the transactions, other economic flows, stock positions, aggregates, or balancing items. For example, in the Statement of Operations, net lending or net borrowing is the basic indicator for the fiscal balance, it be measured from above-the-line inductor as revenue minus expenditure includes expenses plus the net investment in non-financial assets. This fiscal balance can also be measured from below-the-line inductor, it includes the difference between transactions in financial assets and liabilities, it also referred to as financing transactions. From an above-the-line perspective, GFS provides detailed information on revenue sources, and the composition of expenditure, while the below-the-line approach provides detailed information on how governments invest in surpluses or finance deficits (IMF, GFSM, 2014, p. 78).

The Balance Sheet presents data on used fiscal stock position indicators regularly, for example the gross and net debt, and the stock position and also composition of various categories of assets and liabilities. Additional aggregates, such as the maturity breakdown of financial instruments, and the stock position of cash are useful for an analysis of liquidity. Balancing items such as net worth and net financial worth allows for an analysis of the wealth of the government. The chapter uses six fiscal indicators, which were divided into two groups that are directly available from GFSM: (IMF, GFSM, 2014, pp. 79–82).

The public financial indicators include;

- **Gross operating balance (GOB)**: Revenue minus expense, excluding consumption of fixed capital.

$$\text{Revenue} - \text{expense} + \text{consumption of fixed capital} \tag{1}$$

- **Below-the-line transactions**: All transactions in the net acquisition of financial assets, and the net incurrence of liabilities—also referred to as financing transactions. (The main balancing items, such as cash surplus/cash deficit, serve as the "line.")

$$\text{The net acquisition of financial assets} - \text{The net incurrence of liabilities} = \text{net lending/ net borrowing} \tag{2}$$

- **Transfer payments excluding grants**: Transfers to corporations, households, and nonprofit institutions serving households, which comprise subsidies, social benefits, transfers not elsewhere classified, and premiums, fees, and claims related to nonlife insurance and standardized guarantee schemes.

$$\begin{aligned}&\text{The subsidies} + \text{The social benefits} + \text{transfers not elsewhere classified}\\&+ \text{The premiums, fees, and claims related to nonlife insurance}\\&+ \text{The standardized guaranteed schemes}\end{aligned} \tag{3}$$

Wealth and debt indicators include;

- **Gross debt**: Stock position in financial claims that require payment(s) of interest and/ or principal by the debtor to the creditor at a date, or dates, in the future. Includes all liabilities held in debt instruments (i.e., total liabilities excluding equity and investment fund shares financial derivatives, and employee stock options).

$$\text{Total liabilities} - \begin{pmatrix}\text{equity and investment fund shares and financial}\\\text{derivatives} + \text{employee stock options}\end{pmatrix} \tag{4}$$

- **Net financial worth**: Net financial worth equals the stock position in financial assets minus the stock position in liabilities.

$$\text{Financial assets} - \text{stock position in liabilities} \tag{5}$$

- **Change in net worth**: Net worth at the end of the current reporting period minus net worth at the end of the previous reporting period. A split between change in net worth due to transactions i.e., net operating balance and change in net worth due to other economic flows is also analytically useful.

$$\begin{aligned}&\text{Net worth at the end of the current reporting period} - \text{net worth at}\\&\text{the end of the previous reporting period}\end{aligned} \tag{6}$$

3 The Australian experience in evaluating the public sector

Australia's statistics are of a high quality, based on the review of its statistical practices, (IMF, Australia: Report on the Observance of Standards and Codes-Data Module, 2010). The Australian Bureau of Statistics (ABS) was established under the Census and Statistics Act in 1905 as The Commonwealth Bureau of Census and Statistics (CBCS). CBCS was abolished in 1974 and the Australian Bureau of Statistics (ABS) was established in its place in 1975, headed by the Australian Statistician and responsible to the Treasurer (Wikipedia, 2018). The Australian Bureau of Statistics (ABS) is the independent and statutory agency of the Australian Government responsible for the collection and analysis of statistics, and giving evidence-based advice to federal, state, and local governments. The ABS collects and analyses statistics on the economy, population, and environment (Wikipedia, 2018). The ABS strategy responds to opportunities and challenges. These strategies will shift how the ABS collects and protects data, engages with its clients, shapes its workforce, modernizes its technologies, and strengthens its leadership (ABS, ABS Corporate Plan 2022–2023). The ABS aims transformation the balance toward a future by:

- Providing easier access to, and integration of, the data it holds.
- Routinely using alternative data sources to enhance official statistics.
- Actively co-designing solutions with clients for mutual benefit.
- Being an employer of choice that values and develops staff.
- Being the provider of choice for data solutions, big data access, and support for data issues.
- Enhancing data capabilities across government through shared technologies and skills.
- Fostering a culture of high performance and innovation.

> The ABS's purpose is to Inform Australia's important decisions by partnering and innovating to deliver relevant, trusted, objective data, statistics, and insights.

The purpose achieved by focus on three priorities: (ABS, ABS Corporate Plan 2022–2023).

1. Provide high-quality official statistics
2. Transforming the ABS for the future
3. Delivering new statistical solutions to maximize the value of public data.

ABS has released two manuals and Accounting Standards to establish the Australian National Statistics to establish the Australian National Statistics:

- Australian System of Government Finance Statistics: Concepts Sources and Methods, Australia 2015 (AGFS15)
- Australian System of National Accounts (ASNA)
- Australian Accounting Standards (AASB 1049)
- Performance indicators in the General Government Sectors financial reports (ED 142 Draft)

3.1 The Australian System of Government Finance Statistics: (AGFS15)

AGFS15 provides a comprehensive manual of the GFS to be applied in the Australian context.

> The main purpose of the manual is to serve as a reference manual for users of statistics who require a detailed understanding and to assist data providers and compilers of GFS. (ABS, AGFS15, 2015)

The Australian manual updated in 2015 to include the changes in Government Finance Statistics Manual 2014, these updates reflect changes to the international and Australian standards for measure and disclosure of national accounts and to minimizes differences between the statistical and accounting requirements (ABS, AGFS15, 2015).

The Australian manual is intended as a general reference document for users and compilers of GFS, the manual provides a detailed account of the concepts underlying GFS, the employed sources of data, and the used methods to compile the statistics. The manual assists users in obtaining a deeper understanding of financial statistics. The manual is intended to serve as a training aid and as a working reference on matters of public sector financial statistics detail (ABS, AGFS15, Part H, 2015).

3.2 Australian System of National Accounts (ASNA)

The framework of the ASNA is based on the SNA 2008 but does not include all conceptual framework. There are some minor variations that have been adopted in the ASNA to allow for specific data for supply conditions or user requirements.

The ASNA accounting items of the Australian economy are recorded as production, income, consumption, the accumulation of assets and liabilities, and wealth. These items are grouped in a set of accounts and recorded into economic flows and stocks, according to specified accounting rules, for various sectors. The classified sectors comprise groups of units with the same economic role (ABS, Australian System of National Accounts, 2020–2021 financial years).

3.3 Australian Accounting Standards (AASB 1049)

The main sources of GFS data are the accounting system and budget management that foundation public sector accounts, and compliance with Australian Accounting Standards AASB 1049 (ABS, AGFS15, Part D, 2015).

AASB 1049 requires that governments prepare a specified set of financial reports for the whole of government comprising the Statement of comprehensive income, Statement of financial position, Statement of changes in equity, and Statement of cash flows.

3.4 Performance indicators in the General Government Sectors financial reports (ED 142 Draft)

The proposals in Exposure Draft ED 142 Financial Reporting of General Government Sectors by Governments (issued July 2005) relate to performance indicators. Most respondents to ED 142 supported the principles but seemed to interpret the proposals as potentially mandating disclosure of performance indicators in the General Government sector financial reports. Many claimed it would be premature to mandate disclosure of performance indicators (CPA Australia's, ED 142 Draft, 2005).

4 Implementation of the GFSM 2014 in the Sultanate of Oman

Statistical systems in the Sultanate of Oman are recent. Government finance statistics are based on cooperation between the Ministry of Finance, which sets legislation and systems for the work of finance, and The National Center for Statistics and Information (NCSI), which publishes financial statistics. Compatibility between them is the basis for their application.

The Ministry of Finance (MOF) was established in 1941 under the name of the Financial Affairs Directorate and was managed by His Majesty the Sultan until 1971. This directorate continued with the same name during the establishment of the State's Administrative Apparatus in 1970, There were many changes in the structure and mandate of the ministry until 1995, the Royal Decree No. 69/95 was issued, modifying the ministerial structure, whereby financial activity was separated from the economic activity, establishing an independent ministry for each activity, and thus the name of previous Ministry was changed to Ministry of Finance (https://www.mof.gov.om/AboutUs).

The National Center for Statistics and Information (NCSI) is one of the most important sources for the development and sustainability of Oman's economy. It was established in accordance with the Royal Decree No. 31/2012 affiliated with the Supreme Council for Planning. NCSI plays the main role in collecting, refining, processing, and analyzing the data generated by the various authorities in the Sultanate.

> The NCSI Mission to produce the official statistics for the Sultanate of Oman, which will be used to support the decision and policymakers to formulate and design the adopted national policies and programs, as the information disclosure is considered as one of our important goals and a core of our mission.

The responsibility for collecting, processing, and disseminating the statistics is specified. The responsibility to collect, process, and disseminate fiscal data of governments is assigned in the Financial Law, Royal Decree No. 47/1998. The law assigns the MOF the responsibility to deal with all matters related to the financial affairs of the government. These responsibilities include recording revenue, expenditure, financing, and debt-related transactions of the budgetary central government (BCG) and autonomous government agencies. The MOF has the authority to control all government accounts and must issue complete instructions to other government units on the processing and recording of all government transactions. Under the law, the final audited accounts of the government (the State's Final Account) must be made available six months after the end of the fiscal year. The Financial Law also explains the (reporting) responsibilities of the line ministries to the MOF, outlines accountability to the MOF, and stipulates the action required and the penalty scheme in case of financial misconduct (p. 66).

In June 2015, the IMF published a report on the observance of standards and codes (ROSC) in Oman, the report and the report made some different comments about the application of GFSM 2014. Classification issues in this report focus on the nature of current expenditure that cannot be delineated—therefore, data for the use of goods and services include capital expenditure and compensation of employees. For that, it must include delineation in the new Chart of Accounts based on GFSM 2014 (IMF, Oman, 2015, p. 85).

Also in 2017, the Arab Monetary Fund issued a report entitled The Development of Statistical Evidence and Methodologies in the Arab Countries. The report indicated the formation of a working group to implement the Government Finance Manual 2014 in the Ministry of Finance (AMF, 2016, p. 20).

The National Center for Statistics and Information issued the Statistical Yearbook 2022 (NCSI, yearbook 2022, p. 50), which included a set of public finance data that includes revenues and expenditures, and there was no other set available that included non-financial assets, financial assets, and liabilities.

4.1 Government Financial Management Information System (GFMIS) project

The Ministry of Finance of the Sultanate of Oman is establishing the Government Financial Information Management System (GFMIS) project. A modern electronic system for managing public finances, which is used in planning, implementing, and controlling the state's general budget and preparing reports on it and aims to achieve the following objectives: (https://www.mof.gov.om/GovernmentFinancialSystem).

- Enabling decision-making by providing accurate financial data and strengthening financial governance and transparency.
- Developing a modern financial system supports the implementation of an accrual basis of accounting.
- Enhancing the competence of national cadres in the field of public financial management.
- Supporting the implementation of public financial management initiatives, such as Program Based Budgeting (PBB), Treasury Single Account (TSA), and National Asset Register (NAR).

4.2 *Limitations of using fiscal indicators of the Sultanate of Oman*

The chapter relies on the application of the GFSM 2014 for several years, for all items (revenue, expenditure, non-financial assets, financial assets, and liabilities) that are not available in the final accounts of the Sultanate of Oman, for the following Limitation:

- In the statement of government operations, there are differences in the classification of the revenue and expenditure items with the GFSM 2014.
- The balance sheet and its non-financial assets, financial assets, and liabilities are not presented.
- The absence of International public sector Accounting Standards (IPSAS) to present the final accounts.

The foregoing reduces the ability to measure the impact that occurred on the performance of public sector institutions in the Sultanate during the COVID-19 pandemic. Finally; As a result of these limitations and according to the available financial data, only one indicator can be used, the first indicator of the public finance indicators, which is Gross operating balance (GOB).

5 Case Study

5.1 *Data Analysis and Hypothesis Testing*

To achieve the objectives of the chapter, the chapter used some public financial indicators, wealth and debit indicators to test the hypotheses of the chapter, as follows:

5.1.1 *Gross Operating Balance (GOB)*

$$= \text{Revenue} - \text{expense} + \text{consumption of fixed capital}$$

This indicator was used in evaluating the performance of the Australian government and the government of the Sultanate of Oman, noting that the consumption of fixed capital was not used in the final account of the Sultanate of Oman and therefore it was not collected in the equation:

Table 1 and Fig. 2 show that Gross operating balance ($b) decreased significantly in the years, 2019–2020 and 2020–2021, reaching 73.1 and 110, respectively.

Table 2 and Fig. 3 show that (GOB) in the year 2020 achieved a deficit of 2006.1 and achieved a significant increase in the year 2021 with a surplus of 602.1 to compensate for the losses of 2020.

It is clear from the analysis of the performance of the Australian government and the government of the Sultanate of Oman in (GOB); that the performance of the government of the Sultanate of Oman is better in dealing with the COVID-19 pandemic than the performance of the Australian government.

Table 1 Gross operating balance (GOB)—Australia

	2017–2018	*2018–2019*	*2019–2020*	*2020–2021*
Revenue ($b)	657.2	696.3	684.0	730.7
Change in Revenue ($b)	47.6	39.1	−12.3	46.7
Expense ($b)	647.1	679.7	791.9	876.4
Change in Expense ($b)	23.9	32.6	112.2	84.5
consumption of fixed capital ($b)	39.3	5.1	34.8	35.7
Gross operating balance ($b)	49.4	21.7	−73.1	−110

Source Author's calculations, 2022

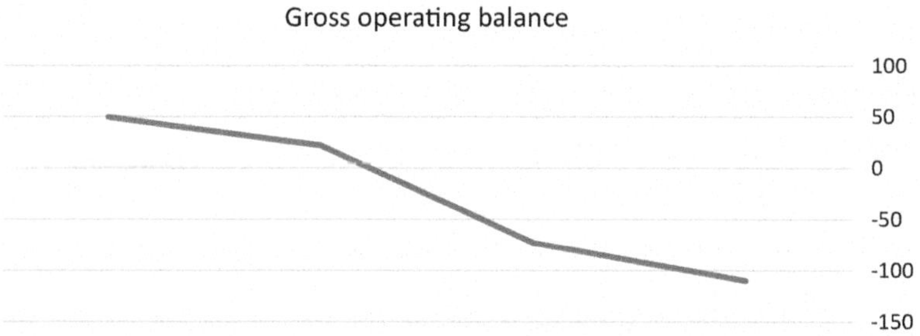

Fig. 2 Gross operating balance (GOB)—Australia (*Source* Author's calculations, 2022)

Table 2 Gross operating balance (GOB) —Oman

	2018	*2019*	*2020*	*2021*
Revenue (RO million)	10,949.6	10,588.7	8503.2	11,194.8
Change in Revenue (RO million)	2435.5	−360.9	−2085.5	2691.6
Expense (RO million)	10,711.1	10,537.3	10,509.3	10,592.7
Change in Expense (RO million)	1092.8	−173.8	−28	83.4
Gross operating balance (RO million)	238.5	51.4	−2006.1	602.1

Source Author's calculations, 2022

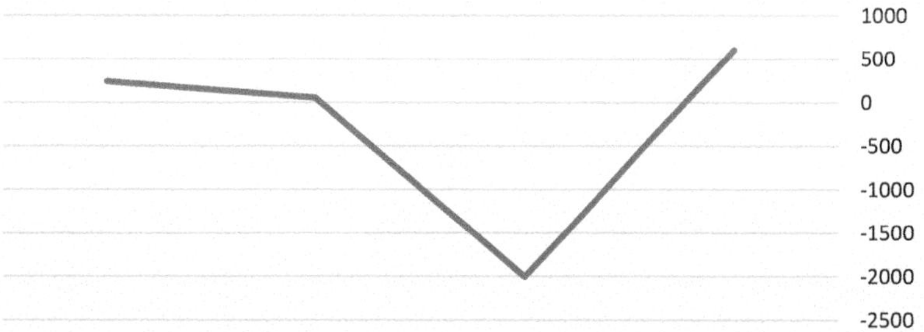

Fig. 3 Gross operating balance (GOB)—Oman (*Source* Author's calculations, 2022)

5.1.2 *Below-the-line Transactions*

= The net acquisition of financial assets – The net incurrence of liabilities
= net lending/ net borrowing

This indicator was used only in evaluating the performance of the Australian government, due to the lack of financial statistics for the government of the Sultanate of Oman.

Table 3 and Fig. 4 show that Below-the-line transactions decreased significantly in 2019–2020 and 2020–2021 reaching -151.5 and -193 respectively.

Table 3 *Below-the-line transactions*—Australia

	2017–2018	*2018–2019*	*2019–2020*	*2020–2021*
The net acquisition of financial assets ($b)	9	16.6	5.54	39.2
The net incurrence of liabilities ($b)	32.5	40.7	157.0	153.8
Below-the-line transactions ($b)	−23.5	−24.1	−151.5	−193

Source Author's calculations, 2022

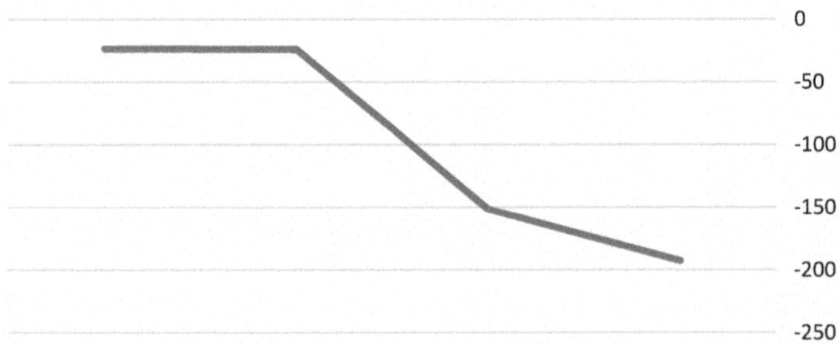

Fig. 4 *Below-the-line transactions*—Australia (*Source* Author's calculations, 2022)

5.1.3 *Transfer Payments Excluding Grants (TP-G)*

$$= \text{The subsidies} + \text{The social benefits} + \text{transfers not elsewhere classified}$$
$$+ \text{The premiums, fees, and claims related to nonlife insurance}$$
$$+ \text{The standardized guarantee schemes}$$

This indicator was used only in evaluating the performance of the Australian government, due to the lack of financial statistics for the government of the Sultanate of Oman.

Table 4 and Fig. 5 show that Transfer payments excluding grants increased significantly in the 2019–20 fiscal year with 113.3, and the increase continued in the 2020–21 fiscal year to become 119.7.

Table 4 Social benefits to households in goods and services—Australia

	2017–2018	*2018–2019*	*2019–2020*	*2020–2021*
(TP-G) ($b)	69,352	77,687	113.3	119,712
Change in (TP-G) ($b)	–	9	36	6
Change in (TP-G) %	–	12%	46%	6%

Source Author's calculations, 2022

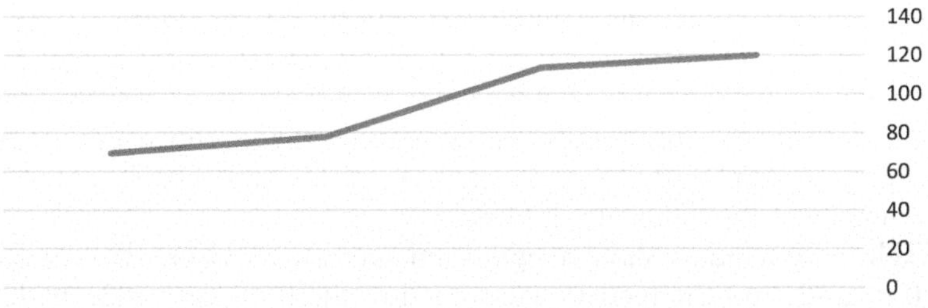

Fig. 5 Social benefits to households in goods and services—Australia (*Note* Disclosing the provision of Transfer payments excluding grants in the Australian Government's operating statement under another name, which is [Social Benefits to households in goods and services]. *Source* Author's calculations, 2022)

Table 5 Gross Debt—Australia

	June 18	*June 19*	*June 20*	*June 21*
Gross debt ($b)	436.2	476.9	633.9	787.7
CHANGE IN debt ($b)	32.5	40.7	157.0	153.8
CHANGE IN debt %	8%	9%	33%	24%

Source Author's calculations, 2022

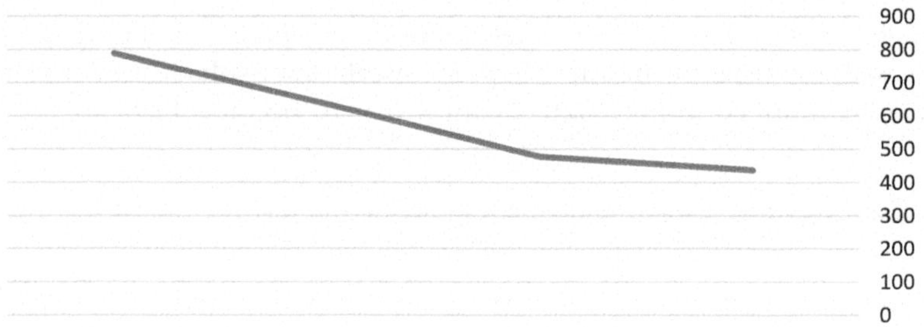

Fig. 6 Gross Debt—Australia (*Source* Author's calculations, 2022)

5.1.4 Gross Debt

$$\text{Total liabilities} - \left(\begin{array}{l}\text{equity and investment fund shares and} \\ \text{financial derivatives} + \text{employee stock options}\end{array}\right)$$

This indicator was used only in evaluating the performance of the Australian government, due to the lack of financial statistics for the government of the Sultanate of Oman.

Table 5 and Fig. 6 show a significant increase in Gross debt in June 2020 of 33%, and the increase continued in the fiscal year 2021 with an additional significant increase of 24%.

5.1.5 Net Financial Worth

$$\text{Financial assets} - \text{stock position in liabilities}$$

This indicator was used only in evaluating the performance of the Australian government, due to the lack of financial statistics for the government of the Sultanate of Oman.

Table 6 Net Finance Worth—Australia

	June 18	*June 19*	*June 20*	*June 21*
Total financial assets ($b)	31.7	33.7	80.9	13.1
Debt securities & other loans & placements liabilities ($b)	−28.7	−51.1	−159.2	−102.7
All other liabilities ($b)	−37.0	−116.1	−41.0	17.4
Net financial worth ($b)	−34	−133.6	−119.3	−72.2

Note In the statement of financial position of the Australian government during the years under chapter, the item stock position in liabilities was divided into two items: Debt securities & other loans & placements liabilities and all other liabilities. *Source* Author's calculations, 2022

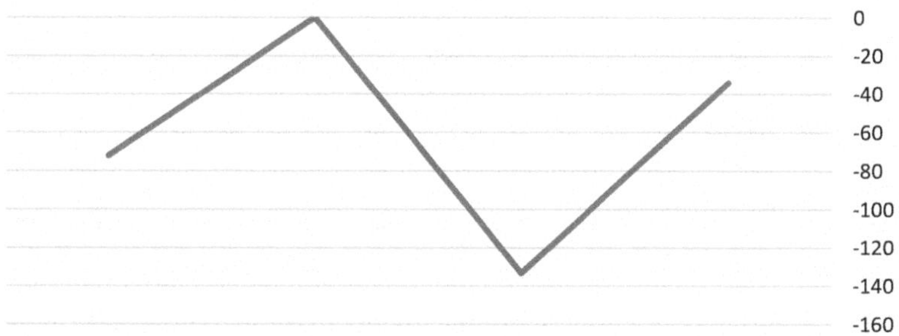

Fig. 7 Net Finance worth—Australia (*Source* Author's calculations, 2022)

Table 6 and Fig. 7 show a significant decrease in Net financial worth in June 2019 by 99.5, the performance improved in June 2020 by 14.2, and the performance improvement continued in June 2021 by 47.1.

5.1.6 *Change in Net Worth*

$$\text{Net worth at the end of the current reporting period} \\ -\text{net worth at the end of the previous reporting period}$$

This indicator was used only in evaluating the performance of the Australian government, due to the lack of financial statistics for the government of the Sultanate of Oman.

Table 7 Changes in Net Worth—Australia

	June 18	*June 19*	*June 20*	*June 21*
GFS Net Worth ($b)	−28.4	−127.0	−113.5	−66.3
Change in Net Worth ($b)	−45.6	−98.6	13.5	47.2
Change in Net Worth %	−265%	−347%	11%	42%

Source Author's calculations, 2022

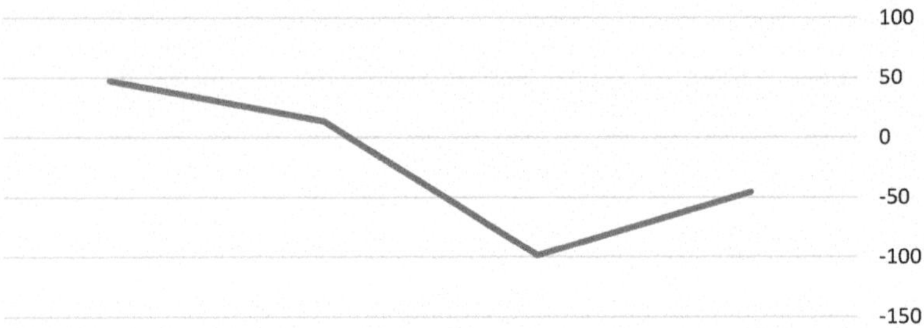

Fig. 8 Changes in Net Worth—Australia (*Source* Author's calculations, 2022)

Table 7 and Fig. 8 show a significant decrease in Net worth in June 2019 by 98.6, and the performance improved in June 2020 by 13.5, and the performance improvement continued in June 2021 by 47.2.

5.2 *Dissection*

5.2.1 *Dissection H1 "The Impact of the COVID-19 Pandemic on the Public Sector can be Assessed Using the Public Financial Indicators"*

- Public financial indicators during the COVID-19 period indicate that the performance of the Australian public sector has followed fiscal policies that have increased expenses significantly, as they rose by 112.2 during the year 2019–2020 and then 84.5 in the year 2020–2021. Revenues were controlled, although they decreased by −12.3 during the year 2019–20, they increased significantly in the year 2020–21 by a value of 46.7, which led to a significant decrease in Gross operating balance in 2019–2020 by 73.1 as well as in 2020–2021 to reach 110.

- In the Sultanate of Oman's performance, the government followed financial policies that led to reducing expenditures, as it reduced them by 173.8 during the year 2019 and then −28 in 2020, and expenditures increased in the year 2021 by a value of 83.4 in the year 2021, which indicates the efficiency of the financial policies followed for expenditures during the period. The pandemic. Revenues also decreased by −360.9 during the year 2019, and by −2085.5 during the year 2020, which led to a significant decrease in the total operating balance by −2006.1. However, it was compensated in the year 2021, as revenues increased by 2691.6, which indicates the efficiency of financial policies for revenues during the pandemic period.
- The Australian government relied on the disposal of financial assets worth 39,158 during the year 2020–2021 and also relied on bearing liabilities extensively during the pandemic. Liabilities increased during 2019–2020 by 157 and in 2020–2021 by 153.8, which significantly reduced Below-the-line transactions in 2019–2020 and 2020 −21 to −151.460 and −192.958 respectively.
- Benchmark from the analysis of the performance of the Australian government and the government of the Sultanate of Oman in (GOB); the performance of the government of the Sultanate of Oman is better in dealing with the COVID-19 pandemic than the performance of the Australian government.

Through the information provided by the government financial statistics system taken from the operating statement and using public financial indicators, the first hypothesis H1 is valid.

5.2.2 *Dissection H2 "The Impact of the COVID-19 Pandemic on the Public Sector can be Assessed"*

- Indicators of wealth and debt during the COVID-19 pandemic show that the Australian public sector has pursued fiscal policies that have increased public debt. The Gross debt index increased by 157.0 in June 2020 and 153.8 in June 2021.
- Liabilities were controlled during the pandemic, despite the increase in stock position in liabilities in June 2020 by 33, the liabilities decreased significantly in June 2021 by 114,9. This resulted in an improvement in Net financial worth during the pandemic period of 23.9 in June 2020, and 47.1 in June 2021.

- The Australian government's fiscal policies led to an improvement in Change in Net Worth. Net Worth improved during the COVID-19 pandemic, In June 2020, performance improved by 13.5, and in June 2021, by 47.2.

Through the information provided by the government financial statistics system taken from the balance sheet and using the indicators of wealth and debt, the second hypothesis H2 is valid.

6 Conclusion

The chapter aimed to measure the impact of COVID-19 on the countries applying GFSM 2014 through a case study of global best practices. To achieve this goal, the chapter used different indicators (Gross operating balance, Below-the-line transactions, Transfer payments excluding grants, Gross debt, Net financial worth, and Change in net worth) to measure the impact of COVID-19 on Australia, which means that, it's possible to measure or assess the impact of COVID-19 on the countries. These findings agreed with the results of the studies of (Pilcher, & Gilchrist, 2019), (Seiferling, 2020), (Zubíková & Smolák, 2022), and (Syahputra et al., 2022) which revealed that the impact of COVID-19 on the countries was measured and assessed using different public financial indicators, wealth and debt indicators. All these findings ensure the accuracy of the chapter's hypotheses which stated that, the impact of the COVID-19 pandemic on the public sector can be assessed using the public financial indicators, and that the impact of the COVID-19 pandemic on the public sector can be assessed using wealth and debt indicators.

The level of implementation of the Government Finance Statistics Manual 2014 in the Sultanate of Oman can be summarized as follows:

- There are some differences in the classification of some revenue and expenditure items with GFSM 2014. The final balance sheet of the Sultanate was not presented, and therefore financial data on non-financial assets and financial assets and liabilities were not available.
- The Ministry of Finance started the GFMIS project, according to the classification of GFSM 2014, and the initiatives it includes.

- There is difficulty in coordinating public finance statistics, namely the Ministry of Finance and the National Center for Statistics and Information.
- The absence of an accounting standard for presenting the final accounts of the Sultanate according to the International Public Sector Accounting Standards (IPSAS).

7 The Results of the Chapter

After completing the case study's analysis, the chapter found the following results:

7.1. Implementation of GFSM 2014 in countries contributes to giving a comprehensive view of the performance of the public sector.
7.2. The analysis of public finance indicators and indicators of wealth and debt gave a balanced view of the performance of the public sector including flows and balances.
7.3. The financial and statistical capacity of countries that implemented GFSM 2014 was able to assess the performance of the public sector during the COVID-19 pandemic.
7.4. The difference between the financial statements and the accounting rules between the government financial statistics and the international accounting standards for the public sector has an impact on the quality of the financial reports of the implementing countries, as they try to harmonize by issuing their financial statements, as they are hybrid statements between them.

8 The Recommendations of the Chapter

Based on the chapter's results, the chapter recommended the following:

8.1. The necessity of full adherence to the analytical framework of GFSM 2014 and its accounting rules to assess the performance of the public sector during crises as is COVID-19 pandemic.
8.2. Harmonizing the public sector accounting standards with the government financial statistics system by building a set of local public sector accounting standards in countries to be able to

reduce the difference between them, according to the experience of the Australian government by establishing the following:

- The Australian System of Government Finance Statistics: Concepts Sources and Methods, Australia 2015 (AGFS15)
- Australian System of National Accounts (ASNA)
- Australian Accounting Standards (AASB 1049)
- Performance indicators in the General Government Sectors financial reports (ED 142 Draft)

8.3. The Government of the Sultanate of Oman seeks to measure, present, and disclose the final accounts of the country according to GFSM 2014 through the following:

- Reclassifying the national accounts of the Sultanate of Oman according to The System of National Accounts 2008 (2008 SNA).
- A photocopy of the state's main final accounts (Government Operations Statement and Balance Sheet).
- Focus on the government financial information management system GFMIS project and the initiatives it includes.
- Increasing coordination in public finance statistics between the Ministry of Finance and the National Center for Statistics and Information.
- Adopting International Public Sector Accounting Standards (IPSAS) for measurement, presentation, and disclosure of the state's final accounts.

References

ABS, Australian System of National Accounts: Concepts, Sources, and Methods, 2020–2021 financial year. https://www.abs.gov.au/statistics/detailed-methodology-information/concepts-sources-methods/australian-system-national-accounts-concepts-sources-and-methods/2020-21/chapter-2-overview-conceptual-framework

Arab Monetary Fund (AMF). (2016). *Development of statistical evidence and methodologies in the Arab Countries.*

Australian Accounting Standards Board. (2020). Whole of Government and General Government Sector Financial Reporting, AASB 1049.

Baum, A., et al. (2020). Managing fiscal risks from state-owned enterprises, IMF. Working chapters, WP/20/213.

CPA Australia's, ED 142 Draft, 2005.

IMF. (2010). *Australia: Report on the Observance of Standards and Codes-Data Module*. https://www.elibrary.imf.org/view/journals/002/2010/343/article-A001-en.xml

International Monetary Fund. (2014). About Government Finance Statistics. https://www.imf.org/external/pubs/ft/gfs/manual/aboutgfs.htm

International Monetary Fund. (2014). Government Finance Statistics Manual 2014.

International Monetary Fund. (2015, June). Oman Report on Observance of Standard and Codes (ROSC).

Ministry of Finance, Sultanate of Oman, https://www.ncsi.gov.om

National Centre for Statistics and Information (NCSI). (2022). Statistical Yearbook 2022, Sultanate of Oman.

National Centre for Statistics and Information (NCSI). Sultanate of Oman. https://www.ncsi.gov.om/Pages/NCSI.aspx

Pilcher, R., & Gilchrist, D. (2019). *Public Sector accounting, accountability and governance: Globalising the experiences of Australia and New Zealand* (pp. 43–54).

Seiferling, M. (2020). Apples, oranges and lemons: Public sector debt statistics in the 21st century. *Financial Innovation, 6*(1), 37.

Silvia, C., & Alexandrina, C. (2021). The link between public management and accounting from the point of view of performance. *CECCAR Business Review, 1*(2021), 60–72.

Syahputra, A., & Saraswati, D. (2022). Explanatory chapter related to the impact of the COVID-19 pandemic in the implementation of public sector accountability for financial reporting quality from SKPD in North Sumatera Province. *Indonesia, International Journal of Research and Review, 7*(7), 17–30.

The Australian Bureau of Statistics. ABS Corporate Plan 2022–2023. https://www.abs.gov.au/about/our-organisation/corporate-reporting/abs-corporate-plan/2022-23/operating-context

The Australian Bureau of Statistics. (2015). Australian System of Government Finance Statistics: Concepts, sources and methods, Part D. https://www.abs.gov.au/statistics/detailed-methodology-information/concepts-ources-methods/australian-system-government-finance-statistics-concepts-sources-and-ethods/2015/17-relationships-other-statistical-systems/part-d-relationship-australian-accounting-standards

The Australian Bureau of Statistics. (2015). Australian System of Government Finance Statistics: Concepts, sources and methods, Part H. https://www.abs.gov.au/statistics/detailed-methodology-information/concepts-sources-methods/australian-system-government-finance-statistics-concepts-sources-and-methods/2015/1-introduction/part-h-purpose-manual; https://en.wikipedia.org/wiki/Australian_Bureau_of_Statistics#cite_note-6; https://www.abs.gov.au/statistics/economy/government/government-finance-statistics-annual/2020-21#data-download; https://www.abs.gov.au/methodologies/government-finance-statistics-annual-methodology/2020-21

The Australian Bureau of Statistics. Government Finance Statistics, Australia, Public sector statements 2020–21. https://www.abs.gov.au/statistics/economy/government/government-finance-statistics-annual/2020-21/55120DO001_202021.XLSX

The Australian Bureau of Statistics. Government Finance Statistics, Australia, Public sector statements 2019–20. https://www.abs.gov.au/statistics/economy/government/government-finance-statistics-annual/2019-20/55120DO001_201920.xls

The Australian Bureau of Statistics. Government Finance Statistics, Australia, Public sector statements 2018–19. https://www.abs.gov.au/statistics/economy/government/government-finance-statistics-annual/2018-19/55120do001_201819.xls

The Australian Bureau of Statistics. Government Finance Statistics, Australia, Public sector statements 2017–18. https://www.abs.gov.au/statistics/economy/government/government-finance-statistics-annual/2017-18/55120do001_201718.xls

Wines, G., & Scarborough, H. (2015). Australian government budget balance numbers the hybrid nature of public sector accrual accounting. *Accounting Research Journal, 28*(2), 120–142.

Zubíková, A., & Smolák, P. (2022). Macroeconomic impacts of the Covid-19 pandemic in the Czech Republic in the period of 2020–2021. *International Journal of Economic Sciences, XI*(1), 117–145.

PART III

The Impact of COVID-19 on Tourism

CHAPTER 11

The Impact of Covid-19 on the Tourism Sector in GCC Countries

Amira Al Salhi

1 Introduction

Tourism entails a purposeful journey that draws a traveler away from the familiar confines of their usual surroundings for a span of less than a year, undertaken with an intention beyond engagement in gainful employment within the visited locale (UNWTO, 2008). The realm of tourism, a vital facet of modern economies, bears a profound significance due to its multifaceted role in diversifying income streams and ameliorating dependence on oil-derived revenues. The dynamic travel and tourism sector, an economic protagonist, leaves an indelible mark through its substantive contributions to the fiscal sector. Its two-fold influence not only unfurls abundant avenues for job creation but also orchestrates a symphony of cultural and social progress within nations (Abbas et al., 2021).

A. Al Salhi (✉)
GCC Statistical Centers, Muscat, Oman
e-mail: aalsalhi@gccstat.org
URL: https://www.gccstat.org

A. Mishrif (ed.), *Economic Effects of the Pandemic*, The Political Economy of the Middle East,
https://doi.org/10.1007/978-981-97-4367-4_11

Within the realm of tourism, a dichotomy emerges, giving rise to two distinct facets: the demand and supply domains. On one hand, the demand spectrum encompasses the flux of various types of travelers, encompassing the local, inbound, and outbound cohorts. Concurrently, the supply facet of tourism encapsulates an intricate tapestry of industries emblematic of the trade, including the aviation sector, the hospitality industry, culinary establishments, reservation agencies, and other interconnected realms (UNWTO, 2008). The ascendancy of tourism within a nation augments its economic fabric, propelling the nation's Gross Domestic Product (GDP) to new heights, while concurrently paving the way for a surge in employment opportunities and heightened investor engagement, which in turn catalyzes the nation's developmental trajectory (Manzoor et al., 2019).

The tapestry of the aviation sector, intricately woven into the broader canvas of the tourism sector, commands a pivotal role in steering the global movement of tourists. A testament to its significance is articulated in a report by International Civil Aviation Organization, which asserts, "aviation's global stature as an economic engine is evident in the statistics. If the global aviation sector were a country, its total contribution (direct, indirect, induced and catalytic) of USD 2.7 trillion to the gross domestic product (GDP), and the 65.5 million jobs it supports, would be comparable to the United Kingdom's economic size and population" (ICAO, 2019).

However, as the sun rose in a new decade, a microscopic adversary emerged, redefining the world's sector. The COVID-19 pandemic, borne of a novel coronavirus hitherto unknown to humanity, surfaced with alarming swiftness. The annals of history will forever mark December 31, 2019, as the day the first case of this pathogen was documented in Wuhan City, Hubei Province, China (MoH, 2021). The International Monetary Fund's (IMF) observations in 2021 underscore the rapidity and profundity of the immediate repercussions, likening the decline in global output during the pandemic's onset to a threefold impact in half the time it took during the global financial crisis (IMF Outlook, 2021).

As the tempest of COVID-19 engulfed the world, its far-reaching repercussions transcended borders and sectors, inducing tremors across the economic, social, cultural, and psychological sectors (Abbas et al., 2021). Among the sectors most acutely sensitive to calamities, whether natural or health-related, is the travel and tourism sector, a domain notorious for both its susceptibility and its role as an unwitting conduit for the dissemination of diseases (Abbas et al., 2021). The world watched as the closure of airports and borders triggered a chain reaction, curbing the pandemic's spread. Yet, these containment measures bore witness to a litany of adverse outcomes, particularly for the tourism sector, exacerbated by the very nature of its operation, mobility prerequisites, and stringent protocols that entailed airport closures and global travel restrictions. The toll incurred by the sector's stakeholders, including businesses, investors, and myriad others, promises a prolonged tenure of pandemic-inflicted loss (Iacus et al., 2020).

As the world adjusted to the paradigm shift instigated by precautionary measures, epitomized by suspended air travel, the reverberations were felt far and wide. The ebb in global travelers set off a ripple effect, enveloping activities synonymous with the aviation sector, encompassing ticket reservations, hospitality services, and ancillary operations. These repercussions reverberated through the socio-economic fabric, driving a surge in job losses and a corresponding dip in the Gross Domestic Product (GDP) of nations (Iacus et al., 2020). The underpinning factor behind the GDP slump lay in the array of preemptive actions undertaken by nations, encompassing social distancing imperatives and mobility curbs (König & Winkler, 2020). Empirical investigations have further illuminated the vulnerability of employees across sectors, with the tourism domain particularly susceptible to job losses amid border closures and industry shutdowns (Fana et al., 2020). However, the pandemic's effects were not limited to the fluidity of global tourism but cast a wide net, enshrouding ancillary industries like the hospitality sector in its somber embrace (Shapoval et al., 2021). The hospitality sector, an expansive realm catering to myriad roles, from employees and customers to intrepid travelers and gastronomes, became an unwitting catalyst for viral transmission, echoing the pandemic's far-reaching influence (Shapoval et al., 2021).

This chapter, poised at the confluence of curiosity and inquiry, is steered by the intention to delve into the ramifications of the pandemic across the Gulf Cooperation Council (GCC) countries, unveiling its impact on the aviation sector, international tourist flows, the hospitality sector, the travel and tourism sector's contribution to the GDP, and the convoluted interplay between the pandemic and employment dynamics within the travel and tourism arena.

2 Methodology: Unraveling the Complex Nexus Between the Covid-19 Pandemic and GCC Tourism

The crux of this chapter revolves around a comprehensive exploration of the intricate interplay between the Covid-19 pandemic and the tourism sector within the Gulf Cooperation Council (GCC). Employing a rigorous analytical methodology, our approach is geared towards dissecting the multifaceted ramifications of the pandemic across a spectrum of crucial indicators. These indicators encompass the intricate dynamics of the aviation sector, the oscillations in international tourist movements, the resilient framework of the hospitality domain, the nuanced contributions to Gross Domestic Product (GDP), and the evolving nuances of employment within the expansive domain of tourism and travel. Through a meticulously constructed framework of quantitative analysis, data-driven insights, and interpretive exploration, this methodology provides a robust bedrock upon which subsequent revelations are woven.

2.1 *Data Collection and Sources*

At the heart of this analytical journey lies the meticulous curation of precise, comprehensive, and contemporaneous data from sources of unwavering credibility. Foremost among these sources stands the Statistical Centre for the Gulf Cooperation Council (GCC-Stat), a venerable repository of official statistics that offers a structured reservoir of information pertaining to tourism indicators across the GCC nations. In addition, the global stage is graced by distinguished contributors such as the World Tourism and Travel Council (WTTC), the International Air Transport Association (IATA), and relevant governmental bodies, each contributing to enrich our analytical panorama with their invaluable datasets.

2.2 *Indicators and Variables*

This methodology undertakes a meticulous deconstruction of an array of indicators and variables, each a crucial fragment in comprehending the pandemic's holistic impact. Among these dimensions are:

- Aviation Sector Analysis: Engaging in an intricate scrutiny of air traffic data, encompassing passenger counts, flight frequencies, and routes, this analysis seeks to discern trends and disruptions coursing through the aviation sector's veins.

- International Tourist Movements: A profound investigation into inbound and outbound tourist flows unfolds, capturing the ebb and flow of shifting travel patterns, evolving visitor demographics, and the ensuing reverberations across the broader tourism ecosystem.
- Hospitality Realm: Delving into the vibrant tapestry of the hospitality sector, this chapter embarks on a meticulous examination of key performance metrics within hotels, restaurants, and allied establishments. Metrics such as occupancy rates, revenue per available room (RevPAR), and restaurant patronage are meticulously scrutinized to shed light on the sector's resilience and recovery trajectory.
- GDP Contributions: A nuanced dissection of the direct and indirect contributions of the travel and tourism industry to the GDP of GCC nations is undertaken. This exploration unravels the economic import of the sector and unveils the far-reaching implications of pandemic-induced disruptions.
- Employment Dynamics: The intricate sector of employment within the tourism and travel sector is meticulously unraveled. This encompasses a panoramic view of direct employment within the sector and its interconnected industries, laying bare shifts in job availability, evolving workforce dynamics, and implications for labor markets.

2.3 *Quantitative Analysis and Interpretation*

The nucleus of this comprehensive methodology rests on quantitative analysis, serving as a robust cornerstone upon which our insights are founded. Employing robust statistical techniques, including time series analysis, regression modeling, and trend identification, our objective is to unearth patterns, anomalies, and causal connections within the data. This quantitative underpinning finds resonance in interpretive exploration, situating our findings within the broader tapestry of socio-economic and geopolitical narratives unique to the GCC region.

2.4 Comparative Assessment and Cross-Validation

To ensure the robustness of our analytical revelations, we embark on a comparative assessment, juxtaposing pre-pandemic data with the contours of post-pandemic trends. This discerning comparison illuminates the pandemic's nuanced impact across diverse indicators. Adding an additional layer of rigor, we cross-validate our findings across a multitude of reputable data sources, elevating the credibility and reliability of our analytical outcomes.

2.5 Limitations and Ethical Considerations

With utmost transparency, we acknowledge that our methodology is not impervious to limitations. The veracity of our findings is inevitably tethered to data availability and the delineated scope of our methodology. Upholding the ethical tenets of responsible data usage, encompassing data privacy and the conscientious handling of sensitive information, remains a steadfast commitment guiding our analytical voyage.

In summation, the depth and breadth of our analytical methodology serve as both guide and compass, illuminating the intricate domain where the Covid-19 pandemic intersects with the GCC tourism sector. Navigating the labyrinthine corridors of data, trends, and insights, this methodology embarks on a journey of discovery, uncovering the intricate dynamics that have not only shaped but fundamentally reshaped the tourism fabric within the GCC countries. The forthcoming sections of this chapter artfully weave together empirical threads and interpretive narratives, culminating in an intricate tapestry that highlights the pandemic's indelible imprints on aviation, international tourism, the hospitality realm, economic contributions, and the ever-evolving sector of employment dynamics.

3 Results: Unveiling the Nexus of Covid-19 Impact and GCC Tourism

3.1 Covid-19 Cases in the GCC Countries

In November 2021, the GCC Statistical Center unveiled a compelling snapshot of the Covid-19 pandemic's toll within the GCC countries. Globally, the confirmed Covid-19 cases had surged to approximately 262.8 million, marking a staggering prevalence of 33.4 thousand cases

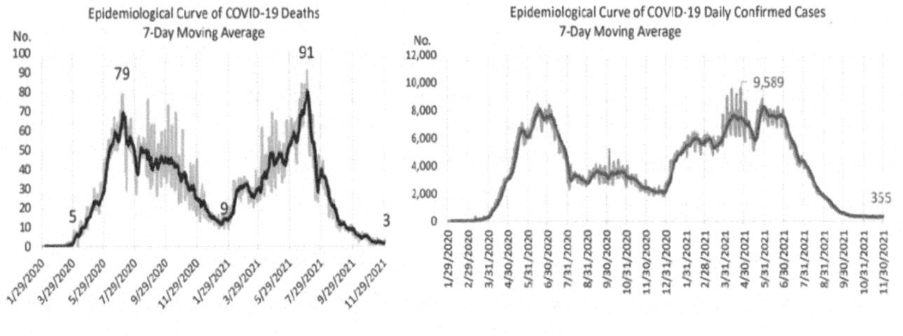

Fig. 1 Covid-19 cases in the GCC countries, November 2021 (*Source* GCCSTAT)

per million population. Zooming into the GCC countries, the cumulative confirmed cases reached 2.5 million, corresponding to approximately 44 thousand cases per million population. Of these cases, a remarkable 98.9% witnessed successful recovery, reflecting a testament to the medical responses and advancements. Tragically, the pandemic led to a loss of 0.8% of confirmed cases, translating to 19.6 thousand deaths attributable to the virus. Notably, the zenith of reported cases occurred in June 2021, with around 9 thousand cases recorded, coinciding with the highest recorded fatalities during the same month, totaling about 91 deaths (Fig. 1).

3.2 *Impact of Covid-19 on the Aviation Sector*

The aviation sector within the Gulf Cooperation Council (GCC) countries has been profoundly and extensively affected by the far-reaching consequences of the Covid-19 virus crisis. The rapid spread of the epidemic, coupled with the unprecedented declaration of a state of emergency to combat it, resulted in an unprecedented upheaval that forced nations to implement sweeping measures, including the suspension or substantial reduction of flight operations. This seismic disruption rippled across the aviation sector, triggering a cascade of unprecedented challenges and transformations.

As depicted in Figure two and elaborated in Table 1, the trajectory of the aviation sector's average daily departures underwent a dramatic evolution during the early stages of the pandemic. In the first quarter of 2020, prior to the appearance of any overt crises in the region, the average daily departures reached a notable figure of approximately 1473 flights.

However, the onset of the pandemic in the subsequent quarter led to an abrupt and staggering decline. In the second quarter of 2020, the average daily departures plummeted by an astounding 93% in comparison to the baseline established in the initial quarter of the same year. This precipitous drop was primarily attributed to the imposition of stringent travel restrictions and the enforced closure of airports across GCC countries, beginning in March 2020.

The third and fourth quarters of 2020 continued to witness a persistent decrease in the average number of daily departures, manifesting a significant decline when juxtaposed with the figures from the first quarter of the same year. The reduction was particularly stark, reaching approximately 310 and 515 flights respectively for the third and fourth quarters, showcasing a respective decrease of 79% and 65% during the same periods in comparison to the first quarter. This cumulative effect of decreased flight operations reverberated through the industry, as airlines grappled with unparalleled challenges to their operations and revenues.

The year 2021 further bore the weight of this tumultuous trajectory. Average daily departures recorded during the first, second, third, and fourth quarters of 2021 illustrated a persistent decline in comparison to the pre-pandemic baseline of the first quarter of 2020. The figures stood at approximately 637, 650, 832, and 1121 flights respectively, signifying a considerable reduction of 57%, 56%, 44%, and 24% across the same periods. Notably, a glimmer of hope emerged in the final quarter of 2021, hinting at a tentative recovery as a marginal increase in the number of

Table 1 Average number of daily departures flights in GCC countries by quarters

Year	*Period*	*Average number of daily departures flights*	*Rate of change (%) compared to Q1 of 2020*
2020	Quarter 1	1473	–
	Quarter 2	104	–93
	Quarter 3	310	–79
	Quarter 4	515	–65
2021	Quarter 1	637	–57
	Quarter 2	650	–56
	Quarter 3	832	–44
	Quarter 4	1121	–24

Source ICAO

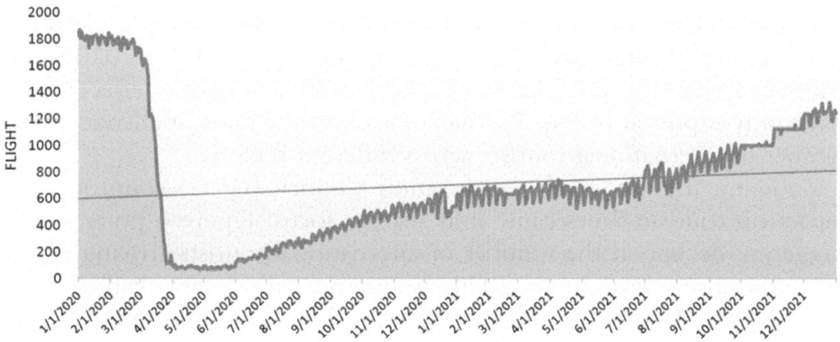

Fig. 2 Average number of daily departures flights in GCC countries (*Source* ICAO)

daily flights departing from GCC countries became evident. This uptick could be attributed to the gradual easing of travel restrictions within the region, albeit still far from returning to the state of normalcy that prevailed prior to the pandemic (Fig. 2).

This data underscores the depth of the impact inflicted by the Covid-19 pandemic on the aviation sector within the GCC countries. The pronounced reduction in the average number of daily flights departing from these nations stands as a testament to the extent of disruption experienced, surpassing the boundaries of mere statistical representation, and this will therefore have deeper effects on the tourism sector than both the supply and demand sides.

3.3 Impact of the Covid-19 Crisis on Tourism Flows within the GCC

A sweeping wave of disruption cascaded through the global tourism sector in the wake of the Covid-19 pandemic. Data released by the United Nations World Tourism Organization (UNWTO) in April 2022 offered a stark testament to the profound impact, revealing a staggering 72% decrease in the number of international tourists worldwide in 2020 as compared to the preceding year. This downward spiral echoed across various regions, with Europe, Asia and the Pacific, Americas, and Africa experiencing declines of 68%, 84%, 68%, and 72% respectively in 2020 in comparison to 2019.

In the Middle East, the repercussions were equally pronounced, as the total number of international tourists plummeted by 73% in 2020 when contrasted with the previous year. The pandemic's seismic effects were poignantly captured in Fig. 3, which illustrates the rates of change in the number of international tourists across different regions.

Zooming into the Gulf Cooperation Council (GCC) countries, the impact on tourism flows came into sharper focus. Figure 4 portrays the staggering decline in the number of international tourists arriving in the GCC countries throughout 2020, beginning with a remarkable 75.4% reduction in March—the advent of the pandemic's widespread propagation. The subsequent months bore witness to a continued decline, an undeniable testament to the substantial impediments placed on international travel due to the closure of borders, airports, and travel restrictions.

The nadir of this decline was evident in May 2020, where the number of international tourists plummeted by a striking 99% in comparison to the same month in the preceding year. Although the decline persisted in 2021 when juxtaposed with 2019, there was a glimmer of hope in the fourth quarter, marked by relatively improved rates of decline owing to the gradual easing of travel restrictions and the partial reopening of borders and airports.

The seismic shifts in tourism flows were further illustrated through the trajectory of total tourist arrivals in GCC countries. In 2019, a total of 47.7 million tourists visited the region, a reflection of the thriving tourism

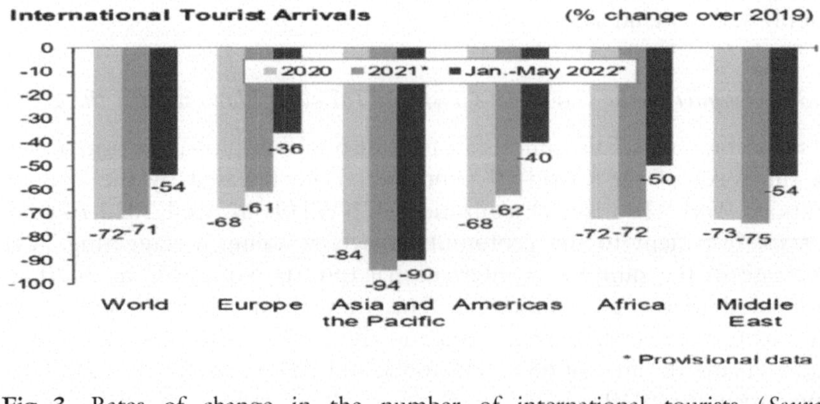

Fig. 3 Rates of change in the number of international tourists (*Source* UNWTO)

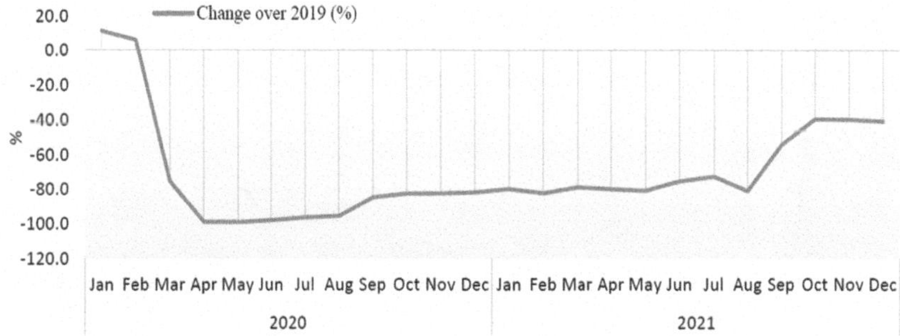

Fig. 4 Rates of change in the number of international tourists coming to GCC countries (*Source* UNWTO)

ecosystem during a period of relative stability. However, as the Covid-19 pandemic took hold in 2020, the total number of tourists plummeted by a staggering 72%, reaching a meager 13.4 million visitors. This downtrend persisted into 2021, with the total number of tourists increasing only slightly to about 13.9 million, reflecting a decline of 71% in comparison to the bustling tourism scene of 2019 (Fig. 5).

With an eye towards the future, the World Tourism Organization outlined two scenarios for recovery, underlining the arduous journey that the tourism sector is expected to undertake. The first scenario anticipates a 29% reduction in the number of international tourists arriving in the Middle East in 2022 when compared to the pre-pandemic levels of

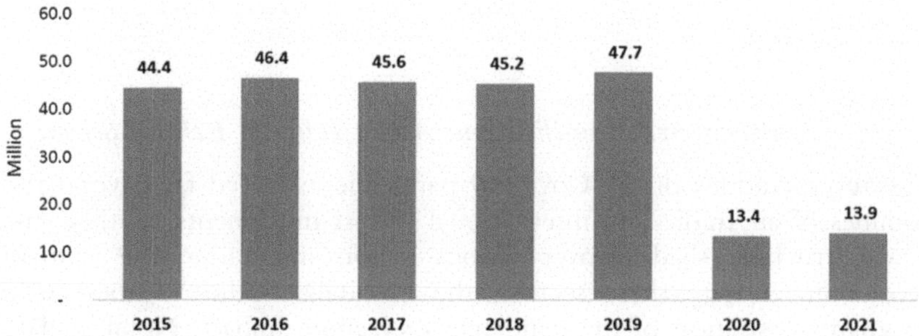

Fig. 5 Total number of international tourists coming to GCC countries (*Source* GCCSTAT)

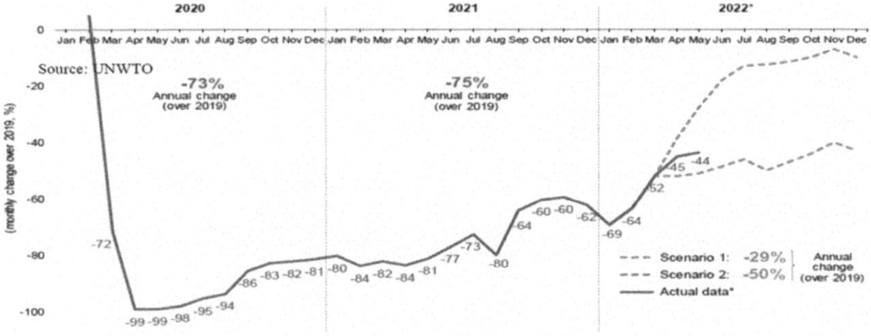

Fig. 6 International tourist arrivals in 2020, 2021, and Scenarios for 2022 in the Middle East (*Source* UNWTO)

2019. Meanwhile, the second, more cautious scenario, envisions a steeper decline of 50% in international tourist arrivals in the region during 2022 as compared to 2019. Figure 6 vividly portrays these potential trajectories, underscoring the challenges that lie ahead as the GCC nations strive to regain their tourism momentum in a post-pandemic world.

In summation, the unprecedented disruption brought about by the Covid-19 pandemic has wielded a profound impact on tourism flows within the GCC and across the globe. The nuances of this impact, the slow journey toward recovery, and the potential scenarios for the future provide a critical backdrop against which policy decisions, economic strategies, and future projections must be crafted. This dynamic sector serves as a poignant reminder of the interconnectedness of global systems and the resilience required to navigate the uncharted waters of a post-pandemic world.

3.4 *Multi-faceted Ramifications Across Tourism-Related Sectors*

The reverberations of the Covid-19 pandemic extended far beyond the confines of air traffic and international tourist movements, as they cast a wide-reaching shadow over various sectors integral to the tourism ecosystem. Among these sectors, the hospitality industry stood as a poignant illustration of the pandemic's sweeping impact. Notably, data presented in Table 2 underscored a significant contraction in the number of accommodations within the GCC countries, plummeting by approximately 9% in 2020 compared to the preceding year.

Table 2 Total number of accommodations in GCC countries

	Total number of accommodations	*Rate of change (%)*
2015	10,480	–
2016	10,519	0.4
2017	10,794	2.6
2018	11,021	2.2
2019	11,421	3.6
2020	10,443	−8.6

Source GCCSTAT

The underlying causes for this decline were manifold, emanating from the substantial losses incurred by the hospitality sector in response to the array of stringent measures implemented to contain the pandemic's spread. The imposition of restrictions on international and local movements, coupled with the transformation of accommodations into quarantine facilities, culminated in a cascading effect that saw many hotels forced to shutter their doors.

A profound consequence of the contraction in the number of accommodations was the ensuing decline in hotel occupancy rates across the GCC countries. In 2020, each GCC nation grappled with a notable decrease in occupancy rates compared to the previous year. Notably, the Sultanate of Oman bore the brunt of this decline, recording the highest drop in occupancy rates across the GCC by a striking 51%. In contrast, Saudi Arabia showcased a comparatively milder decrease, with occupancy rates contracting by approximately 9% (Fig. 7).

The ramifications of these fluctuations were profound, as they manifested in the form of reduced revenue streams, strained operational viability, and challenges in sustaining a skilled workforce. The hospitality sector, a cornerstone of the broader tourism tapestry, grappled with the intricate interplay between global health exigencies and the evolving demands of the market, painting a vivid portrait of the sector's resilience and adaptability in the face of adversity.

It is imperative to underscore that the consequences of these shifts extended beyond the confines of the hospitality industry itself, with ripple effects impacting employment, local economies, and the broader tourism supply chain. As GCC countries navigated the ever-shifting sector, characterized by a delicate equilibrium between public health imperatives and

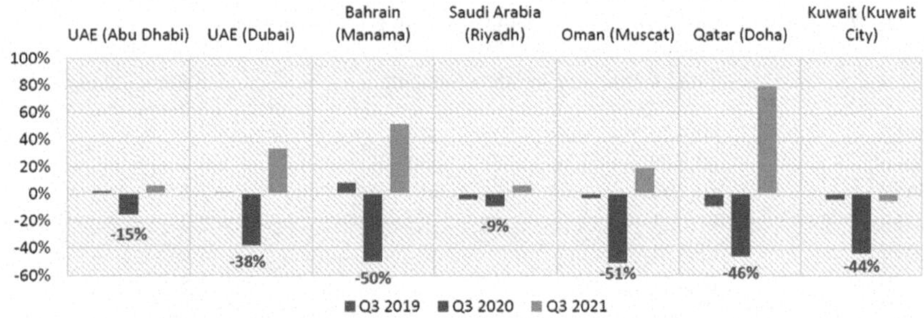

Fig. 7 Rates of change in hotel occupancy rates in the GCC countries (year-on-year change) (*Source* Colliers)

economic rejuvenation, the implications of these multifaceted changes underscored the sector's interconnectedness and its integral role in the region's socio-economic fabric. The subsequent sections delve deeper into the ramifications of these fluctuations, offering a comprehensive analysis of the implications on GDP contributions, employment dynamics, and the broader tourism ecosystem within the GCC countries.

The repercussions of the pandemic were not confined solely to air travel and international tourism. The hospitality sector bore the brunt as well, experiencing a contraction in line with pandemic-induced disruptions. With the closure of numerous establishments, including hotels repurposed as quarantine centers, the number of accommodations within the GCC dwindled by about 9% in 2020, relative to the previous year. This resulted in a concomitant reduction in occupancy rates across the GCC, with the Sultanate of Oman experiencing the most profound decline at 51%.

3.5 *Covid-19's Influence on Employment in the Tourism Sector*

The Covid-19 pandemic profoundly impacted employment within the tourism sector. The pandemic's cascading effects reverberated across a myriad of industries crucial to tourism, such as hotels, restaurants, travel agencies, and other associated enterprises, catalyzing a domino effect that led to a staggering reduction in global tourism activities.

As nations grappled with the necessity of suspending global tourism movements to curb the pandemic's spread, a somber cascade of closures unfolded. Hotels, restaurants, travel agencies, and others once bustling with visitors, become stood empty.

Within the GCC countries, the turbulence in employment dynamics within the tourism sector during the pandemic years was starkly evident. In the pre-pandemic sector of 2019, the sector stood as a robust source of livelihood, providing 2.98 million jobs. However, as the pandemic unfurled its relentless course, the numbers began to ebb, ultimately culminating in a 20.5% reduction in 2020, leaving 2.37 million jobs remaining in the sector, as depicted in Fig. 8. This precipitous drop in employment was a poignant testament to the formidable challenges that the tourism industry confronted during the tumultuous period.

The subsequent year, 2021, painted a similar tale of decline, albeit with a less pronounced trajectory. The number of jobs in the tourism sector dwindled further, reaching 2.51 million jobs, reflecting a 15.8% decrease compared to the vibrant employment sector of 2019. The echoes of lockdowns, restricted movements, and the broader economic upheaval resonated through these numbers, underscoring the far-reaching implications of the pandemic on employment prospects within the GCC countries.

It is pivotal to emphasize that the reverberations of the pandemic were not uniform across the GCC countries. The lockdown measures and their intensity varied from nation to nation, engendering differing degrees of impact on employment within the tourism sector. The figures in Fig. 8 bear witness to this nuanced reality, with each nation charting its unique trajectory through the challenging terrain of the pandemic's economic fallout.

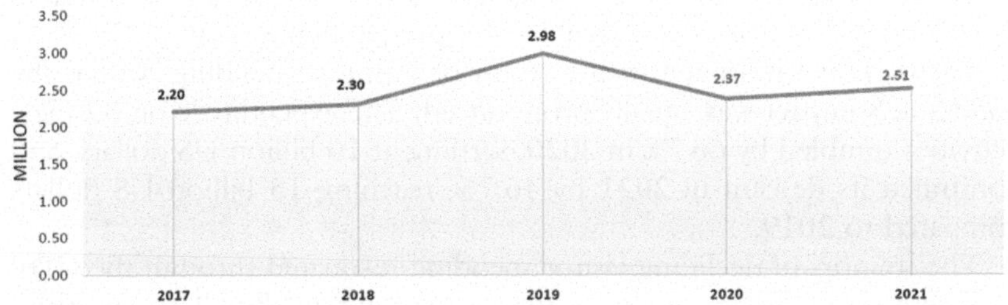

Fig. 8 Total number of jobs in the travel and tourism sector in GCC countries (*Source* WTTC)

As the pandemic's unyielding grip receded in some quarters, and with cautious steps taken to revive economic activities, a glimmer of recovery appeared. However, the journey to a complete return to pre-pandemic levels remained a complex endeavor, fraught with uncertainties and a need for measured approaches.

3.6 GDP Contribution and Spending Shifts

The Covid-19 pandemic unleashed a relentless torrent of disruptions, fundamentally altering the dynamics of the travel and tourism sector within the GCC countries. The far-reaching implications extended beyond the confines of tourism movements, permeating the very fabric of economic transactions and reshaping spending patterns. At the nexus of these shifts lies the contribution of the travel and tourism sector to the Gross Domestic Product (GDP), a pivotal metric that serves as a barometer of the sector's economic resonance.

A cornerstone of the travel and tourism sector's economic vitality lies in the spending patterns of international and domestic visitors. The pandemic's unrelenting grasp manifested itself in a dramatic reduction in visitor spending, reverberating through both entertainment and business expenditures. As the world grappled with the pandemic's repercussions, the spending sector transformed, echoing the tumultuous journey that characterized the period.

As Fig. 9 vividly illustrates, the spending on entertainment by both domestic and international visitors painted a stark narrative. In 2020, the total expenditure on entertainment plummeted by a staggering 56.2%, amounting to 45.4 billion US dollars. This decline further deepened in 2021, culminating in a 40.2% reduction, with total spending reaching 62 billion US dollars compared to the pre-pandemic year of 2019. A similar narrative unfolded in the realm of business spending, where the pandemic's impact was equally pronounced. The expenditure on business activities tumbled by 66.7% in 2020, settling at 10 billion US dollars, and continued its descent in 2021 by 46.7%, reaching 15 billion US dollars compared to 2019.

The tremors of declining visitor spending resonated through the GDP contribution of the travel and tourism sector within the GCC countries. The pre-pandemic sector of 2019 witnessed a robust contribution, with the sector adding a substantial 166 billion dollars to the region's GDP. However, the pandemic's effect was akin to a seismic shift, resulting in a

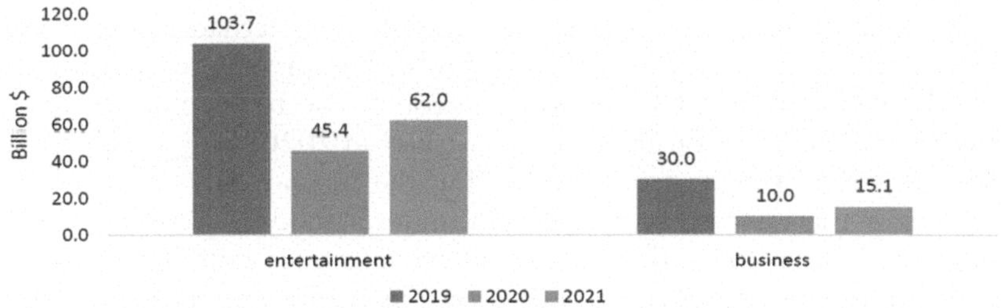

Fig. 9 Spending of domestic and international visitors in GCC countries by main purpose of the tour (*Source* WTTC)

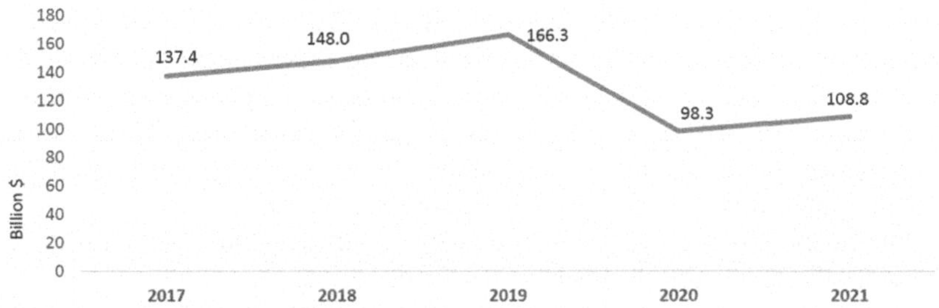

Fig. 10 Contribution of travel and tourism sector to GDP in GCC countries

remarkable 40.9% reduction in the sector's GDP contribution in 2020, as it dwindled to 98.3 billion dollars. This contraction endured, albeit with a slightly moderated pace, in 2021, with the sector's contribution declining by 34.6% compared to 2019, culminating in a figure of 108.8 billion dollars (Fig. 10).

4 Discussion: Navigating the Complex Interplay of Covid-19 and GCC Tourism

The intricate web of effects brought about by the Covid-19 pandemic on the Gulf Cooperation Council (GCC) tourism sector is undeniable. This discussion section delves into the multifaceted repercussions of the pandemic on various dimensions of GCC tourism, highlighting both challenges and potential avenues for recovery.

The aviation sector, serving as the backbone of international tourism, found itself at the epicenter of disruption. The precipitous decline in daily departures from GCC countries mirrors the sector's vulnerability to external shocks. The near collapse of air travel in 2020, with a staggering 93% reduction in daily departures during the second quarter, reverberated across the tourism ecosystem. Although a modest recovery began to emerge in late 2021, the path ahead remains uncertain. The aviation sector's resurgence hinges on coordinated global efforts to restore traveler confidence, harmonize health protocols, and stimulate demand.

The contraction of international tourist flows in GCC countries parallels the global decline, emphasizing the sector's interconnectedness and susceptibility to global events. The imposition of border closures, travel restrictions, and lockdowns led to a drastic 73% decrease in international tourists in the Middle East during 2020. Despite the emergence of recovery in 2021, the World Tourism Organization's projections caution that a full return to pre-pandemic levels may be protracted. The path to rejuvenation demands a cautious balance between health considerations and the imperative to reinvigorate the tourism sector.

The hospitality sector, deeply interwoven with tourism, faced a unique set of challenges. Hotel closures, declining occupancy rates, and transformed roles as quarantine facilities underscored the sector's resilience. However, the path to recovery requires innovative strategies that marry health and safety with guest experience. Embracing technology, recalibrating services, and fostering sustainable practices can propel the hospitality sector towards a resurgence that fosters renewed traveler interest and investment.

The Covid-19 pandemic exacted a heavy toll on employment in the tourism sector. The sharp decline in jobs by 20.5% in 2020 and 15.8% in 2021 underscores the sector's role as a major employer within GCC countries. The symbiotic relationship between tourism and employment further highlights the urgency of a concerted recovery. The contraction in the travel and tourism sector's contribution to GDP accentuates the sector's economic significance and underscores the need for targeted interventions to restore its vibrancy.

Rebuilding GCC tourism demands a comprehensive and adaptive approach. Collaborative efforts between governments, international organizations, and private sector stakeholders are paramount. Strategies should encompass building traveler confidence through clear health protocols, digital innovation to enhance the traveler experience, and initiatives to promote sustainable and responsible tourism practices.

The diversification of tourism offerings, with an emphasis on local and regional tourism, can also play a pivotal role in driving recovery. Encouraging domestic and intra-regional travel can help mitigate the impact of external shocks while fostering a sense of pride in local destinations.

This study is not without limitations. The reliance on quantitative data may overlook nuanced qualitative aspects. Future research endeavors could delve deeper into understanding post-pandemic traveler behavior, exploring the potential for experiential and transformative tourism, and investigating the evolving role of technology in shaping tourism experiences.

5 Conclusion: Forging a Resilient Future Amidst Uncharted Terrain

In the ever-evolving saga of human progress, the Covid-19 pandemic unfurled an unprecedented chapter in the annals of Gulf Cooperation Council (GCC) tourism, leaving an indelible imprint on every facet of the sector's vibrant tapestry. As the globe grappled with the relentless waves of uncertainty, the GCC's tourism sector bore witness to the profound interplay between crisis and resilience, vulnerability and innovation, disruption and adaptation. The symphony of data and analysis presented herein, encompassing the stark realities of plummeting aviation trajectories, cascading tourist flows, vacillating hotel occupancy rates, dwindling job numbers, and the nuanced fluctuations in the sector's contribution to GDP, serves as a mosaic that paints a vivid portrait of the pandemic's impact. Yet, within the depths of challenge, glimmers of hope and opportunities for renewal emerge. The journey through the pandemic became a crucible for introspection, a canvas on which the colors of sustainable practices, transformative experiences, and technological prowess have been applied with purpose. This chapter closes with a resounding call to action—a call for unity, collaboration, and strategic foresight that transcends borders and industry silos. It urges the GCC countries, as architects of their own destiny, to harness the lessons learned and the potential untapped to usher in a renaissance of GCC tourism. A renaissance marked not only by recovery but by transformation, where authenticity, sustainability, and human connection take center stage. This is the moment to reshape the narrative of GCC tourism, weaving threads of resilience, innovation, and empathy into the fabric of a sector poised to rise anew, driven by the collective determination to chart a course towards a future where the allure of exploration, discovery, and cultural exchange flourishes once more. As the sun sets on this chapter, the dawn of a resilient and reimagined GCC tourism industry beckons, illuminating the path ahead with the promise of rekindled wanderlust, redefined horizons, and a horizon aglow with the radiance of a promising and resilient tomorrow.

References

Abbas, J., Mubeen, R., Iorember, P. T., Raza, S., & Mamirkulova, G. (2021). Exploring the impact of COVID-19 on tourism: Transformational potential and implications for a sustainable recovery of the travel and leisure industry. *Current Research in Behavioral Sciences, 2*, 100033. https://www.sciencedirect.com/science/article/pii/S2666518221000206!

Fana, M., Pérez, S. T., & Macías, E. E. (2020). Employment impact of Covid-19 crisis: From short term effects to long terms prospects. *Journal of Industrial and Business Economics, 47*(3), 391–410. https://link.springer.com/article/10.1007/s40812-020-00168-5

Iacus, S. M., Natale, F., Santamaria, C., Spyratos, S., & Vespe, M. (2020). Estimating and projecting air passenger traffic during the COVID-19 coronavirus outbreak and its socio-economic impact. *Safety Science, 129*, 104791. https://www.sciencedirect.com/science/article/pii/S0925753520301880

International Civil Aviation Organization. (2019). *Aviation benefits report*. https://www.icao.int/sustainability/Documents/AVIATION-BENEFITS-2019-web.pdf

International Monetary Fund. (2021). *World economic outlook*. https://www.imf.org/en/Publications/WEO/Issues/2021/10/12/world-economicoutlook-october-2021.

König, M., & Winkler, A. (2020). Monitoring in real time: Cross-country evidence on the COVID-19 impact on GDP growth in the first half of 2020. *Covid Economics, 57*, 132–153. https://www.researchgate.net/publication/346025617_Monitoring_in_real_time_Cross-country_evidence_on_the_COVID-19_impact_on_GDP_growth_in_the_first_half_of_2020

Manzoor, F., Wei, L., Asif, M., Haq, M. Z., & Rehman, H. (2019). The Contribution of Sustainable Tourism to Economic Growth and Employment in Pakistan. *International Journal of Environmental Research and Public Health, 16*(19), 3785. https://www.ncbi.nlm.nih.gov/pmc/articles/PMC6801594/

Ministry of Health. (2021). *Corona virus disease (Covid-19)*. https://www.moh.gov.om/en/ebola

Shapoval, V., Hägglund, P., Pizam, A., Abraham, V., Carlbäck, M., Nygren, T., & Smitha, R. M. (2021). The COVID-19 pandemic effects on the hospitality industry using social systems theory: A multi-country comparison. *International Journal of Hospitality Management, 94*, 102813. https://www.ncbi.nlm.nih.gov/pmc/articles/PMC8631802/

World Tourism Organization. (2008). *International recommendations for tourism statistics 2008*. Retrieved from https://www.e-unwto.org/doi/book/10.18111/9789211615210

World Tourism Organization. (2018). *UNWTO Tourism Highlights*. Retrieved from http://www2.unwto.org

CHAPTER 12

Impact of COVID-19 Pandemic on Travel and Tourism Industry of India and Middle East Nations

Issac P. Elias

1 Introduction

Tourism is defined as an economic, social, and cultural Phenomenon that entails the movement of people to countries or places outside their usual place of residence for personal or business purposes (UNWTO—United Nations World Tourism Organization). As an economic activity, the tourism sector comprises of several industries. The Travel and Tourism sector is one of the sectors most affected by the Covid-19 pandemic across the world. The pandemic continued globally for several months claiming the lives of millions of people and drastically affected almost all economies in the world and has led to multi-dimensional challenges to nations across the world. The loss of life and livelihood caused by the Covid-19 pandemic was unprecedented in history and adversely affected all areas of

I. P. Elias (✉)
School of Business and Management, Christ University, Bangalore, India
e-mail: issac.p.elias@christuniversity.in

A. Mishrif (ed.), *Economic Effects of the Pandemic*, The Political Economy of the Middle East,
https://doi.org/10.1007/978-981-97-4367-4_12

socio-economic activities of human life. The report of UNWTO 2020, has commended the *unparalleled and fast-evolving nature of the crisis, it is extremely challenging to estimate the impact of the Covid-19 pandemic on international tourism*. Nothing prepared us for the pandemic and hence policymakers and advisors rushed to board rooms to make some protocols to face it. In fact, the pandemic challenged the survival of human beings globally. The repeated lockdowns announced by various governments across the world to control the spread of the pandemic led to the stoppage of all economic and social activities for a longer period.

In the last two decades of the new millennium the Tourism Industry has experienced enormous growth and popularity all over the world. Across the world, the Tourism industry plays a significant role in the overall well-being of every country. The tourism sector has contributed 10.4% of the GDP of the Global economy, and it was reduced to 5.5% in the year 2020. In the year 2019, just before the Covid-19 pandemic, the Travel and Tourism sector supported 10.6% of global employment opportunities (334 million jobs). But in the year 2020, due to the spread of the pandemic sixty-two (62) million people in the Tourism industry have lost their jobs. The pandemic has drastically and adversely affected all branches of the travel and tourism industry across the world such as Airlines, Transportation, Cruise lines, Hotels and Restaurants, Event management, tourist attraction spots like heritage sites, Museums and Zoos, Travel agencies, etc. In addition to these areas, sectors like cottage industries which are indirectly dependent on the Travel and tourism sector are also adversely affected by the outbreak of the Pandemic. In fact, all activities directly and indirectly related to tourism have been adversely affected by the Pandemic.

India and Middle East nations are among the countries that have been worst affected by the pandemic. The Middle East nations are always one of the most favorable tourist destinations in the world. The MENA (Middle East and North Africa) region has a variety of natural, cultural heritage, and religious assets. This region is home to many of the ancient monuments and archaeological sites listed in the World Heritage List published by the United Nations Educational, Scientific and Cultural Organization (UNESCO). The region is also blessed with access to famous Beaches, Cruises, Shopping venues and Man-made attractions. The contribution of the Travel and Tourism sector to the employment market of the MENA region is very significant. At present many of Middle East countries are focusing on diversification of the sources of national revenues and to reducing the dependence on Oil fields. In this context, the role of the Tourism industry is of cardinal importance to the Middle East Region.

India is one of the most popular tourist destinations in the world which attracts millions of tourists every year. The cultural diversity and natural beauty are the main factors attracting tourists from all over the world to India. India is a beautiful destination surrounded by cold mountains, dry deserts, vast plains, hot and humid plateaus, beautiful beaches, and tropical islands. To everyone who visits India, there is something new for a lifetime memory in every nook and corner of the country. The Tourism sector is economically very significant to India because it is one of the main sources of revenue to the nation. Further, it is the largest service sector industry, where a greater number of youth and women are employed in the country. In the financial year 2019–2020, the direct contribution of the Tourism sector to the GDP of India is 2.7% and 6.7% to the total employment in the country.

Travel and Tourism is one of the business sectors across the world that experienced the devastating effect of the Covid-19 Pandemic. All activities related to tourism have been drastically affected in an unprecedented manner due to the pandemic. The repeated lockdowns imposed by several countries in the world to arrest the spread of the disease brought all economic activities to a standstill for a long period. The countries which are highly reliant on the tourism sector for economic growth, have been seriously affected by the Pandemic. During the year 2020, due to the impact of the Covid-19 Pandemic and incidental restrictions to international mobility for the long term, the Travel and Tourism industry globally suffered losses of USD 4.5 trillion and its contribution to the global GDP declined by 49.1% compared to the year 2019 (Report of the World Travel and Tourism Council, 2022). Through this chapter, the author has tried to examine the impact of the Covid-19 Pandemic on the Travel & Tourism sector of two prominent tourist locations in the world, India and the Middle East. Further, it focusses on the strategies to revive the industry in the *new normal* situation, even though there is uncertainty and challenges in the road ahead.

2 Review of Literature

The Tourism industry facilitates balanced regional development and uplifts the economic growth of nations (Ranjbarian & Zahedi, 2010). The manifold benefits of Tourism such as employment opportunities, attracting foreign exchange, and strengthening of infrastructure are important to every country (Jarvis & Stoeckl, 2016). Many underdeveloped countries focus on tourism as a way for growth, development and a source of foreign exchange (Andrades & Dimanche, 2017). Tourism has played a significant role in history and may play in the future also the same in society, although it can bring adverse socio-economic effects if managed poorly (Marković & Klarić, 2015). The Covid-19 Pandemic has adversely affected the financial system worldwide and caused a substantial reduction in the arrival of foreign tourists (Pawan Kumar, 2021). Since Travel Tourism is one of the most vulnerable industries in the service sector (Khare & Sathe, 2021) it is very much sensitive to various national and international crisis such as war, terrorism, deadly diseases, political unrest, natural calamities etc. (Jawabreh, 2020). Political instability, investment in tourism infrastructure, and maintenance of an acceptable cost of living are some of the factors holding down tourism advancement in the Middle East countries. Morakabati (2013) is of the opinion that the wealth of heritage and range of leisure resources provides a competitive advantage to the Tourism industry of the Middle East countries. Hidayat et al. (2019) have pointed out that understanding the characteristics and behavior of tourists helps the service providers in the industry to know their market segment in a better manner and adjust their services in par with the needs and desires of tourists. Zhamgaryan has rightly pointed out that the growth of Abu Dhabi and Dubai as important business centers in the middle east region increases the importance of business tourism in UAE. Tourism represents a major economic pillar for the Middle East MENA economies and a key component of economic diversification for oil-exporting countries. The World Travel and Tourism Council (WTTC) report, in the year 2019, the travel and tourism sector accounted for 5.3% of GDP growth and 6.7 million jobs across the Middle East and North Africa (MENA) region.

The number of international tourists to Middle east nations has increased tremendously in the last two decades. The religious tourism, one of the strong Pillars of the economy of the Kingdom of Saudi Arabia declined significantly due to the Covid-19 pandemic impact (Kernshi &

Waheed, 2021). In the context of the Pandemic, Kassem et al. (2021) have identified five dimensions of Tourist Social Responsibility (TSR) namely, Responsibility for legal and social aspects, Responsibility for health issues, Responsibility for Altruism and solidarity, Responsibility for support towards socially responsible businesses and Responsibility for environmental impacts. Kenny and Dutt (2022) stated that Government Regulations and Corporate Crisis Management plans are the important factors that influenced the response of the hotel industry against the pandemic to ensure the continuity of business. Across the world Tourism industry and allied activities are at a halt in March 2020, with an international ban on travel and public gatherings which affected more than 90% of the world's population (Al-Qasem, 2021).

Hadi and Hadi are of the opinion that there is a close relationship between trade freedom and Tourism demand in Middle Eastern countries. A 10% increase in trade freedom leads to a 7% increase in tourist demand which requires improvement in foreign trade regulatory policies. The formation of policies with trade freedom has a positive impact on the tourism industry in Middle Eastern nations. The Covid-19 pandemic has caused a direct loss of 5 million Omani Riyals to the Tourism sector of Oman (Habiba Muhammed et al., 2022). Further, there is a reduction in customer demand at national and international levels, disruption in the logistics and distribution channels, and relationship with suppliers, customers, and employees. The social impact includes depression, anxiety, and stress among people especially businessmen. The Covid-19 pandemic has adversely affected the performance of the Tourism sector of the Sultanate of Oman Hadi and Hadi are of the opinion that there is close relationship between trade freedom and Tourism demand in Middle east countries. A 10% increase in trade freedom leads to a 7% increase in tourist demand which requires improvement in foreign trade regulatory policies. The formation of policies with trade freedom has a positive impact on tourism industry in the Middle east nations. The Covid-19 pandemic has caused direct loss of 5 million Omani Riyals to the Tourism sector of Oman (Habiba Muhammed et al., 2022). Further, there is a reduction in customer demand at national and international level, disruption in the logistics and distribution channels, and relationship with suppliers, customers, and employees. The social impact includes depression, anxiety and stress among people especially with businessmen. The Covid-19 pandemic has adversely affected the performance of the Tourism sector of the Sultanate of Oman Al-Hasni, 2021). There has been increased unemployment and a decline in the purchasing power of people. Among the Small and Medium Enterprises (SME) segment in Oman, the most affected are in the Tourism sector (Al-Hanai & Matriano, 2021).

Tourism governance could be an effective tool for managing the tourism sector in Egypt due to the fact that the Tourism sector is composed of activities that involve multiple interrelationships among various stakeholders intervening in the production of goods and services consumed by tourists (Ramzy, 2017) Since there is involvement of both public and private sectors with different visions and approaches to tourism, there is need of a unified planning efforts for the betterment of Tourism sector. As regards the issue of Sustainable tourism, three principles of development, namely Economy, Environment and Society are of cardinal importance (Shalan, 2005). The Red Sea region of Egypt has high potential for sustainable and nature-based tourism, by adopting environmentally sound policies and practices to avoid degradation of the natural heritage of the county for the sake of present and future generations.

The economic growth of Saudi Arabia creates opportunities for sustainable tourism in the country (Ekiz et al., 2017) In order to have a sustainable tourism sector, there is a need of educating the young generation about the significance of tourism. One of challenges of the Saudi Arabian tourism is the diversification of the sector rather than depending exclusively on one-dimensional development based on religious Tourism. Tourism is an alternative source of revenue for the Kingdom of Saudi Arabia. The Country has its own uniqueness with reference to history, monuments, peaceful atmosphere, culture, and hospitality, and has great potential to develop as one of the best tourist locations in the world (Basendwah & Rahman, 2021).

Cultural tourism is one of the biggest attractions of tourists to India. As a country with diversified culture and heritage, India can be an unmatchable mark on the global tourism destinations if taken care of properly (Menon et al., 2021). One of the opportunities for the Indian Tourism sector in the post covid rea is investment in health and well-being tourism (Vijay Raj & Jayanthila Devi, 2021).

As per the information provided by the International Civil Aviation Organization (ICAO), the Number of international Passengers to Middle East nations are drastically declined due to covid-19 Pandemic (Table 1).

Table 1 Number of international passengers to Middle East

Year	*No. of international passengers (million)*
2019	147
2020	39
2021	45

Source ICAO Report 2021

The United Nations Conference on Trade and Development focuses on three major areas for the betterment of the Tourism sector in the light of future uncertainties.

(a) Bring back the confidence of travelers who are concerned about health and the risk of being stranded overseas. (b) Minimize the socio-economic impact on livelihoods of those who are associated with the travel and tourism sector. (c) Consider the long-term implications of the covid-19 pandemic with reference to the tourism sector.

3 UAE Tourism and Covid-19

UAE is the country with the leading share of Tourism spending in the Gulf Cooperation Council (GCC) region. The tourism industry has established itself as a major amplifier of economic divergence in the United Arab Emirates. The Travel and Tourism sector of the United Arab Emirates (UAE) provides employment to Lakhs of people and contributes significantly to the GDP (13%) of the country (IATA Report, 2019).

The Covid-19 pandemic has adversely affected the Air Travel sector of UAE, which has five Airline companies namely Emirates Airlines, Etihad Airways, Air Arabia, Fly Dubai, and Wizz Air Abu Dhabi. All these companies have incurred heavy losses due to the stoppage of their operation during the pandemic period. Further, thousands of the employees of these companies were jobless during the pandemic period. The stoppage of Flights into and out of the UAE had a direct impact on the Tourism industry also. The number of tourists to UAE fell drastically as compared to the period before the Covid-19 Pandemic. The Dubai Expo2020, which attracts millions of international tourists to the UAE has been postponed by one year due to Covid-19 which resulted in the loss of millions of dollars. The Hospitality sector also suffered great losses because of the Lockdown during the pandemic period. The average room occupancy rates at hotels came as low as 20% (Table 2).

Table 2 Tourists to Dubai from 2015–2021

Year	*No. of Tourist to Dubai*
2015	14,200,000
2016	14,900,000
2017	15,790,000
2018	15,920,000
2019	16,730,000
2020	5,510,000
2021	7,280,000

Source Dubai Tourist Annual Visitors Report-2021

The prominent economies in the UAE Dubai and Abu Dhabi have taken a holistic approach to the revival of the economy during the post-Covid period. In the first phase, they announced a stimulation package of US$ 79 billion for the private sector business and further decided to relieve those business houses which are subject to administrative penalties. The UAE government has issued guidelines for the revival of business activities in the Emirates and has been efficiently handling the challenges passed by the Covid-19 pandemic and continuing as a role model in the Middle East in protecting the population and reopening the economy.

The Emirates Airlines has implemented bio-safety measures in their flights, namely aircraft cleaning, disinfecting of toilets in every 45 minutes, wearing of personal protective equipment for Cabin crew and Airport employees, distribution of hygiene kits to passengers, delivery of Food and drinks in bento-style boxes to reduce interaction between cabin crew and passengers. Emirates is the first airline company to introduce Covid-19 insurance coverage to passengers, and accordingly, if a passenger is subject to covid while traveling Emirates flights, the company will pay medical bills up to EUR 150,000 and quarantine costs of EUR100 per day for 14 days.

4 Saudi Arabia Tourism and Covid-19

Saudi Arabia is the largest religious tourism location in the Middle East Region. Every year millions of people across the world visit Makkah and Medina, the two holy places in the Kingdom of Saudi Arabia for performing the religious rituals of Umrah and Hajj. Thousands of flights are coming to the country carrying these pilgrim tourists from various parts of the world, which in turn results in huge amounts of revenue and foreign exchange. The contribution of the Tourism sector to the GDP of Saudi Arabia is very significant and occupies a position next to oil exports. In the job market of the KSA also the contribution of the Tourism sector is very significant, especially in the private sector.

On account of the cancellation of the annual Hajj pilgrimage in the year 2020, Saudi Arabia lost millions of Dollars in terms of foreign exchange. Generally, around 2 million Muslim Pilgrims from across the world visit Saudi Arabia every year to perform Hajj and Umrah. The VISION 2030, program of Saudi Arabia has allotted $50 Billion worth of projects to the travel and Tourism sector of the country in order to increase the number of Hajj and Umrah visitors by providing them with better infrastructure and other amenities.

5 Oman Tourism Sector and Covid-19

Covid-19 has drastically affected the Travel and Tourism sector of Oman. The rate of unemployment has increased and purchasing power of people declined due to a reduction in income (Al-Hasani, 2021). The tourism sector of Oman experienced a direct loss of 5 million Omani Rials and adversely affected the mental health of businessmen in the Tourism and Hospitality sector. The Room occupancy rate of hotels was also significantly reduced due to the pandemic. As compared to the year 2019, Omani hotels experienced a more than 50% decline in the room occupancy rate during the year 2020. To overcome the adversities in the Tourism sector of Oman due to the Covid-19 pandemic, remedial measures from both the government and private sector are significant. Loss of revenue and the drastic reduction in the room occupancy rate of hotels are the main issues being faced by the Omani tourism Industry during the Pandemic period. One of the strategies for the recovery of the Tourism sector is the marketing of Oman as the best tourist destination in the Middle Eastern region through national and international channels of media (Al-Hasani, 2021).

6 Tourism in Egypt and Covid-19

Tourism is considered as one of the main pillars of the economic resurgence of Egypt in recent years. The tourism sector recorded its highest revenue earning in the financial year 2018. According to the estimate of the International Food Policy Research Institute, the revenue loss from the Tourism sector accounts for two third of the total losses in the GDP of Egypt due to the crisis. In addition to revenue loss, Egypt experienced loss of foreign exchange earnings also due to the spread of the Pandemic. Further, remittance from citizens abroad and payment from the Suez Canal contribute to 14.5% of the national economy of Egypt. Further, lower tourism spending adversely affected even food processing and agriculture sectors in Egypt. As per the report of the UNCTAD, Egypt is one of the nations most affected by GDP losses due to a decline in the Tourism sector during the Covid-19 Pandemic period across the world. The Central Bank of Egypt introduced special credit lines for Tourism enterprises and a scheme of debt rescheduling. Exemptions from Tourism levies and other fees. Hotels are allowed to reopen for domestic tourists at 50% capacity under strict protocols of safety and hygiene.

7 Tourism in India and Covid-19

India is one of the most favored tourist destinations in the world, known for its traditions, cultural heritage, and hospitality. During the financial year 2019–2020 the direct contribution of travel and tourism sector to the GDP of India is 2.7% and to the total employment of the country is 6.7%. The decline of tourist arrivals to India started in the month of February 2020. The Covid-19 Pandemic drastically affected the Travel and Tourism sector of India. As a result of the lockdown imposed by the Government on account of the pandemic 14.5 million jobs have been lost during the period 2020–2021 in addition to loss of income and foreign exchange earnings. The Archaeological Survey of India (ASI) has 3691 notified tourist locations in India out of which 38 are world heritage sites. As per the information provided by the ASI, the total revenue from these ticketed tourist spots was Rs. 247.89 crores in the year 2019 and Rs. 302.34 crores in 2019. In a normal economic situation, the tourism sector has a significant contributor to the GDP of the country. As per the Tourism Satellite Account (TSR), the tourism sector contributes 5.2% of the GDP of India and provides 12.4% of the employment in the country and facilitates foreign exchange earnings (FEE). To increase the Foreign Exchange Earnings of the country the tourism sector-related policies need to be restructured because the arrival of foreign tourists is one of the key factors of FEE. To attract foreign tourists the existing resources are to be utilized in an efficient manner rather than investing in new resources in the sector (Jaipuria et al., 2021) (Tables 3 and 4).

As Per the report of the United Nations World Tourism Organization, based on their global survey on the Impact of Covid-19 on the Tourism sector, the factors weighing on the recovery of international tourism during the post-pandemic period include (a) economic environment prevailing in nations (b) travel restrictions imposed by countries, (c) higher transport cost and accommodation cost (d) uncertainty about Russia-Ukraine war (e) low confidence level of travelers and (f) lack of coordinated response among nations.

Table 3 Foreign tourists arrival in India during the last 10 years and Foreign Exchange Earning

Year	*Number of foreign tourists visited India (No. In Lakhs)*	*Foreign exchange earnings (Rs. In Crores)*
2011	57.8	83,036
2012	63.1	95,607
2013	65.8	107,563
2014	69.7	120,367
2015	76.8	134,844
2016	88	154,146
2017	100.4	177,874
2018	105.6	194,881
2019	109.3	211,661
2020	27.4	50,136

Source Report of Ministry of Tourism Government of India

Table 4 GDP contribution of travel and tourism sector of India

Year	*GDP contribution (US-$ billion)*
2013	172.91
2014	185.63
2015	201.43
2016	219.72
2017	232.01
2018	247.37
2019	191.3
2020	121.9

Source Report of the Ministry of Tourism—India

8 Sustainable Tourism in Post Covid-19 Period

The World Tourism Organization defines Sustainable Tourism as "Tourism that takes full account of its current and future economic, social and environmental impacts by addressing the needs of visitors, industry and host communities." The topic of sustainable tourism is highlighted in the United Nations' 2030 Agenda for Sustainable Development, adopted by member countries. The essence of sustainable tourism is the promotion of tourism and allied activities in a manner that provides the best and most memorable experience to the travelers but protect the natural environment, natural heritage, and biodiversity, respecting the socio-culture of the host communities, and facilitating long-term employment opportunities for the local people. In fact, sustainable tourism focuses on better tourism today without compromising the future.

9 Discussion on Recovery Strategies in Post Covid Period

The Covid-19 Pandemic has drastically affected the Travel and Tourism sector and Economy of the Middle East countries and India. The Travel and Tourism sector is an important contributor to the GDP of Middle East countries and India. The Pandemic was a cause for considerable decline in the GDP of these countries during the years 2020 and 2021. The Tourism sector is one of the largest service sectors which provide employment to a greater number of youth and women across the world. As a result of the Covid-19 pandemic, Millions of people have lost their employment and livelihood. Both India and Middle East Economies have experienced considerable decline in their Foreign Exchange Earnings during the financial years 2020 and 2021 due to the Covid-19 Pandemic. The timely and effective intervention of the governments of both India and Middle East nations are successful in managing the issues in relation to the covid-19 pandemic to a great extent and revive the tourism sector, though there are several restrictions and concerns still prevailing across the world.

Building up confidence among travelers at national and international levels is important for Tourism Promotion during the post-covid era and to achieve the same, the joint effort of the Ministry of Health and Ministry of Tourism will be solicited. The public relations department of the Ministry of Tourism must highlight the various measures taken for the safety of tourists. For the promotion of tourism, proper co-operation between Airline companies, the Hospitality sector, and tour operators must be facilitated by the policymakers and authorities. It is advisable that Middle East nations, focused exclusively on religious Tourism, have to think about diversification of the sector in collaboration with private sector investors. As part of the recovery framework and promotion of sustainable tourism, the development of a standard protocol for both domestic and international tourists keeping in view the various issues and challenges in the light of the Covid-19 pandemic is highly appreciable. Application of Technology in the best possible manner while providing products and services to the Tourism sector should be part of the recovery strategies. The Governments may take the initiative to introduce Degree programs in Tourism and Hospitality Management in various Universities. The Economic growth of countries in the Arab region mainly depends on Oil price fluctuations at the international level. However, the argument for the ban of petroleum using vehicles and the introduction of electric vehicles due to environmental issues is a threat to the economy of Middle East nations. In this context, sustainable development of tourism as an alternative source of revenue to the economy must be a policy matter of cardinal importance to the Middle East nations. The government's response to the new situation is very significant in the light of global call to reduce or avoid the use of oil as a source of energy. In fact, it is an opportunity to develop tourism as the main source of revenue for Middle East countries. Further, the authorities may consider establishing tie-ups with insurance companies to introduce competent products for tourists in order to win their confidence. Public Private partnership (PPP) model projects and Foreign Direct Investment (FDI) in the field of tourism seems to be a better option for Middle East countries for the promotion of tourism as a main source of revenue.

10 Conclusion

A collective and resilient approach is required from governments, market players and work-force for the recovery of the tourism industry in a sustainable manner during post-pandemic period. In order to maintain sustainable tourism, it is desirable to give importance to both the supply and demand sides of the market and policy decisions (Carrasco & Carvao, 2022), which will affect the society and economy. It is advisable that all policies and programs in Tourism development are to be framed keeping in view the Sustainable Development Goals of the United Nations. The policymakers and service providers in the tourism industry are expected to be oriented towards communal harmony, the beauty of diversity, and environmental and social justice. Though there are threats and challenges on the road ahead, Middle East nations and India are expected to emerge as the most favored and competitive tourist locations, in the coming years.

References

Al-Hanai, Y., & Matriano, D. M. T. (2021). Issues and challenges faced by SMEs in Sultanate of Oman during Covid-19: A case study of the Tourism Sector. *Advances in Social science Research Journal, 8*(9), 1–17.

Al-Hasani, Z. S. (2021). Identifying and prioritizing way to improve Omans's Tourism Sector in the Corona period. *Journal of Intercultural Management, 13*(1), 144–176.

Al-Hasni, Z. S. (2021). The economic impact of Covid 19 on the Oman Tourism Sector. *Psychology and Education Journal, 58*(2), 824–830.

Al-Qasem, A. (2021). Impact of pandemic Corona Virus Disease (Covid-19) on UAE Tourism Industry. *PJEE, 18*(7), 2556–2570.

Andrades, L., & Dimanche, F. (2017). Destination competitiveness and tourism development in Russia: Issues and challenges. *Tourism Management, 62*, 360–376.

Annual Review. (2019). International Air Travel Association.

Basendwah, M., & Rahman, S. (2021). A review on the importance of tourist satisfaction and destination image in Kingdom of Saudi Arabia. *PalArch's Journal of Archaeology of Egypt/egyptology, 18*(1), 4191–4200.

Carrasco, B., & Carvao, S. (2022, March). *United Nations World Tourism Organizations (UNWTO) and Asian development bank report on Covid-19 and the future of Tourism in Asia-and the Pacific.*

Ekiz, E., Öter, Z., & Stephenson, M. L. (2017). Tourism development in the Kingdom of Saudi Arabia: Determining the problems and resolving the challenges. In *International Tourism Development and the Gulf Cooperation Council States* (pp. 124–139). Routledge.

Habiba Muhammed, S. A., Bhaskar, P., & Alazri, A. K. (2022). The economic and social impact of Covid-19 on Tourism and hospitality industry. A case study from Oman. *Journal of Public Affairs, 22*, e2786.

Hidayat, T., Damanik, J., & Soeprihanto, J. (2019, June). Characteristics and behaviors of tourists: Case of Middle East Tourists in Puncak Cianjur, Indonesia, from Tour Guides' Perspective. *Advances in social science, education, and humanities research (ISOT 2018)* (Vol. 259, pp. 326–329). Atlantis Press.

Jaipuria, S., Parida, R., & Ray, P. (2021). The impact of COVID-19 on tourism sector in India. *Tourism Recreation Research, 46*(2), 245–260.

Jarvis, D., & Stoeckl, N. (2016). The impact of economic, social and environmental factors on trip satisfaction and the likelihood of visitors returning. *Tourism Management, 52*, 1–18. Elsevier.

Jawabreh, O. (2020). Management of tourism crisis in the Middle East, chapter 7. *Book-Public Sector Crisis Management*.

Kassem, A., Ragab, A. M., Alomran, A., Alotaibi, E., Ahmed, T. A., Shaker, E., & Alajloni, A. (2021). Underlying factors of tourist social responsibility (TSR) within the COVID-19 context: An empirical investigation of the Saudi tourism market. *Sustainability, 13*(23), 13342.

Kenny, J., & Dutt, C. S. (2022). The long-term impacts of hotel's strategic responses to COVID-19: The case of Dubai. *Tourism and Hospitality Research, 22*(1), 71–85. https://doi.org/10.1177/14673584211034525

Kernshi, A. S., & Waheed, R. (2021). COVID-19 and tourism sector: A perspective of Saudi Arabia. *International Journal of Advanced and Applied Sciences, 8*(9), 58–62.

Khare, A., & Sathe, S. (2021). A study of tourism choices by tourists in India in new normal. *International Journal of Engineering, Management, and Economics, 10*(5), 54–64.

Kumar, P. (2021, September). Impact of Covid-19 pandemic on Indian Tourism & Hospitality Industry. *World Wide Journal of Multidisciplinary Research and Development, 7*(9), 22–26.

Ladki, S., Abimanyu, A., & Kesserwan, L. (2020). The rise of a new tourism dawn in the Middle East. *Journal of Service Science and Management, 13*(4), 637–648.

Menon, S., Bhatt, S., & Sharma, S. (2021). A study on envisioning Indian tourism–Through cultural tourism and sustainable digitalization. *Cogent Social Sciences, 7*(1), 1903149.

Morakabati, Y. (2013). Tourism in the Middle East: Conflicts, crises and economic diversification, some critical issues. *International Journal of Tourism Research, 15*(4), 375–387.

Marković, I., & Klarić, Z. (2015). Attitudes of local population of tourism impacts on destination sustainability: Case of Croatia. *Turizam, 19*(3), 98–110.

Rafiei Darani, H., & Asghari, H. (2018). Study of international tourism demand in Middle East by panel data model. *International Journal of Culture, Tourism and Hospitality Research, 12*(1), 80–88. https://doi.org/10.1108/IJCTHR-03-2017-0030

Ramzy, Y. (2017). Managing Egyptian tourism through tourism governance. *Journal of Social Sciences (COES&RJ-JSS), 6*(2), 196–210.

Ranjbarian, B., & Zahedi, M. (2010). *Tourism recognition* (3rd ed.). Charbagh Publications.
Report of Ministry of Tourism, Government of India 2021.
Shalan, I. M. (2005). Sustainable tourism development in the Red Sea of Egypt: Threats and opportunities. *Journal of Cleaner Production, 13*(2), 83–87.
United Nations Department of Economic and Social Affairs-17 SDGs (2015).
United Nations World Tourism Organizations (UNWTO) Global survey on Tourism Report-2021.
Vanzetti, D., & Peters, R. (2021). Covid-19 and tourism: An update. United Nations Conference on Trade and Development (UNCTD).
Vijay Raj, B. V., & Jayanthila Devi, A. (2021). Restoring Tourism Industry in India after Covid-19. *International Journal of Case Studies in Business, IT and Education*, *5*(2), 284–298.
World Travel and Tourism Council (WTTC) Report 2022.

CHAPTER 13

Implications of the Pandemic for Economic Development

Ashraf Mishrif

1 Introduction

The experience of the COVID-19 pandemic has weakened the current global economic system. The growth rate of the global economy declined by as high as minus –6% in 2020 and global recession reached unprecedented levels in the aftermath of the pandemic. Global supply chains were also affected by the border closures and reduced capacity for shipping and transportation of goods, except for vital medical equipment and goods during the pandemic (Mishrif & Khan, 2022b). The disruption of the global value chains network, particularly from China and the Far East affected so many manufacturing companies around the world, most of these companies were unable to fulfil the demands of their consumers. The reduction in supply and demand resulted in a sharp decline in the GDP of many industrialized countries, while oil exporting

A. Mishrif (✉)
Humanities Research Centre, Sultan Qaboos University, Muscat, Sultanate of Oman
e-mail: ashraf.mishrif@gmail.com

A. Mishrif (ed.), *Economic Effects of the Pandemic*, The Political Economy of the Middle East,
https://doi.org/10.1007/978-981-97-4367-4_13

countries suffered from lack of demand in the energy markets, subsequently decreasing oil demand due to the closure of many factories and plummeting oil prices to as low as US$30 per barrel in 2020.

The experience of the pandemic also highlighted the interdependence of the global value chains network to the extent that any disruption in one chain could have spillover effects on other chains and subsequently deteriorate the global economy. For example, the disruption of the value chain in China affected negative several related industries such as the textile and apparel industry in East Asia. This was evident in the effect of closing some Chinese factories on the production and export of apparel in South Korea which decreased by 27% and the lay off workers and closure of factories in Bangladesh (Mishrif & Khan, 2022a; Sen et al., 2020; Yoo, et al., 2020). Another example of economic interdependence was seen in the effect of the pandemic on the airline industry, which suffered from the closure of airports and air travel restrictions. The negative spillover effects of this industry spread to related industries including airlines, airport authorities, air cargo providers, inflight food caterers, aircraft spare parts manufacturers, and maintenance and repair companies. Rahman et al. (2020) argued that passenger/cargo, food catering, parts manufacturing, maintenance, and repairs were the hardest hit in the aviation industry. Data analysis revealed that airports lost a large chunk of their revenue, with Asia/Pacific suffering the highest revenue loss (42%), followed by North America (34%), and the Middle East (11%) (International Civil Aviation Organization, 2020). Mishrif and Khan (2022a, b) stressed that air transport mobility was reduced by more than 89%, however cargo traffic saw an increase in some cases due to the supply of medical equipment.

The aim of this chapter is to provide concluding remarks on the findings of the examinations presented in this book and provide some recommendations for governments to minimize the effects of any similar crises in the future. In the following sections, a summary of the sectoral survival and the lessons learned from this crisis for governments to develop alternative strategies to effectively deal with similar crises in the future.

2 Implications for Geo-Political and Economic Development

The COVID-19 pandemic has left a lasting impact on the global economy. Although most countries have officially declared the end of the pandemic, the political, economic, and social consequences of the pandemic are still affecting all walks of life. The pandemic effects have not only affected people's lives and cost a significant loss in lives and livelihoods but have also reduced income and increased poverty rates in many low- and middle-income countries. They also affected the development process in emerging markets in Asia and Latin America, as the breakdown of global supply chains resulted in goods and services scarcity, decreased purchasing power and increased inflation.

Other consequences of the pandemic are the energy and food security challenges. The sharp reduction in global demand for oil and fluctuation in oil prices have had direct impacts on the oil exporting countries. For example, the GCC countries suffered from the decline in oil revenues, forcing many of them to borrow from the international financial markets to meet their basic needs. Oman was forced to borrow at high interest rates from international lenders, increasing its foreign debts from around 30% of GDP in 2016 to over 70% of GDP in 2022. Almost all GCC countries experienced budget deficits during the pandemic.

Moreover, the disruption of the global supply chains has caused huge concerns about food security. These concerns are heightened by the outbreak of the Russian-Ukrainian war in February 2022. With both Russia and Ukraine contributing around 40% of global supply of wheat and other agriculture commodities, the war has stopped or reduced much of this supply, creating a huge shortage in food and basic commodities that are essential for many countries and increasing the prices of these commodities in international markets. The sanctions imposed against Russia has affected the Russian economy due to the suspension of importing advances technology that vital for its industrial development and prevented it from selling its oil in the international markets at the market price, putting a huge pressure on its balance of payment and public expenditure. The war also affected Russia's relations with the European Union countries, as Russia suspended the oil and gas supply to Europe, forcing the latter to forge new relations with major gas and oil exporters, particularly in the Middle East.

Indeed, the multiple exogenous shock to the economy has caused many concerns to the global economy, especially emerging and least developed economies that have limited fiscal capabilities. While developed economies were able to spend about 28% of their GDP to help their markets, low-income countries spent only around 2–7% of their GDP to support their companies to survive the pandemic. The experience of the pandemic has also underscored the great disparity between developed and developing countries in responding to the crisis and pace of recovery. There are also differences in the inflation rates, which recorded around 10% in the USA and EU countries, while these rates reaching unprecedented levels in developing countries such as Turkey and Egypt those inflation stood around 65% and 40%, respectively, in August 2023. To address the persistent inflation, central banks are forced to increase interest rates and adopt forceful monetary policy measures. Many countries are forced to depreciate their national currencies, adding additional pressure to these markets. Although the pandemic was a global crisis, different countries adopted different approaches to recover from the pandemic. Some countries focused on supply chain intervention and infrastructure spending, while others focused on putting money in the hands of people and providing a social safety net.

Furthermore, the implications for macroeconomic development were reflected in the adverse macroeconomic shocks that most countries experienced during the pandemic. Most European countries expected a wide-spread pessimism across different sectors of the economy, while many economic agents anticipated a surge in inflation facing the pandemic shock. Similar adverse expectations are recorded in terms of the employment situation, with unemployment reaching unprecedented levels during 2020 and 2021. These behaviors and expectations are found in almost all countries regardless of the number of deaths and infected cases. The analysis also revealed that although COVID-19 caused a significant contraction in economic activities and negatively affected all economic sectors, contact-intensive services suffered the most. It found stiffnesses in the adjustment of expectations and the presence of asymmetric inconsistencies in the responses of economic agents towards the pandemic shock.

When the inflation and unemployment were examined in the case of Malayasia, the analysis found that inflation was asymmetrically correlated with Malaysia's unemployment rate, which indicated that unemployment reacted differently to the changes in inflation rate. The results suggest that unemployment was more sensitive to the decrease in inflation compared to the increase. However, our analysis revealed that there was no long run cointegration between the unemployment rate and the inflation rate in Malaysia. Thus, policy makers should pay more attention to reducing the unemployment rate by creating new job opportunities or assisting the unemployed to obtain a job. They should investigate an improved reward mechanism compared to the existing apprenticeship programs by creating new vacancies for the jobless and adopting the type of monetary policies that attract foreign direct investment and enhance job market performance.

3 Implications for Consumption in the GCC Countries

The COVID-19 pandemic has also underlined significant changes in the patterns of consumption at the household and country levels. In terms of household consumption behavior, our analysis reveals that consumers shifted their consumption patterns, with many consumers incurring high costs in spendings on face masks, sanitizers, testing kits and other COVID-19 related medications. This was at the expense of reduced expenditure for necessity-based shopping. The belonged lockdown that forced people to stay at home increased both food consumption and expenditure on groceries. There was also a significant decline in vehicle maintenance, travelling, gatherings, and weddings expenditure. However, our analysis indicated that these changes are temporal and people's consumption behavior returned to the pre-pandemic behaviors once the restrictions removed.

In fact, the pandemic has encouraged many scholars and researchers to examine the phenomenon and assess people' reaction and responsiveness in dire situations such as COVID-19. It is also important to evaluate the capacity of the state and its institutions to prepare themselves for the absorptive capacity of shocks. There is a need to determine innovative methods and strategies to optimize the dependence on our natural resources and fossil fuels in the development process, while enabling governments to set up policies that would safeguard the welfare of entities involved in the food and beverage industry, logistics and supply chain and the medical sector of the nation for future crises.

Water consumption was another critical factor brought about by the pandemic. Our analysis shows that almost all GCC countries experienced an increase in households' water consumption. The rise in consumption was caused by the COVID-19 lockdown and WHO instructions asking people to increase the frequency and duration of handwashing. This significantly affected water consumption in the GCC courtiers in 2020 compared to 2019. Statistics show that the highest rate of water consumption coincided with the lockdown and closure of commercial centers and factories, particularly in March, April, and May 2020. However, our analysis also identified other factors such as population growth, hot climate, and the high standard of living that contributed to an increase in water consumption, mainly for washing, showering and laundry in the GCC countries.

Thus, it is advisable that GCC countries should focus on sustainable management of resources, in particular water and energy, as well as putting in place alternative strategies to deal with similar situations in the future. GCC countries must also consider availing and sustainably managing water for all in line with sustainable development goal 6 (SDG 6) and considering socioeconomic conditions and factors when compiling statistics of water consumption to achieve a better government planning for water supply and production. We also recommend that GCC countries should conduct studies to investigate peak times of water demand and then use the results for a more sustainable and informed water supply process, while using the experience of COVID-19 to raise awareness about water conversation.

4 Implications for the Finance and Banking Sectors

The impact of COVID-19 was severe and caused significant stress on the finance and banking sectors across the world. In the case of Oman, efficiency ratio of the financial institutions was negative as Oman Central Bank imposed a ceiling on the interest rates commercial banks can charge on personal loans. This, however, did not prevent banks from increasing their loan rates due to the stive competition from other banks. Banks' profits, which lost 19% of their profitability during the pandemic, were also affected by the slow economic growth and high inflation. The effect of inflation on bank's profitability was obvious when the deposit and lending interest rates had varying sensitivity to inflation. This forced some banks to offer prize schemes to attract deposits with low-interest rates. Omani banks profitability was also affected by the fall in oil prices that were direly needed for enhancing banks' profits and increase revenues. This underlined the extent to which the pandemic caused volatility in oil prices and subsequently affected the operations of financial institutions in the country.

Meanwhile, there were also some positive effects of the pandemic as banks were forced to create business continuity plans or improve their existing ones to better serve their employees and customers during the pandemic. Banks were effective in keeping smooth daily operations, while accelerating the use of e-services, fintech, and other technological advancements. They were also efficient in community support and services provisions, hence stabilizing the financial system and the economy. The pandemic offered an opportunity for us to think of new ideas to strengthen the banking system at the time of crises by having sufficient capital reserves to cover their potential losses, focusing on improving business strategies and making investments as means of maintaining profitability. Banks should abide by the rules and regulations and focus on meeting the needs of their customers during crises. They should assist the government in its efforts to accelerate economic diversification since oil price fluctuations have a direct effect on the performance of the banking sector.

In terms of accounting and finance, this book examined the effect of the pandemic on the performance of the public sector when implementing government finance statistics manual. Our analysis revealed that the implementation of the government finance statistics manual, together with the analysis of public finance indicators, provided a comprehensive assessment of the public sector performance during the pandemic. It also indicated that the difference between the financial statements and the accounting rules and between the government financial statistics and the international accounting standards for the public sector has a direct impact on the quality of the financial reports. The findings of this book stress the necessity to fully adhere to the analytical framework of government finance statistics manual and its accounting rules to properly assess public sector performance during the pandemic. It is also recommended that countries should harmonize the public sector accounting standards with the government financial statistics system by building a set of local public sector accounting standards.

5 Implementation for the Tourism Industry

The hospitality, travel and tourism industries were among the most affected sectors from the COVID-19 pandemic. In fact, these industries form a major part of the services sector that provides employment to a huge number of people, generates income revenues, and contributes to GDP. Our analysis revealed that the pandemic drastically affected the travel and tourism sectors, causing millions of people to lose their jobs and livelihood, reducing foreign exchange earnings, and triggering a significant decline in the GDP in India, Oman, the Gulf countries, and the wider Middle East between 2020 and 2023.

The recovery strategy depends on the capacity of the country to contain the virus and build confidence among travelers through joint efforts between the Ministry of Health and Ministry of Tourism and developing effective tourism promotion campaigns in the post-pandemic era. The joint efforts among different ministries, public authorities, and private sector tourist companies enabled Saudi Arabia to boost religious tourism and attract more than 3 million pilgrims for Hij and Umra in 2022. Several successful events in the Gulf countries were held, including FIFA World Cup 2022 in Qatar and EXPO2023 in Dubia, which attracted hundreds of thousands of people from around the world. Among the recommendations to promote tourism in the region are adopting technology to provide tourist products and services and introducing a single visa for up to three months to those wanting to visit the Gulf and Middle Eastern countries.

6 Conclusion and the Way Forward

This timely book offers an interesting perspective on the economic consequences of the COVID-19 pandemic, with particular focus on key strategic sectors such as finance and tourism. The impact of the pandemic was also severe on the global economy, affecting both developed and developing countries with an average contraction of minus −5% in 2020. The performance of the productive sectors was negatively impacted by the disruption of the global value chains, restriction of flow of capital, goods and services, and layoff of workers during the pandemic years. After four years of fear, illness and death of millions of people and disruption to all walks of life, the economic impact of COVID-19 has not faded away and many macroeconomic indicators have yet to return to the pre-pandemic levels. The international community is currently struggling with several crises emanating from the pandemic including energy, food security, climate change, migration, and poverty.

The economic impact of the pandemic is also observed in the new economic strategies that focus mainly on green economy and sustainable development to help improve the quality of life in the post-pandemic era. The shift towards green economy is accelerating to reduce the destructive environmental effects on human lives such as global warming, environmental pollution, and the depletion of natural resources. Digitization of the economy, automation, electric vehicles, and several aspects of industry 4.0 technologies are now featuring in the global economy. Although the pandemic is officially ended, its negative and positive effects are like to shape our lives for many years to come.

References

International Civil Aviation Organization. (2020). *Revenue loss of airports*. https://data.icao.int/icads/. Accessed 20 December 2020.

Mishrif, A., & Khan, A. (2022a). Examining the effects of COVID-19 on logistics and supply chain networks in Oman. *Journal of Emergency Management, 21*(7), 299–306.

Mishrif, A., & Khan, A. (2022b). Shipping and transportation traffic of medical and non-medical goods before and during COVID-19 in Oman. *Procedia Computer Science, 201*, 223–230.

Rahman, N., Rahim, S., Ahmad, M., & Hafizuddin-Syah, B. (2020). Exploring COVID-19 pandemic: Its impact to global aviation industry and the key strategy. *International Journal of Advanced Science and Technology, 29*(2020), 1829–1836.

Sen, S., Antara, N., Sen, S., & Chowdhury, S. (2020). The unprecedented pandemic "COVID-19" effect on the apparel workers by shivering the apparel supply chain. *Journal of Textile and Apparel, Technology and Management, 11*(3), 1–20.

Yoo, J.-H., Park, S.-K., & Cheong, I.-K. (2020). The impact of COVID-19 and Korea's new southern policy on its global value chain. *Journal of Korea Trade, 24*(8), 19–38.

Index

A. Mishrif (ed.), *Economic Effects of the Pandemic*, The Political Economy of the Middle East,
https://doi.org/10.1007/978-981-97-4367-4

SPRINGER NATURE

GPSR Compliance

The European Union's (EU) General Product Safety Regulation (GPSR) is a set of rules that requires consumer products to be safe and our obligations to ensure this.

If you have any concerns about our products, you can contact us on ProductSafety@springernature.com

In case Publisher is established outside the EU, the EU authorized representative is:

Springer Nature Customer Service Center GmbH
Europaplatz 3
69115 Heidelberg, Germany

The manufacturer's authorised representative in the EU is Springer Nature Customer Service Centre GmbH, Europaplatz 3, 69115 Heidelberg, Germany. If you have any concerns regarding our products, please contact ProductSafety@springernature.com

Printed and bound by CPI Group (UK) Ltd, Croydon, CR0 4YY
01/10/2026
02226249-0007